IMAGES
*of America*

# Austin's Montopolis Neighborhood

I0810082

**ON THE COVER:** The original truss bridge across the Colorado River that connected the city of Austin with the village of Montopolis was constructed by the King Bridge Company for Travis County in 1888–1889. It consisted of six spans of lengths varying between 110 and 280 feet. This iron bridge was the last of five bridges washed away by infamous Austin floods and was destroyed in June 1935. Federal assistance was requested, and a replacement bridge was completed in February 1938 at a cost of about $232,000. This historic bridge is still in use and serves as the southbound frontage road to the Montopolis Drive exit. Plans are underway to preserve the bridge in place as part of the Lance Armstrong Bikeway. It was added to the National Register of Historic Places in 1996. (Courtesy of the Austin History Center.)

IMAGES
*of America*

# Austin's Montopolis Neighborhood

Fred L. McGhee, PhD

ARCADIA
PUBLISHING

Copyright © 2014 by Fred L. McGhee, PhD
ISBN 978-1-4671-3176-6

Published by Arcadia Publishing
Charleston, South Carolina

Printed in the United States of America

Library of Congress Control Number: 2014937881

For all general information, please contact Arcadia Publishing:
Telephone 843-853-2070
Fax 843-853-0044
E-mail sales@arcadiapublishing.com
For customer service and orders:
Toll-Free 1-888-313-2665

Visit us on the Internet at www.arcadiapublishing.com

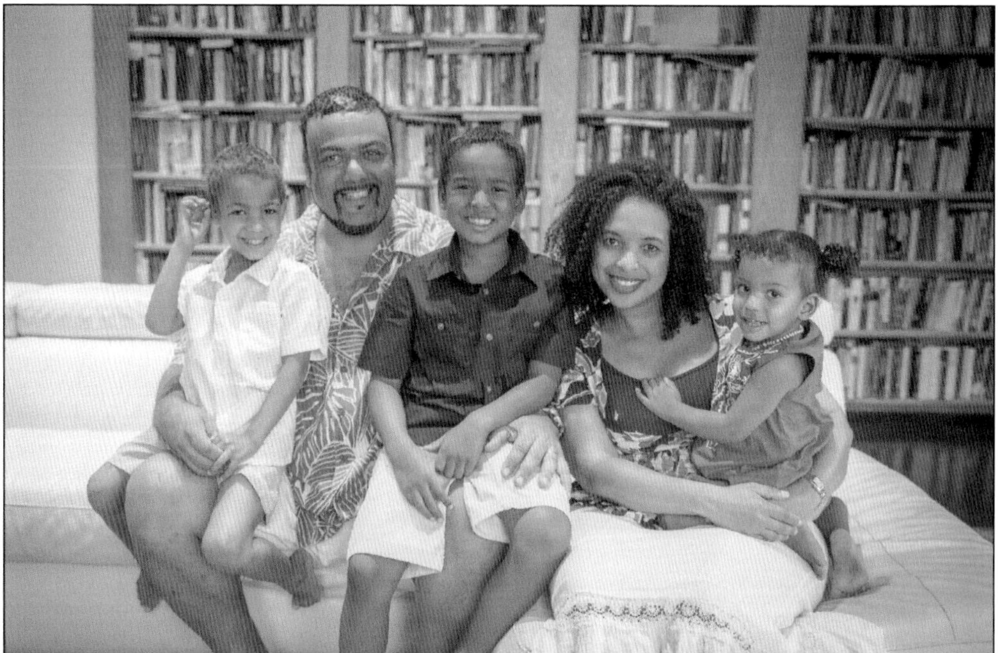

This book is dedicated to Alexander, Carmen, and Thelonious McGhee, true children of Austin's "City on a Hill." (Courtesy of Casey Chapman-Ross Photography.)

# Contents

# Acknowledgments

The writing of a book is never a solo venture, and I am indebted first and foremost to my friends and neighbors in Montopolis, Del Valle, and Dove Springs for sharing their stories. Glenn Scott and her team at People's History in Texas produced a fine oral history in 1985 about Montopolis for the City of Austin, and I would like to thank the late Stephanie Neely of the Dan Ruiz Branch of the Austin Public Library for bringing the film to my attention.

Heartfelt gratitude to the staff of the Austin History Center and my colleagues at the Austin History Center Association for their professionalism, goodwill, and dedication. A special note of thanks to my wife, Lisa Goddard, and our three children, who gave me the time and space to write this book, and to the staff at Arcadia Publishing, Laura Bruns, and Suzanne Lynch, who understood the challenges posed by my impossibly busy schedule.

Unless otherwise credited, all images in this book are courtesy of the Austin History Center.

# INTRODUCTION

Annexed by the City of Austin relatively recently, the sleepy southeast Austin neighborhood of Montopolis is a tightly knit community nestled along the Colorado River amid pine and cedar forests, wetlands, rolling hills, and farmland. Long visited by various indigenous peoples, the area entered Euro-American history when Jessie Cornelius Tannehill (sometimes spelled "Jesse"), a Kentucky-born settler coming from Tennessee, established a townsite atop a hill along the Colorado River in 1830. He named the area Montopolis, Greek for "City on a Hill."

The land containing today's Montopolis community officially entered public records in 1832 when Santiago del Valle, a nobleman from Monclova in the Mexican state of Cohuila y Texas, was granted official title to the Travis County land "at the mouth of Onion Creek." Del Valle paid 1,100 pesos for 10 leagues of land—roughly 35,000 acres—designated as lying between Onion Creek, or Burro Creek, and the Colorado River, southeast of Austin. Benjamin Milam was the impresario who handled the tract, and Samuel Williams, representing Don Santiago del Valle, was the attorney who filed for the land with alcalde Horacio Chriesman (Chriesman was one of Stephen F. Austin's "Old Three Hundred"). The deeds were signed on June 12, 1832. Del Valle's grant includes the present-day communities of Montopolis, Del Valle, and Dove Springs, as well as others.

Del Valle's land grant, written in Spanish, was recorded in the office at San Felipe de Austin, which is not the Austin of today. Del Valle never set foot in his real estate venture, subdividing it to men such as A.C. Horton, Nathaniel H. Watrous, Bartlett Sims, Michael Menard, and Thomas F. McKinney instead. Travis County did not yet exist; the region was part of Bastrop County and was populated by wild Buffalo and "wild" Indians, feared by the Anglo settlers.

Montopolis never developed into the metropolis that Tannehill had hoped. Against the vigorous protestations of Tannehill and others, subsequent Euro-American settlement began to cluster around the settlement known as Waterloo, located about four miles upriver and chosen as the new capital of the Republic of Texas in 1839. A small and crude ferry crossed the Colorado River between Montopolis and Austin, and the Old Bastrop Road, which ran from Bastrop to San Antonio and Austin, was little more than a dirt road that would turn into an impassable mud bog after moderate rain.

The period between the 1840s and the 1890s saw the gradual establishment of plantation agriculture in the Montopolis and Del Valle area. Pioneer settlers during this time period included John W. Cloud, James S. Shaw, James Bascom Norwood, James Baker, Neilam Soules, Robert Jones, and Lewis and William Hancock, who established themselves as small-scale planters and introduced slavery and, later, sharecropping into the area. The primary cash crop was cotton. Cattle husbandry was also popular, as the Montopolis and Del Valle prairie was a stop on the Old Chisholm Trail route, which drove immense herds of cattle from South Texas to Kansas via Gonzales and Lockhart.

John W. Cloud, who purchased his land in 1867, was the first commissioner of Precinct 4 on the Travis County Commissioners Court, and was instrumental in the location and construction of the original Montopolis Bridge in the late 1880s. He was followed in 1874 by William Givens, who moved to the area from Kentucky and built a small general store. The store proved successful, and by 1878, Givens also became the first postmaster for Del Valle. The Givens General Store, open day and night, became the heart of the Del Valle and Montopolis area in the late 1800s and early 1900s. Montopolis briefly had its own post office from 1897 to 1902, but the community's population proved too small to support permanent postal service. With the new bridge in place, mail began to be routed to Austin or Del Valle instead.

With the introduction of a cotton gin in the 1880s, the agricultural economy of the area eventually grew, and the census of 1900 reported the population of Montopolis at 142 persons. Del Valle's stood at 75. The Montopolis-Del Valle area had a common school district, Colorado District 36, which was renamed the Del Valle Independent School District in 1963. In 1907, District 36 had a one-teacher school for 9 white students and a one-teacher school for 108 black students. In 1952, when the City of Austin began annexing the Montopolis portion of the district, enrollment stood at about 600 students. The Montopolis boundary between the Austin and Del Valle Independent School Districts remains chaotic to this day; portions of Montopolis are part of the Del Valle Independent School District, while other areas are part of Austin's school district.

The African American legacy of Montopolis is reflected in such institutions as St. Edward's Baptist Church, the oldest black Baptist church still in operation in Travis County, and the Burdett Prairie Cemetery, which is the final resting place of the enslaved African Americans owned by local planter Jesse F. Burditt and their descendants.

Significant Mexican migration to the rural outskirts of Austin, including Montopolis, began in the 1920s. By the 1930s, in order to service the increasingly Mexican population of the area, the Fathers of the Holy Cross Congregation in Austin began regular visits to the Catholic families of Montopolis. Fr. James W. Donahue and Fr. Frank Weber baptized many of the children and blessed the Catholic couples that had been married under civil law. This eventually led to the construction of a new church, Nuestra Señora de Siete Dolores (Our Lady of the Seven Sorrows), and the establishment of Dolores Parish as distinct from the San Jose Mission (constructed in 1941) in present-day South Austin. The "seven" was eventually dropped, and the church is today known simply as Nuestra Señora de Dolores.

The establishment of the church and the construction of Del Valle Army Air Field (later Bergstrom Air Force Base) in 1942 radically altered life in Montopolis. When the US government purchased most of the farming property in Del Valle in order to construct the air base, many residents of the area lost their jobs working on the farms and migrated into Montopolis, where they not only built their homes, but also operated businesses that catered to the servicemen stationed in the area. The legacy of this can be seen in businesses such as the Landing Strip, an adult entertainment establishment that primarily catered to members of the military.

In the 1960s, the Dolores Parish, under the leadership of Fr. Fred Underwood, was instrumental in public advocacy to address long-standing infrastructure and educational needs in Montopolis. Roads were finally paved, traffic lights were installed, water and drainage infrastructure problems began to be addressed, and youth programs were put into place, culminating with the construction of the Montopolis Recreation Center by the parish in the mid-1960s. Father Underwood labeled Montopolis "Poverty Island" and worked tirelessly with local, state, and federal officials such as Sargent Shriver to ensure that "War on Poverty" funding flowed into the neighborhood in order to address longstanding needs. Father Underwood remained at Dolores Parish into the 1980s before assuming leadership of San Jose Church and supervising the construction of the cathedral that exists there today.

Although it still has a "secret beach" and other undercover gems, today's Montopolis is no longer as hidden as it once was. The neighborhood is facing increasingly speculative real estate development, as well as ongoing infrastructure expansion, including the Bergstrom Expressway project and the East Riverside Corridor plan, parts of which would entail the installation of rail service from downtown Austin to Bergstrom Airport, bisecting the current neighborhood.

This book is not just offered as a documentation and remembrance of things past, but also as a historical guide for planners and newcomers to the neighborhood. As Austin continues to urbanize, public education about the city's rural origins and its fascinating ethnic and working-class history becomes more important. Montopolis is not a blank slate; it is a proud community with a rich history that predates Austin's. It is the author's hope that readers will not only be informed, but also engaged by this book.

# *One*

# Beginnings

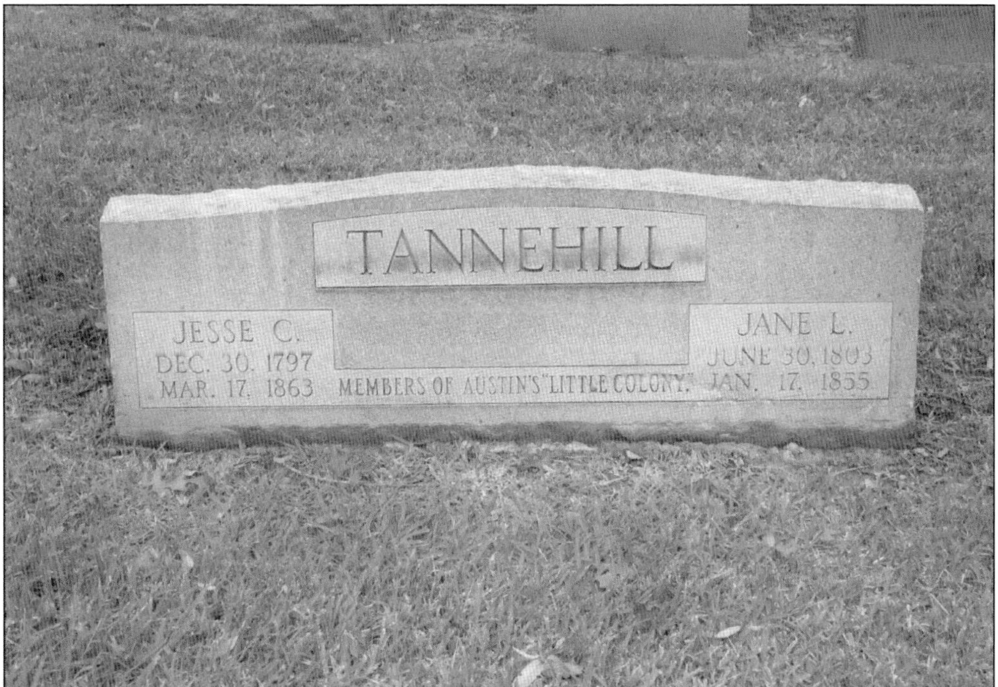


Born in Kentucky, Jessie Cornelius Tannehill (1797–1863) came to Texas with his family in 1827 and established the Montopolis settlement along the Colorado River in 1830. When surveyors began laying out a townsite to be called Waterloo farther up the river in the late 1830s, Tannehill and his settlers protested and argued vigorously that Montopolis should be chosen for the fledgling republic's capital instead. Tannehill was the father of seven children and was buried in the family plot near his house until he and his wife were reinterred in the Texas State Cemetery in 1965. (Courtesy of the author's collection.)

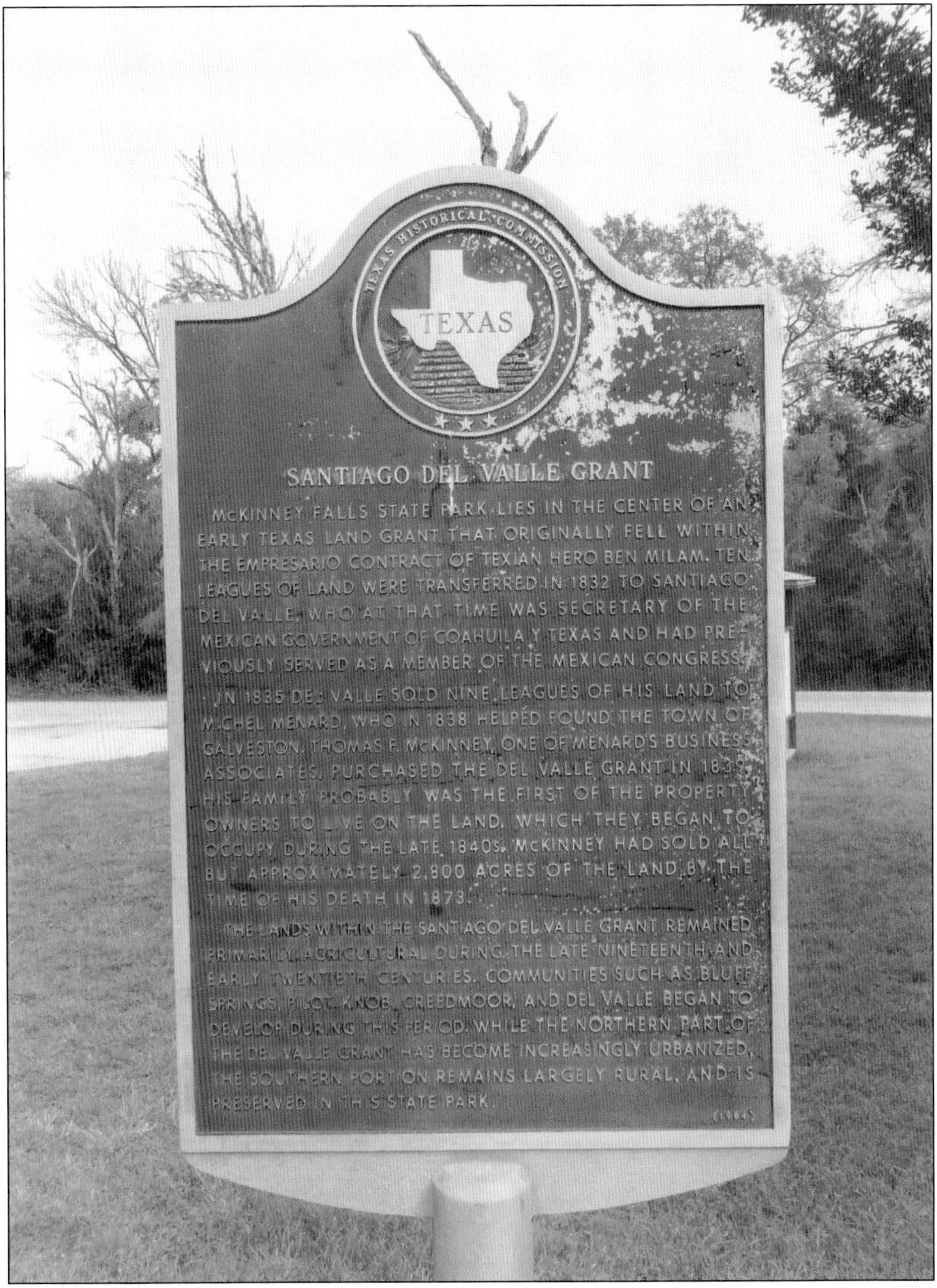


One of the original Mexican federalists and speculators in Texas land, Santiago Del Valle was a *hacendado* from Cohuila who was associated with Thomas F. McKinney and Samuel May Williams through the Banco de Comercio y Agricultura and the Galveston City Company. Del Valle is named for him. Almost all of southeast Austin, including Montopolis, lies in the Del Valle land grant. (Courtesy of the author's collection.)

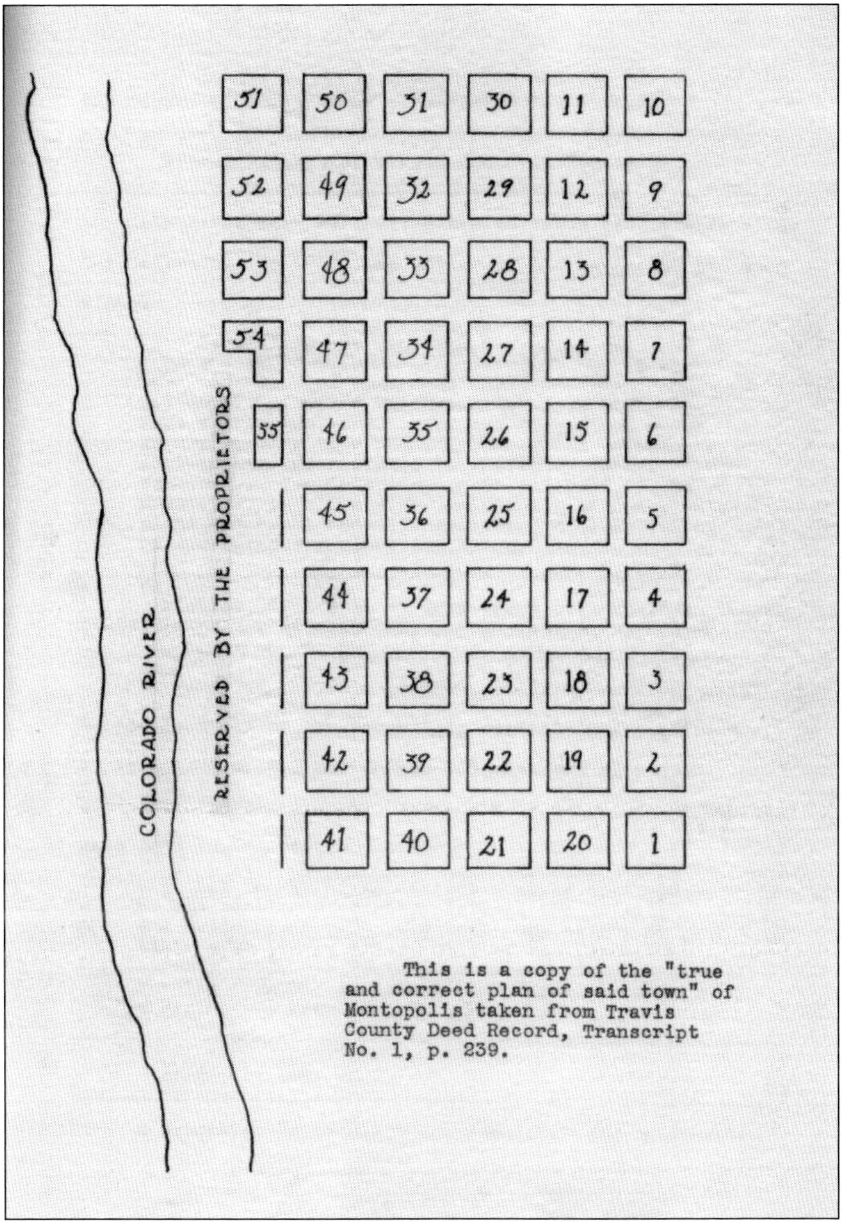


Jessie Tannehill's original 1830 Montopolis settlement essentially consisted of a log cabin and little else. By 1839, about 20 families lived in Montopolis. With competition from the newly founded—and properly surveyed—Waterloo settlement, located about three miles upriver, Tannehill and his associates decided to do the same for their settlement, which, they stressed, was the oldest Euro-American outpost along this portion of the Colorado River. The 55 blocks depicted here were officially recorded by the following individuals: J.C. Tannehill, J.S. Lester, William M. Eastland, James Smith, J.L. Lynch, and Silas Dinsmore. Blocks 5, 6, 15, and 16 were set aside for churches or "seminaries of learning." Tannehill was able to sell a few of his Montopolis lots, but as soon as 1840, two of his buyers sold back their purchases and bought new ones in Waterloo instead. As Waterloo continued to grow and was renamed Austin, Montopolis remained rural and isolated. (Courtesy of the author's collection.)

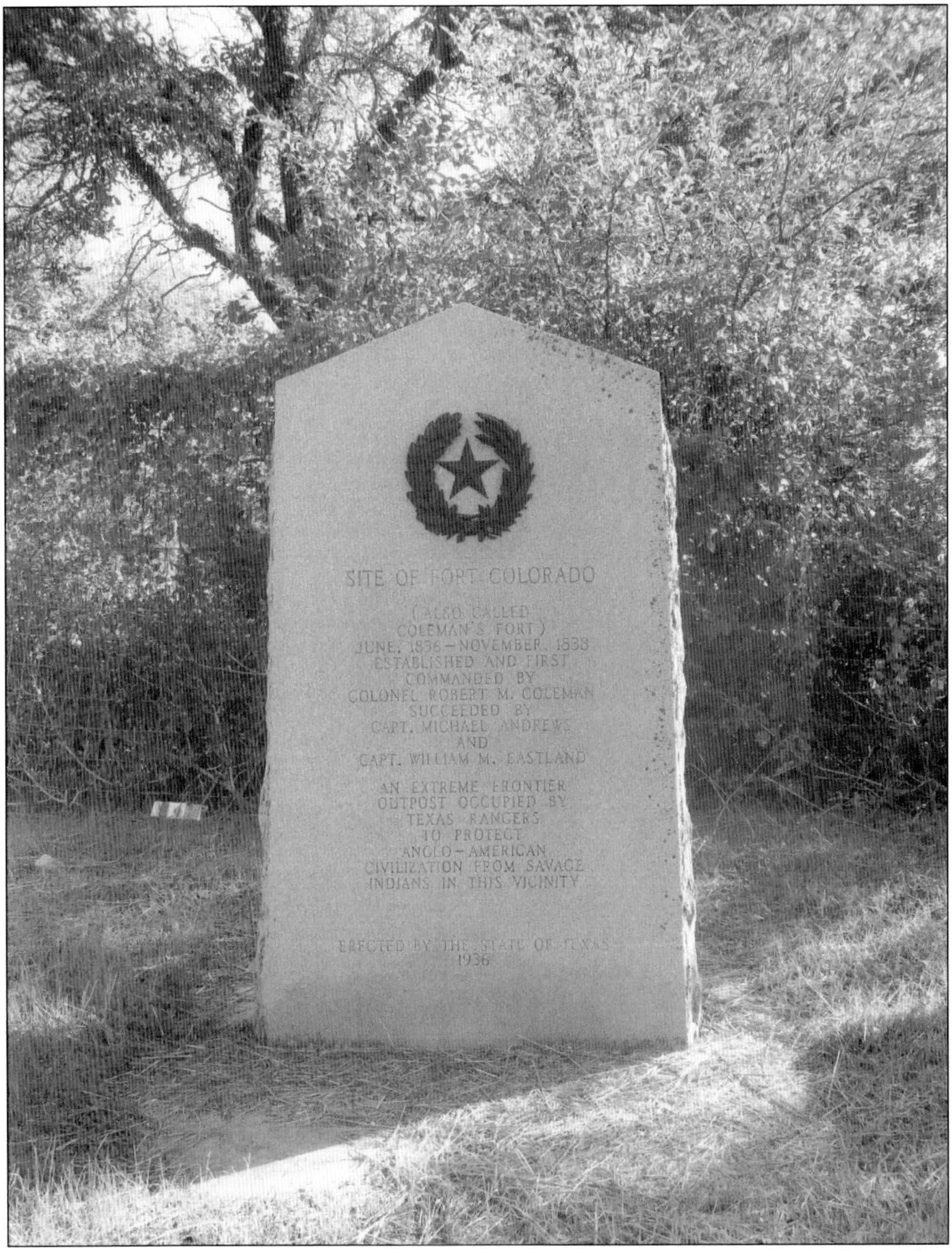


In 1839, Tannehill built a two-story house in Montopolis using logs from Fort Colorado, the fort described in this historical marker. The marker, which is along East Martin Luther King Drive in Austin, is not located at the site of the fort. The fort itself was located along the north bank of the Colorado River, a site now occupied by the Driveway Austin Motorsports Academy and Retreat. The marker reveals as much about racial attitudes Texans held toward Indians in 1936, when the marker was erected, as it does about the fort. It describes the fort as "an extreme frontier outpost occupied by Texas Rangers to protect Anglo-American civilization from savage Indians in this vicinity." (Courtesy of the author's collection.)

Who were some of the "savage Indians" Euro-American settlers felt so paranoid about? At right is an image of Campo, a Tonkawa Indian said to be 123 years old at the time this photograph was taken in January 1873. Campo is also said to have fought in the Texas War of Independence and the Mexican War. Below is Placido, a chief of the Tonkawa Indians in Texas.

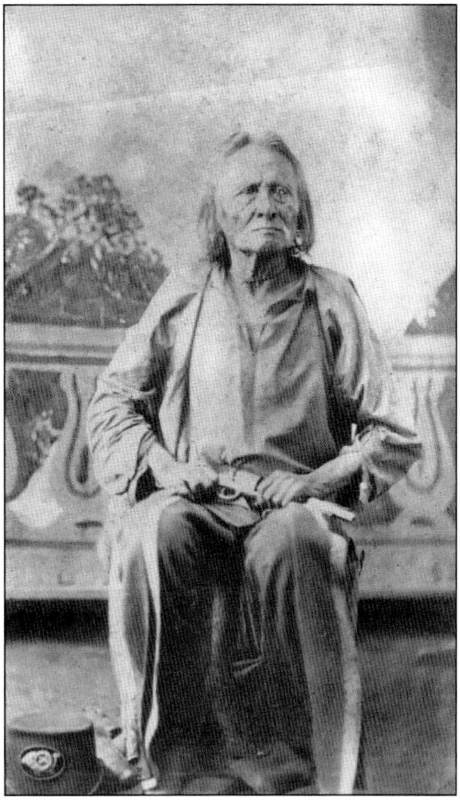

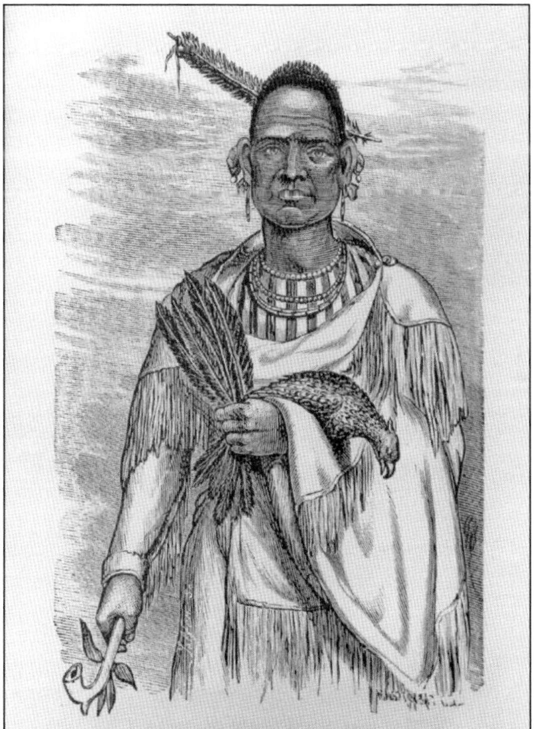

PLACIDO, CHIEF OF THE TONKAWA.

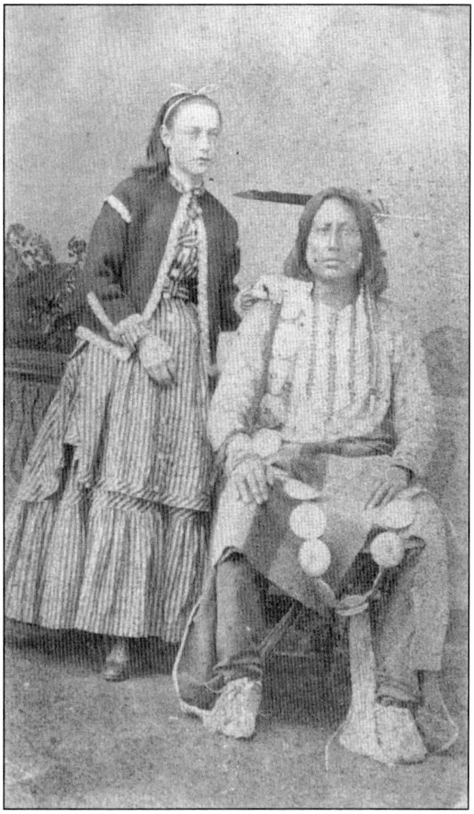

Seen at left is a photograph from between 1865 and 1872 of a woman named Ida and a Tonkawa Indian named Johnson. Below is an image of another Tonkawa chief, Castile. Chief Castile was a scout and guide for the US Army and the Texas Rangers in the 1860s and 1870s in their pursuit of "hostile" Comanches and Kiowas.

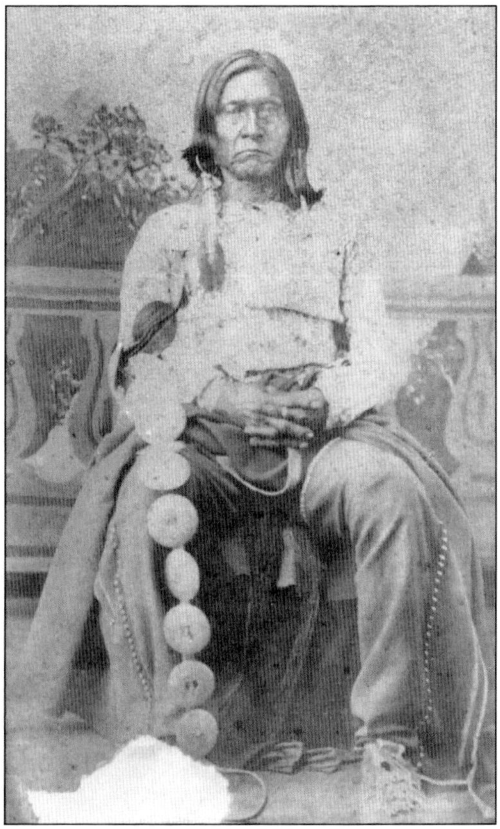

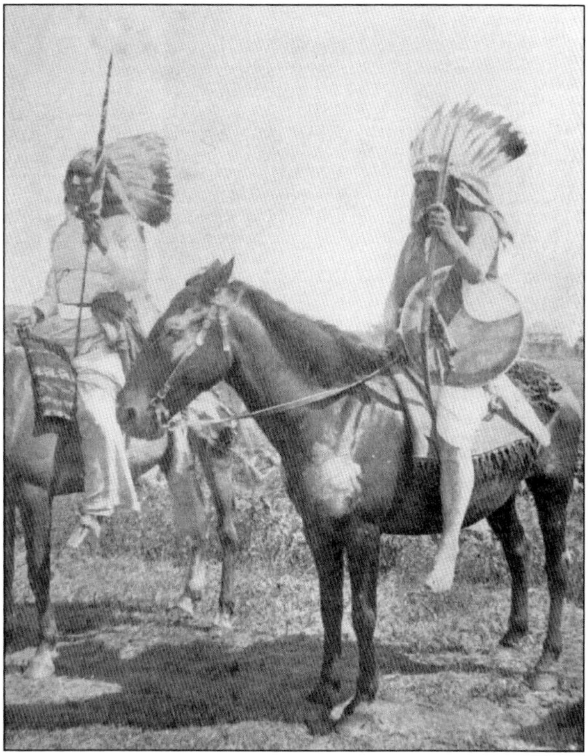

Pictured at right are Comanche warriors on horseback. Seen below is an unknown Indian.

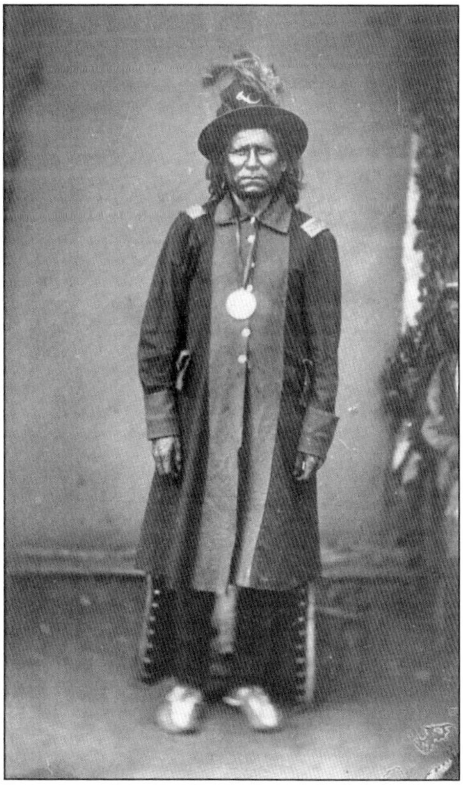

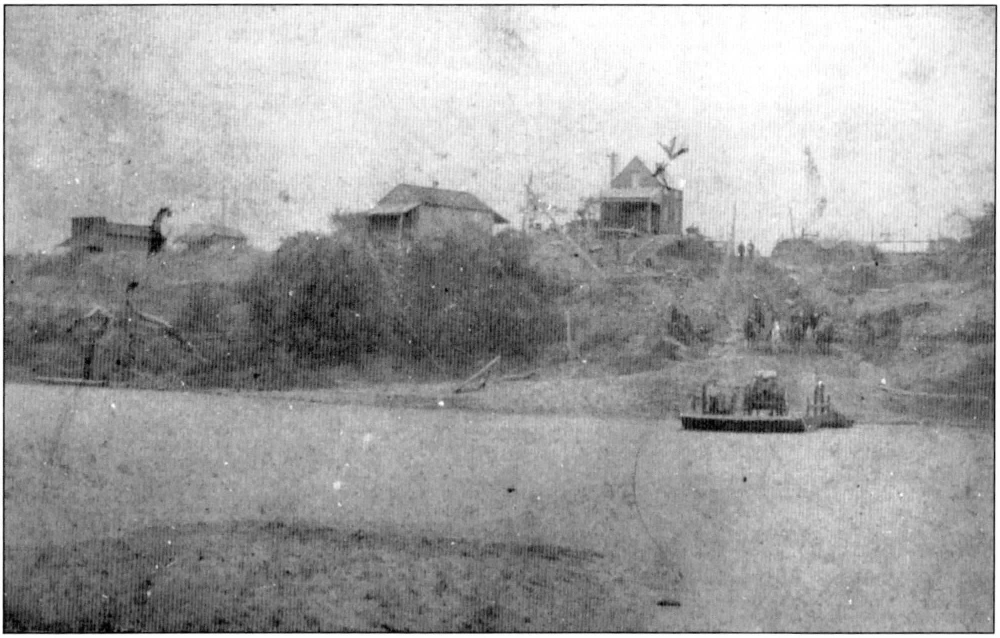

After the settlement of Montopolis, and later, Austin, Colorado River ferry crossings were a fixture in the 1830s and 1840s. Until construction of the first Montopolis bridge in the 1880s, the ferry was the only way to cross the river at the Montopolis crossing. The Montopolis ferry was authorized in 1840, with Wesley Hunt as ferryman.

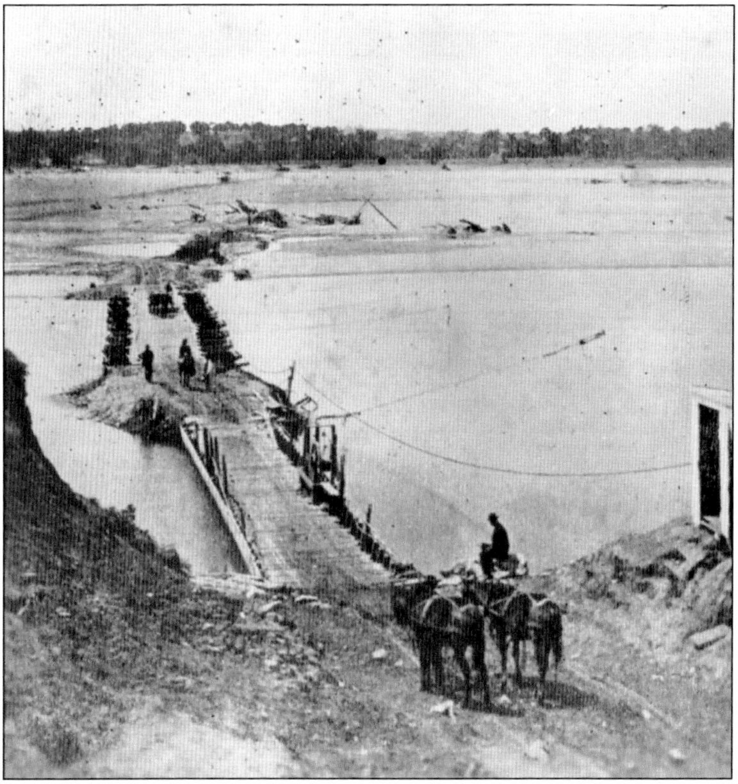

Before the construction of proper iron bridges, pontoon river crossings across the Colorado River were also tried.

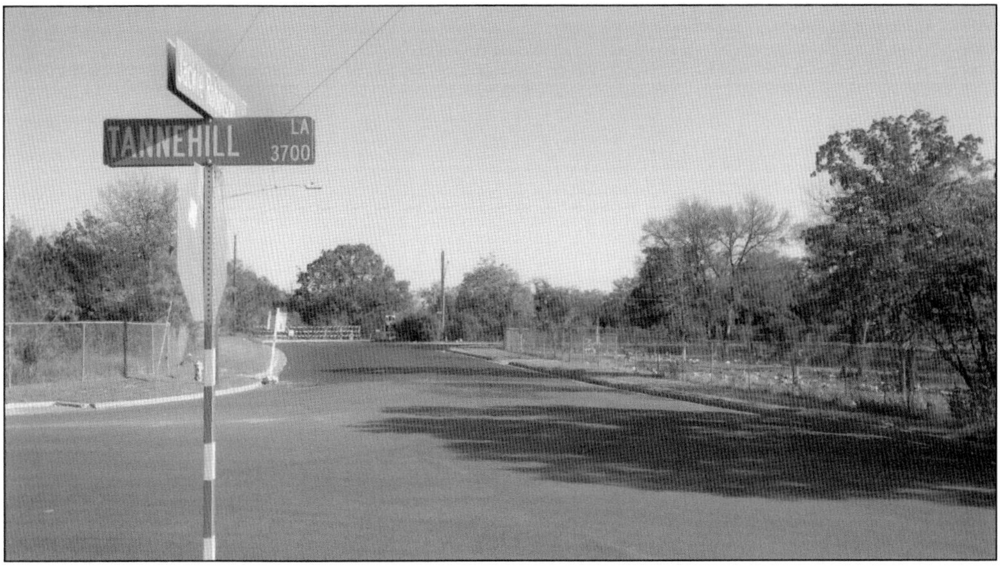


Jessie Tannehill also has an Austin street named for him. Tannehill Lane is a north-south street that parallels Highway 183 (Ed Bluestein Boulevard) between East Martin Luther King Boulevard and Jackie Robinson Street. Jackie Robinson's connections to Austin are deep and long-standing. While stationed at Fort Hood, Robinson would often travel to Austin to visit the Rev. Karl Downs, then president of Samuel Huston College (now Huston-Tillotson University). After being discharged by the US Army for refusing to sit at the back of a bus, Robinson briefly served as the head basketball coach for Samuel Huston College before going on to break Major League Baseball's color barrier with the Brooklyn Dodgers in 1947. (Courtesy of the author's collection.)

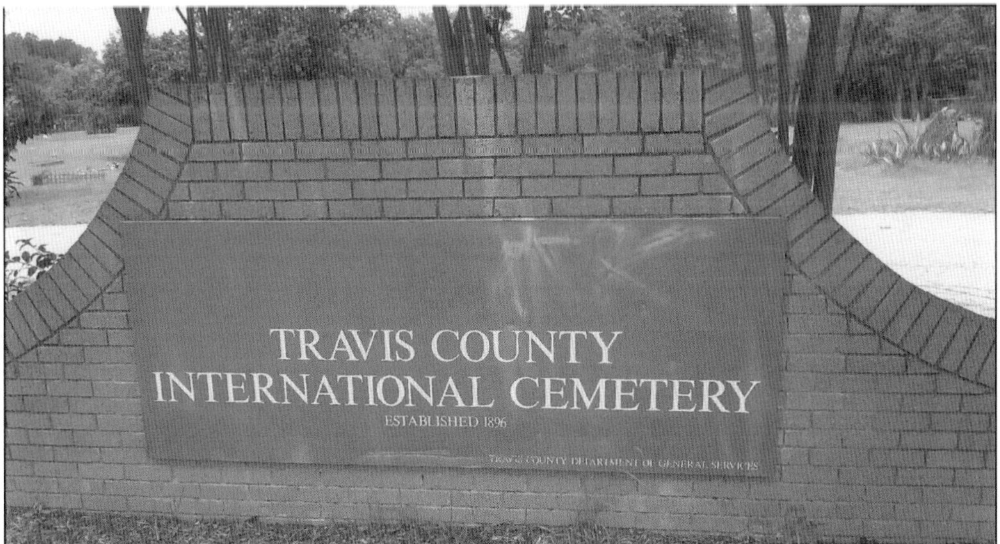


The intersection of Tannehill Lane and Jackie Robinson Street is also noteworthy because it marks one of the boundaries of the Travis County International Cemetery, the county's cemetery for the indigent. Many early Mexican settlers in Travis County are buried in this "international" cemetery. In operation since the late 1800s, the cemetery is now full, and the county now buries its indigent dead at the Wells School Road Cemetery in Manor. (Courtesy of the author's collection.)

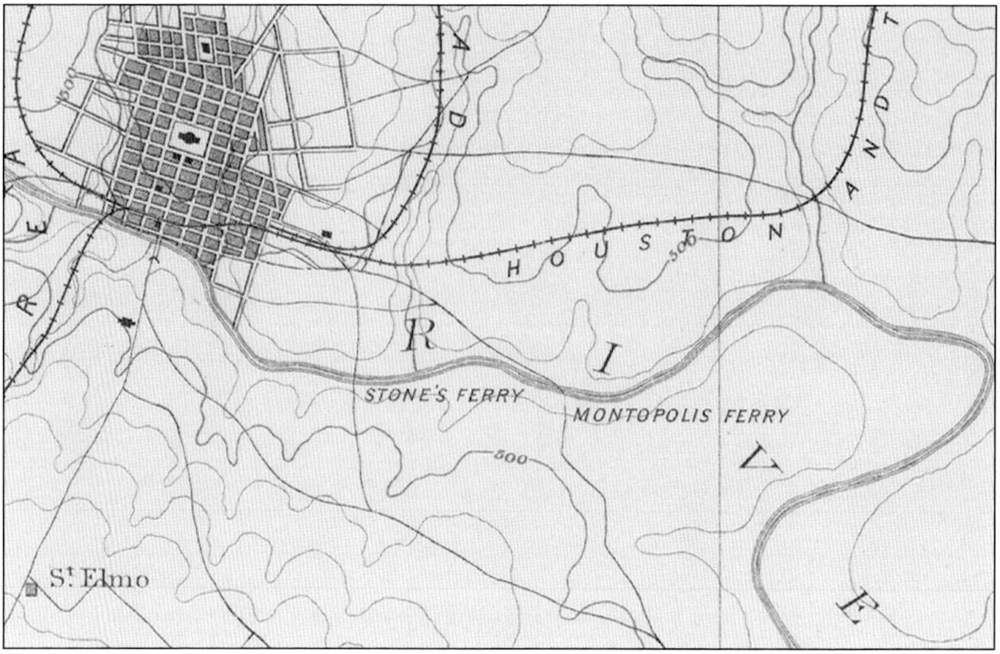


The name *Montopolis* did not show up on official government maps until the late 1800s. This 1894 US Geological Survey topographic map of Austin shows the approximate location of the Montopolis ferry. (Courtesy of the author's collection.)

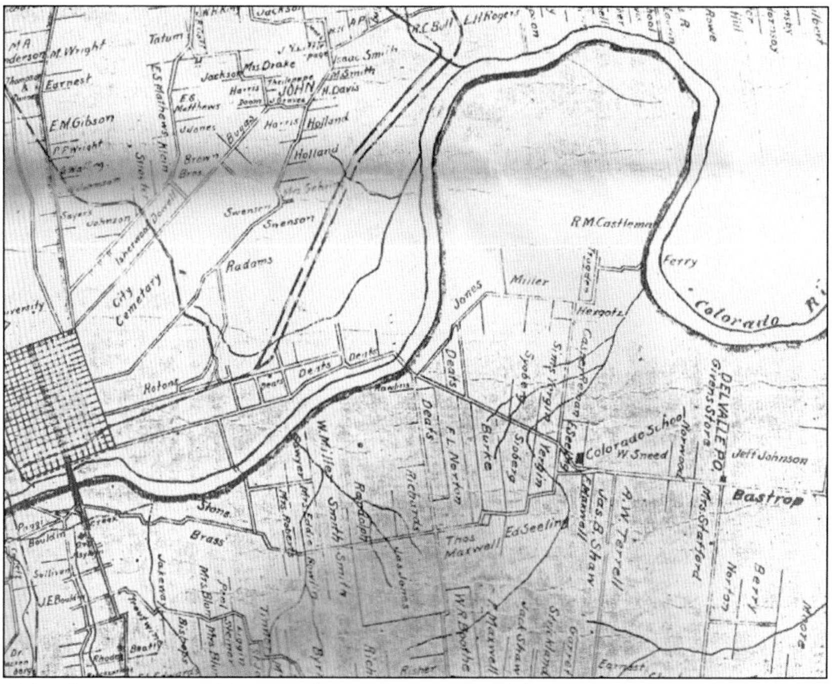


This 1898 land grant map of Austin shows the names of landowners in Montopolis, as well as the approximate locations of important landmarks such as the Colorado School and the Givens General Store. However, it does not identify the Montopolis community itself. (Courtesy of the author's collection.)

This 1910 map of Austin was the first to identify the Montopolis neighborhood by name. (Courtesy of the author's collection.)

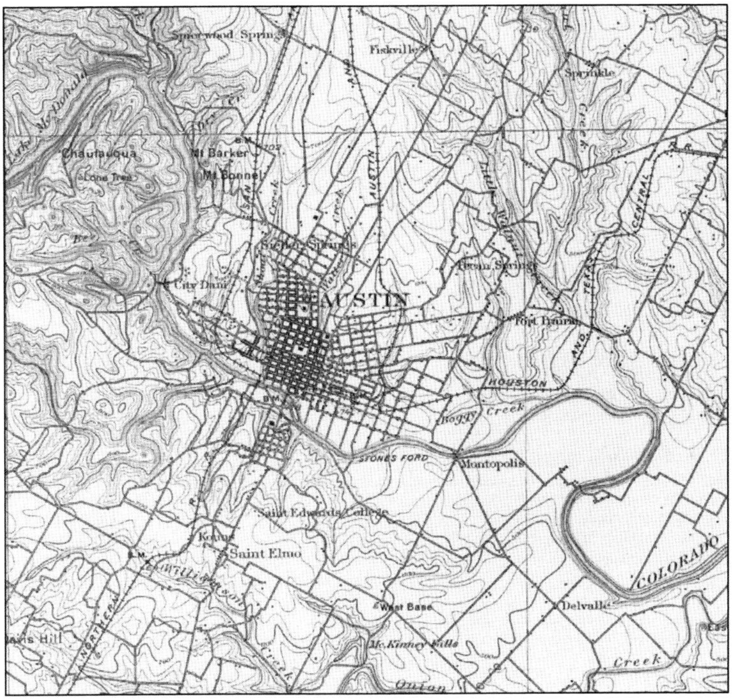


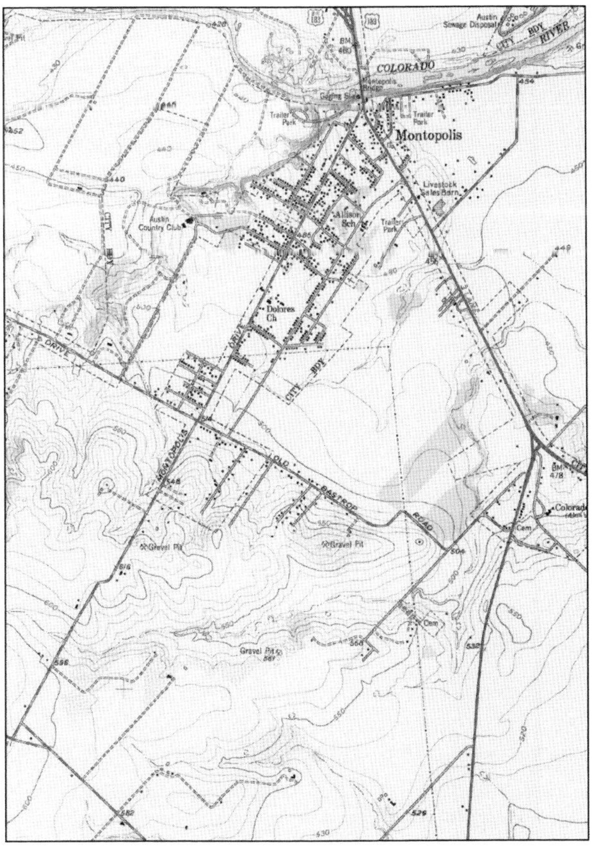


This 1955 topographic map of Montopolis is useful for determining the extent of the City of Austin's annexation of the neighborhood at the time, as well as identifying the locations of important land features in the early years of Route 183, before the extension of Riverside Drive along Old Bastrop Road. (Courtesy of the US Geological Survey.)

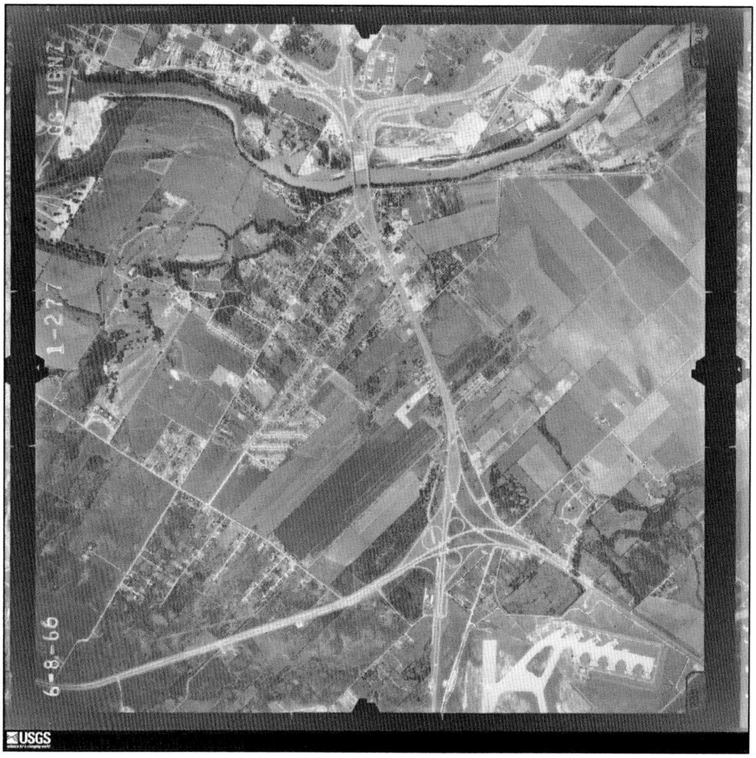


This 1966 aerial photograph of Montopolis shows the extent of rural land use at the time. Montopolis Drive, then still a dirt road, was the primary north-south thoroughfare, and Dolores Catholic Church had just built a new recreation center across the street. (Courtesy of the US Geological Survey.)

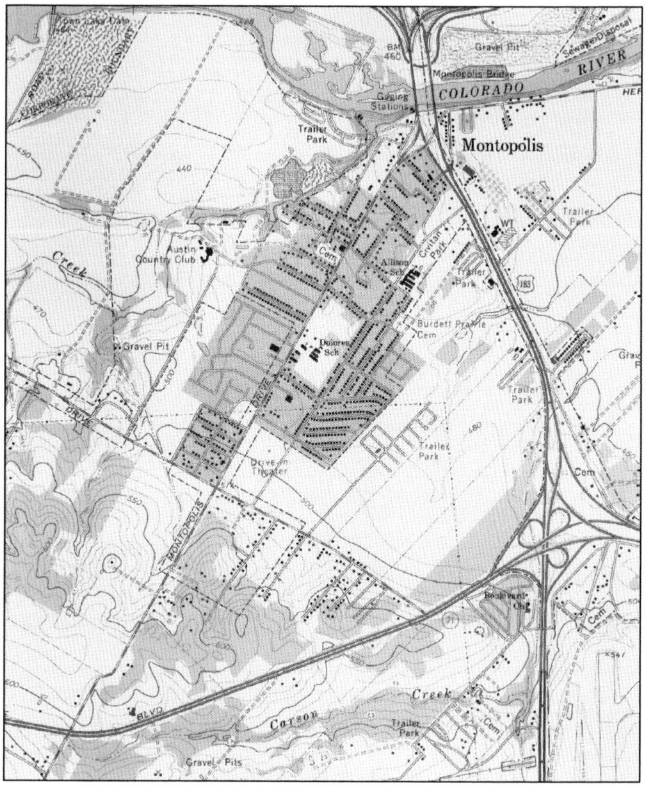


The most recent US Geological Survey topographic map of Montopolis, from 1995, shows the neighborhood's major landmarks, including Dolores Church, the Burdett Prairie Cemetery, and the San Jose Cemetery, as well as previous land uses such as the drive-in theater on the corner of Riverside and Montopolis Drives and some now-gone trailer parks. (Courtesy of the US Geological Survey.)

# *Two*

# Growth

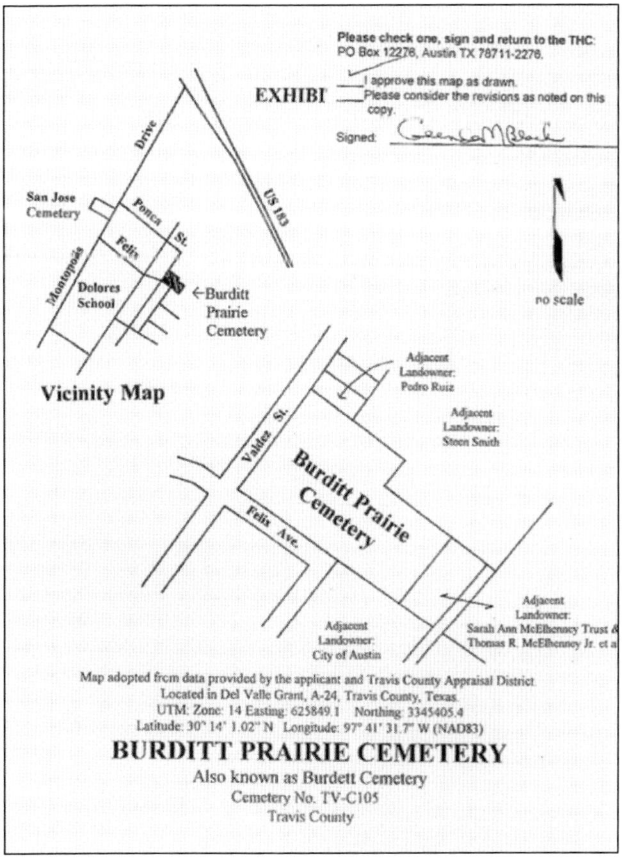


The full extent of the Burdett Prairie Cemetery became apparent in the early 1990s when the City of Austin began to explore the feasibility of installing a sports complex. The cemetery bears the name of Jesse F. Burditt (also spelled "Burdett" or "Burdette" in historical records), an early Euro-American settler and supporter of the Texas Revolution who settled in Montopolis in 1844 and established a cotton plantation. The 1850 census shows that the plantation was overseen by three of Burditt's grown sons and was worked by 25 slaves, ages 1 to 66. Burditt's other three sons moved north of the Colorado River and established cotton plantations near Fiskville in Austin, where they and their parents are buried. Burdett Prairie Cemetery was established in 1850 and is one of the most historical cemeteries in Austin. (Courtesy of the Texas Historical Commission.)

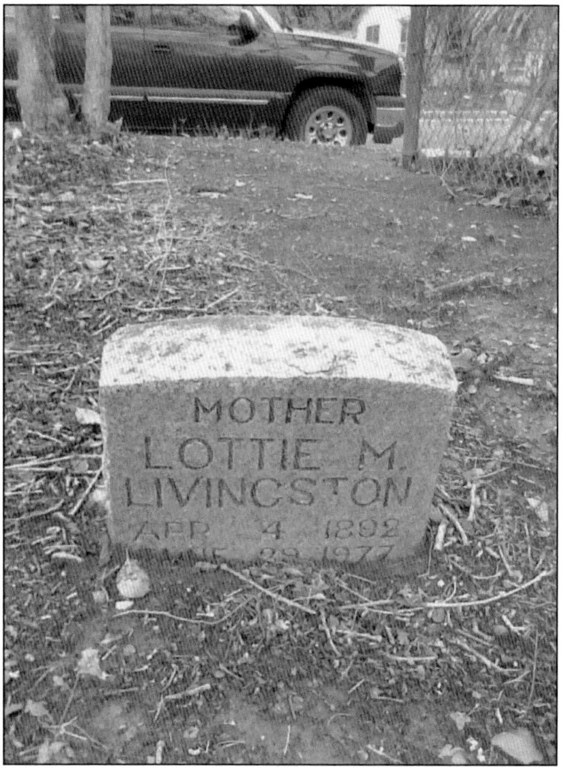


The Burdett Prairie Cemetery, still in active use, is the final resting place of dozens of former slaves and emancipated African Americans and their descendants. The full geographical extent of the cemetery is still unknown, as the eastern portion of the cemetery remains heavily vegetated and has not been properly archaeologically surveyed to date. (Courtesy of the author's collection.)

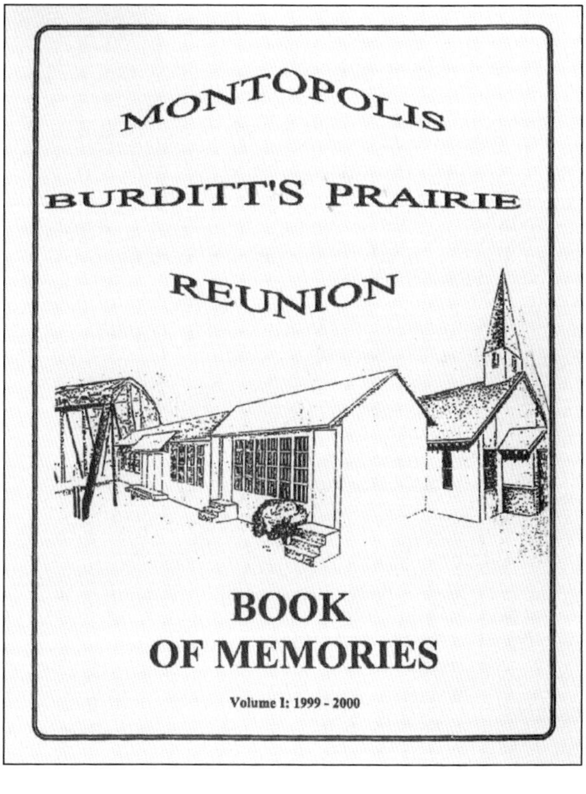


Burditt's Prairie eventually developed into a rural freedmen's settlement, with St. Edward's Baptist Church, founded in 1863, as its focal point. In addition to the church, Burditt's Prairie School educated the settlement's newly emancipated children. The school appears in records as early as the 1870s, but it was renamed the Colorado School at Burditt's Prairie in the 1920s and then simply Colorado School by the 1930s. In 1999, the church sponsored a reunion, the program of which is seen here. (Courtesy of St. Edward's Baptist Church.)

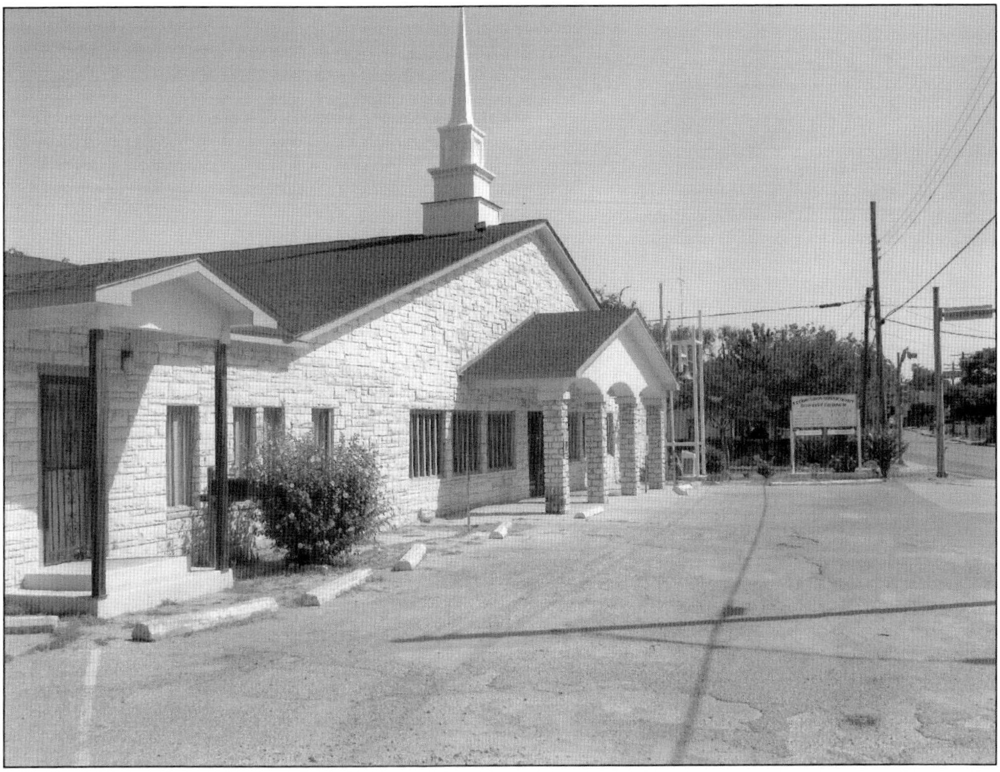

St. Edward's Baptist Church is the oldest continually operating African American Baptist church in Travis County. Many of its parishioners have strong family ties to Montopolis or are descendants of its historic black community. The original church was built closer to the cemetery, near the home of Rose Edwards, a Burditt family slave and the church's namesake. (Courtesy of the author's collection.)

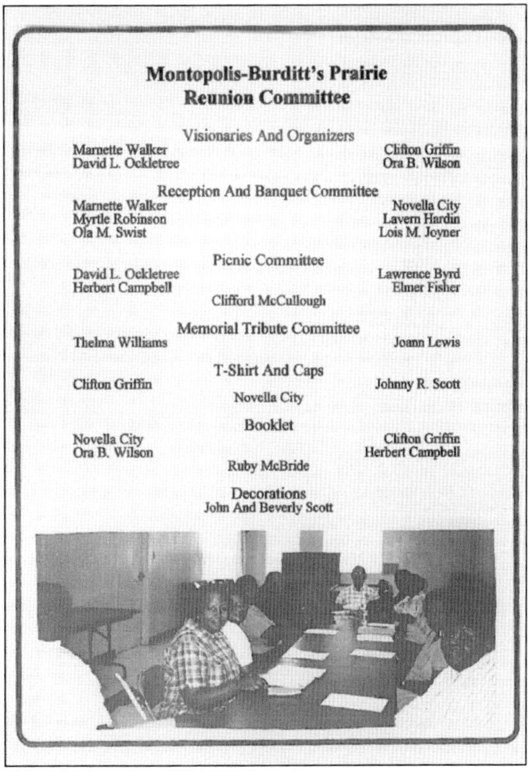

**Montopolis-Burditt's Prairie**
**Reunion Committee**

Visionaries And Organizers
Marnette Walker
David L. Ockletree
Clifton Griffin
Ora B. Wilson

Reception And Banquet Committee
Marnette Walker
Myrtle Robinson
Ola M. Swist
Novella City
Lavern Hardin
Lois M. Joyner

Picnic Committee
David L. Ockletree
Herbert Campbell
Lawrence Byrd
Elmer Fisher
Clifford McCullough

Memorial Tribute Committee
Thelma Williams
Joann Lewis

T-Shirt And Caps
Clifton Griffin
Johnny R. Scott
Novella City

Booklet
Novella City
Ora B. Wilson
Clifton Griffin
Herbert Campbell
Ruby McBride

Decorations
John And Beverly Scott

After attending numerous funerals of former classmates, four people with roots in the Montopolis community, Ora B. Wilson, Marnette Walker, David Ockletree, and Clifton Griffin, began a discussion about organizing a Montopolis school reunion. An organizing committee, consisting of those four classmates, was formed in April 1999. People came from all over Austin and the rest of Texas, as well as several other states, to attend. The highlight of the reunion was the participation of Delores Merriweather, a teacher in the 1940s. (Courtesy of St. Edward's Baptist Church.)

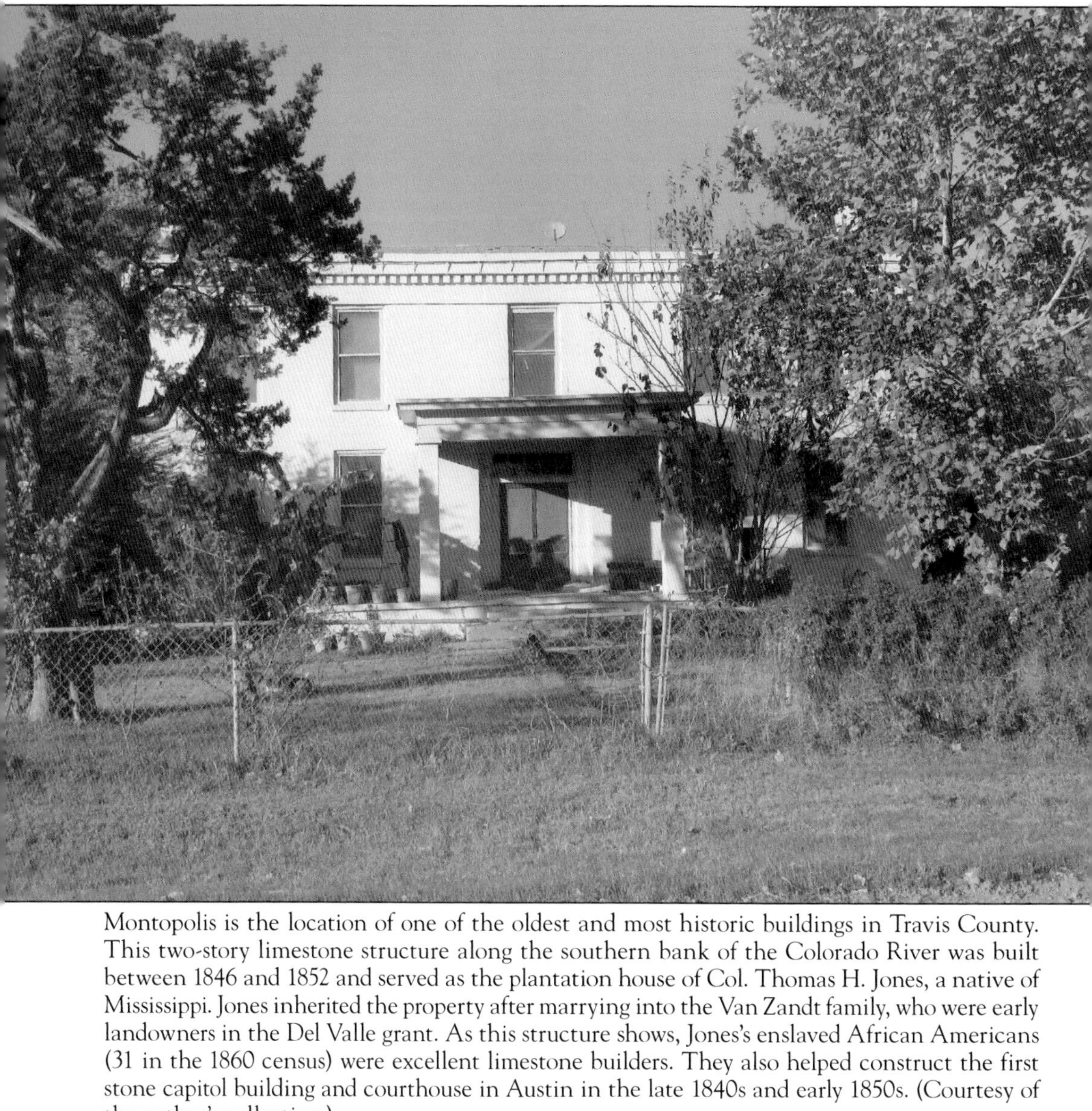

Montopolis is the location of one of the oldest and most historic buildings in Travis County. This two-story limestone structure along the southern bank of the Colorado River was built between 1846 and 1852 and served as the plantation house of Col. Thomas H. Jones, a native of Mississippi. Jones inherited the property after marrying into the Van Zandt family, who were early landowners in the Del Valle grant. As this structure shows, Jones's enslaved African Americans (31 in the 1860 census) were excellent limestone builders. They also helped construct the first stone capitol building and courthouse in Austin in the late 1840s and early 1850s. (Courtesy of the author's collection.)

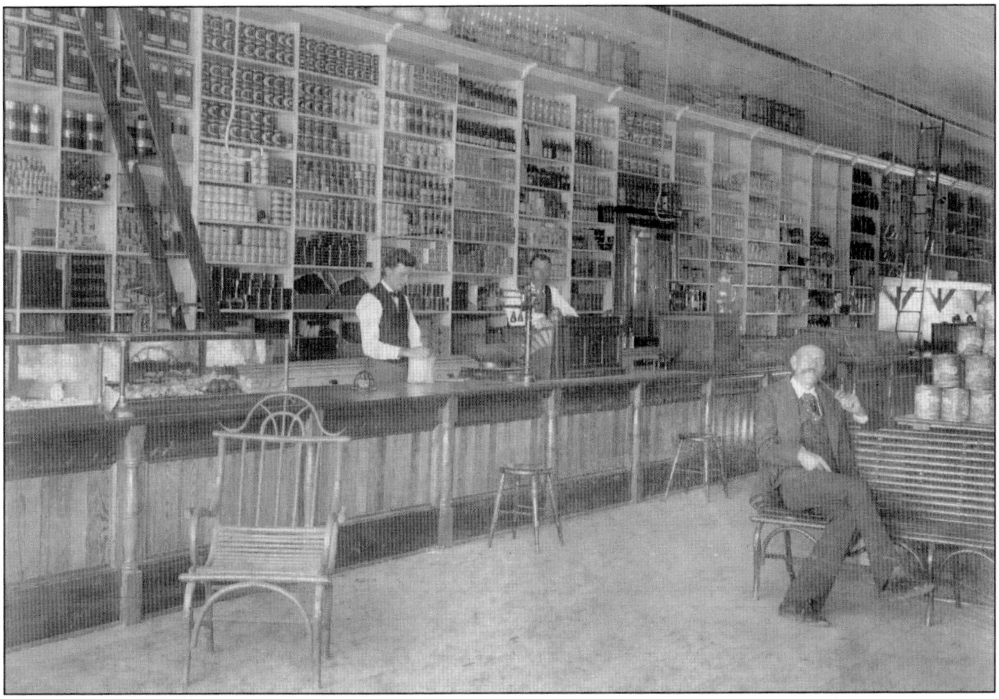

William M. Givens (1850–1933) came to the Montopolis–Del Valle area in 1874 and established the Givens General Store, which became a focal point for the region in the late 1800s and early 1900s. He is seen here seated at right.

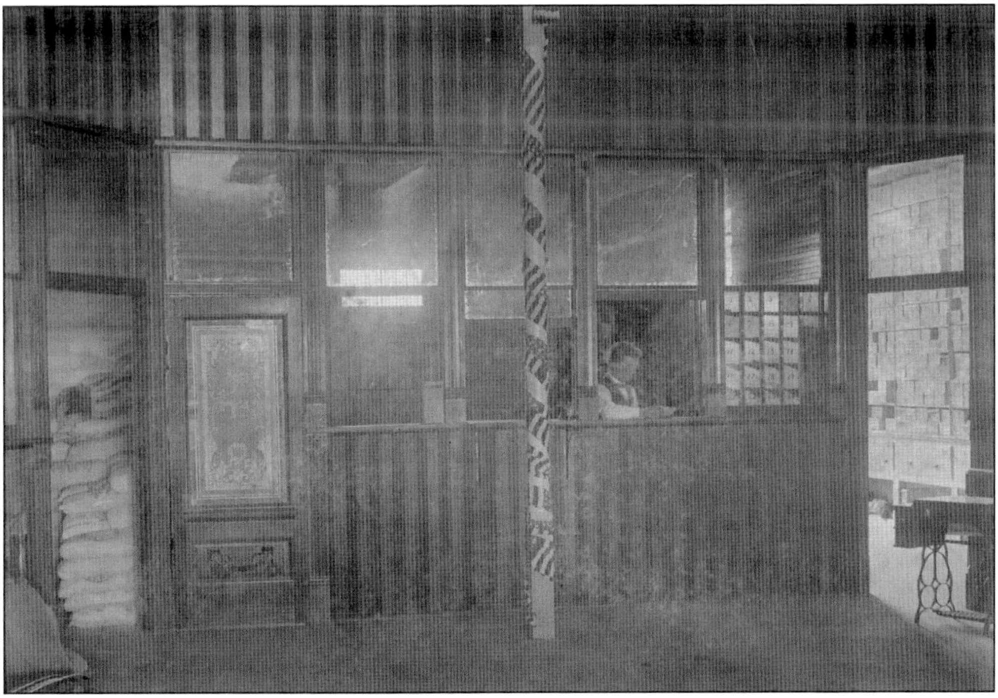

The Givens General Store also housed the Del Valle post office. This late-1800s photograph shows Eugene A. Murchison, the post office clerk.

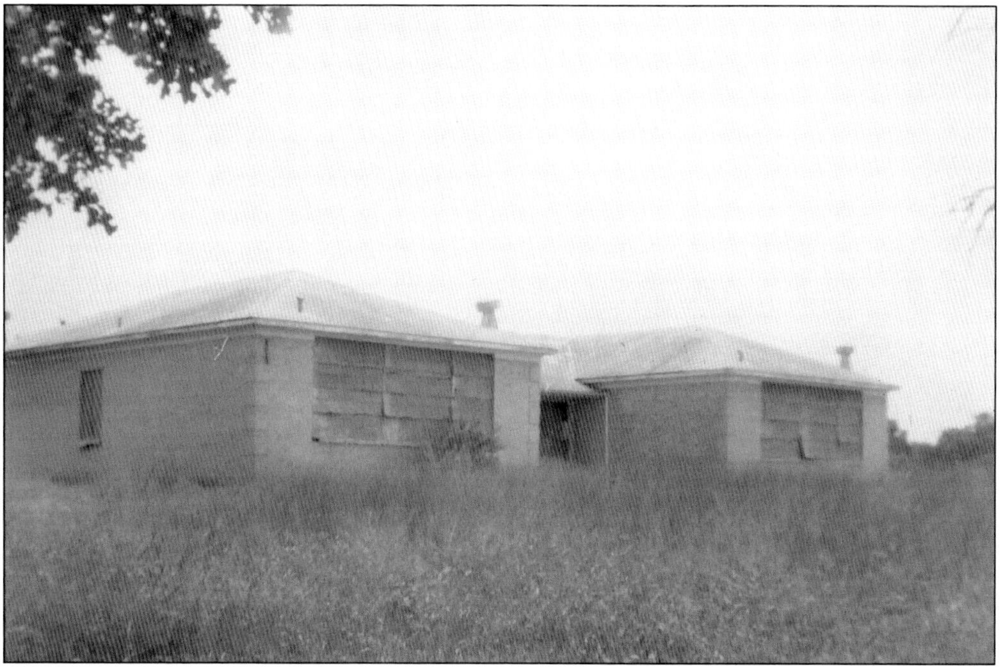

The Colorado Negro School, also known as the Colorado School for Negro Children and the Montopolis Negro School, educated the post-emancipation children of the rural area's sharecropping workforce.

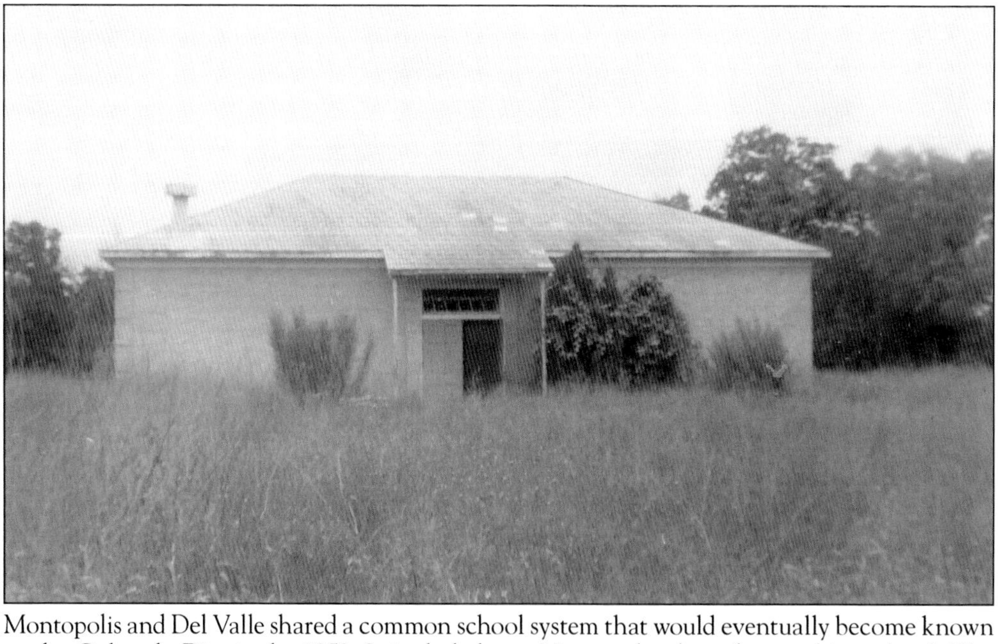

Montopolis and Del Valle shared a common school system that would eventually become known as the Colorado District by 1952. It included two Negro schools and one white school. The children of Mexican sharecroppers often were not required to attend school, but, when they did, they mostly attended church schools, or, occasionally, one of the Negro schools. However, the J.B. Norwood Mexican School was eventually established near Moore's Crossing to service the area's increasing Mexican population.

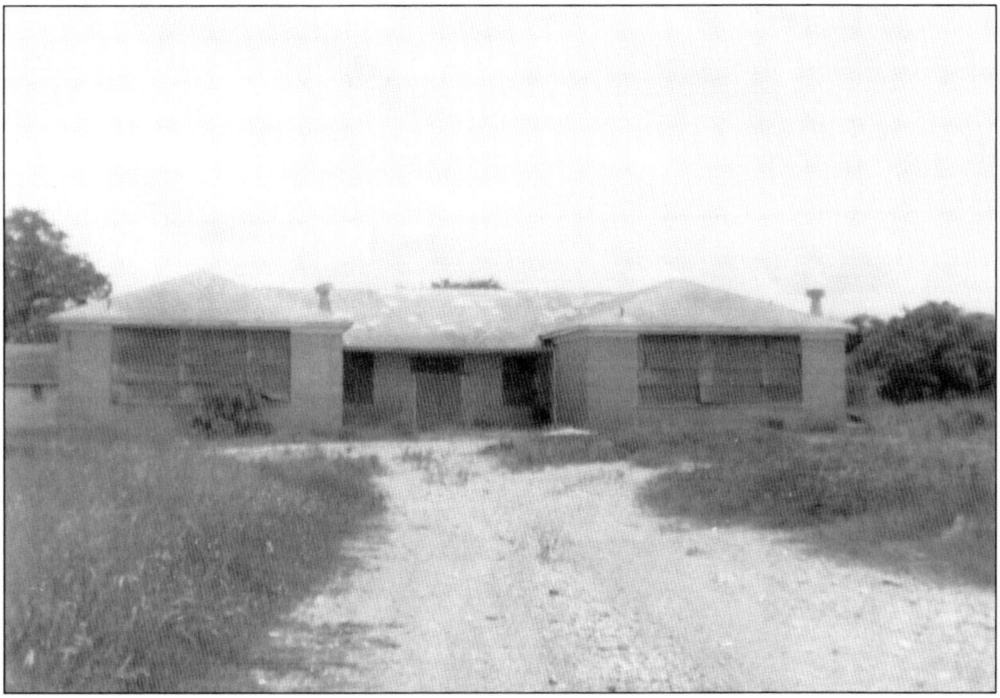

In 1952, Austin began annexing the northern portions of the Montopolis neighborhood. The move produced educational confusion because, as a rural community south of the Colorado River, Montopolis children were educated alongside peers from neighborhoods such as Del Valle, Creedmoor, Pilot Knob, and Elroy. After a series of consolidations, the Colorado District eventually became the Del Valle Independent School District in 1963. Pictured here are school structures in the Colorado District around 1958.

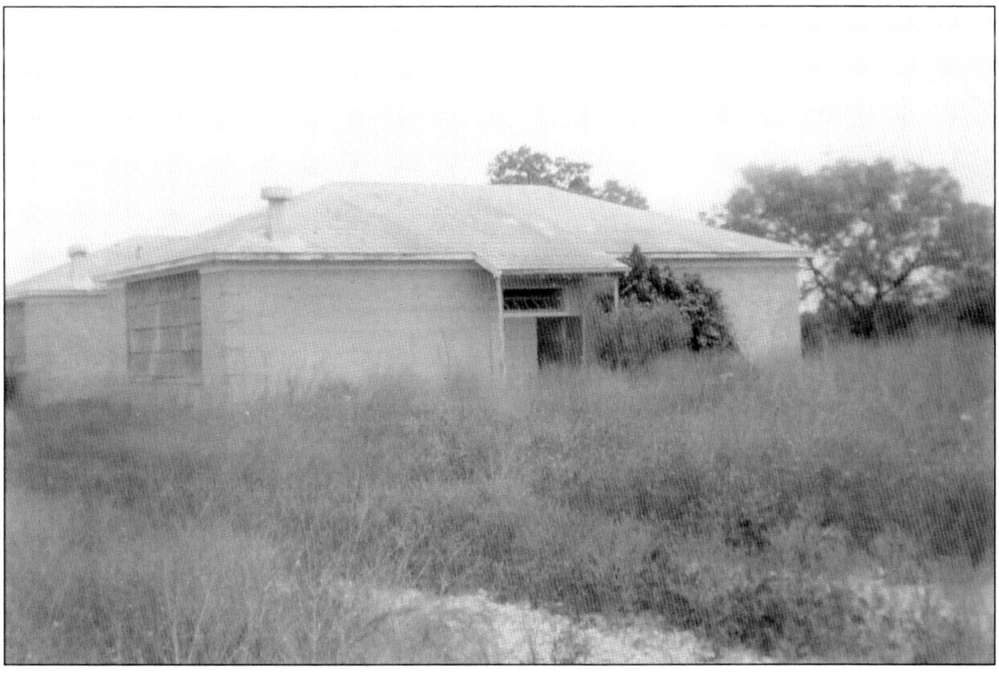

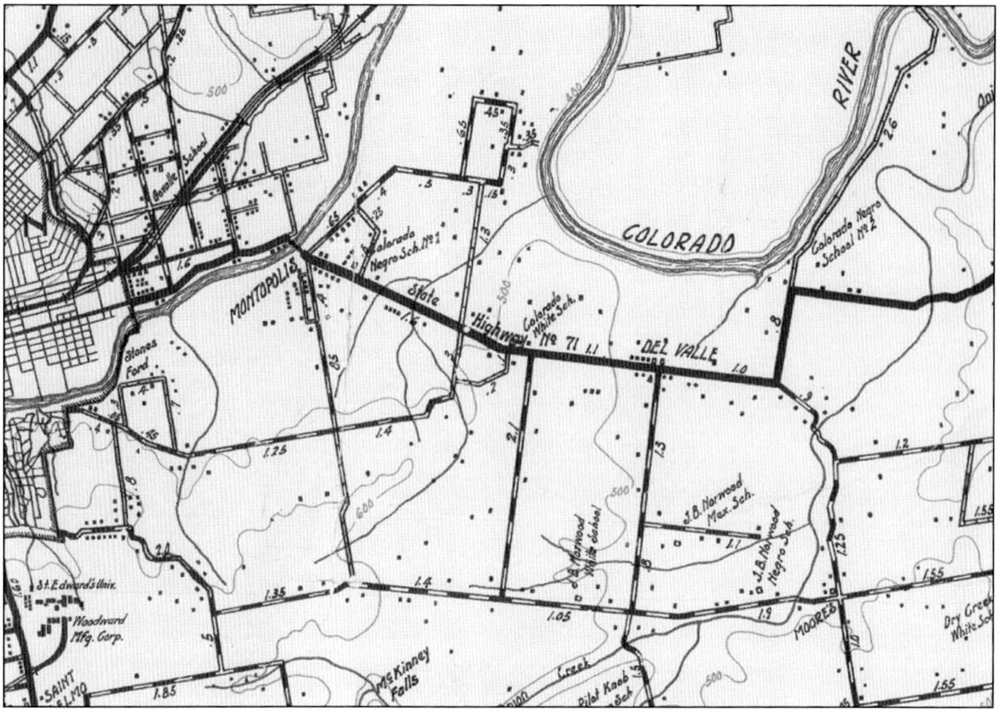


The 1932 topographic and road map of Travis County, prepared by the county engineering department, shows the locations of schools in Montopolis and Del Valle. The two Colorado black schools, as well as the Colorado white school, were located north of Highway 71, whereas the J.B. Norwood schools were located south of the highway towards Moore's Crossing. (Courtesy of Travis County.)

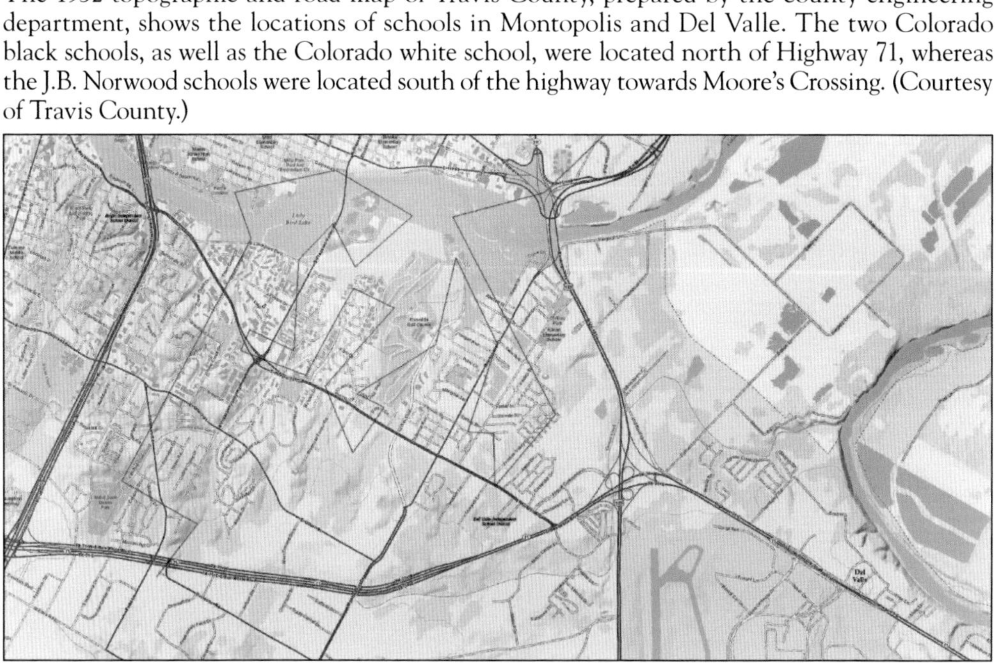

The boundary between the Austin and Del Valle Independent School Districts is a studied example of gerrymandering. Because of the Montopolis neighborhood's quirky location in the southeastern outskirts of Austin and its historical associations with Del Valle, Dove Springs, Creedmoor, and similar locales, some of the neighborhood's children attend Del Valle schools while a sizable number attend Austin schools. (Courtesy of the US Department of Education.)

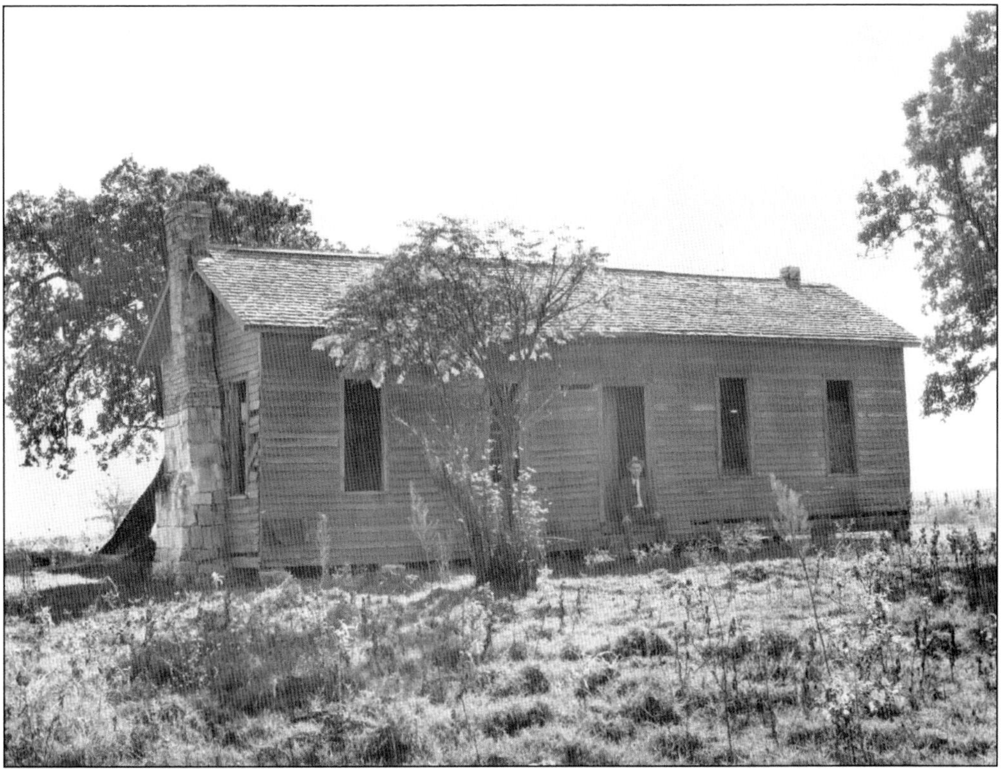

By the early 1900s, almost all of the original buildings in Montopolis, built in the mid-1800s, were gone. Some survived, however, including the old Montopolis Courthouse, said to have been the first courthouse in Travis County. This photograph shows Sgt. Leslie J. Fox of the Austin Police Department in the doorway of the courthouse in November 1937.

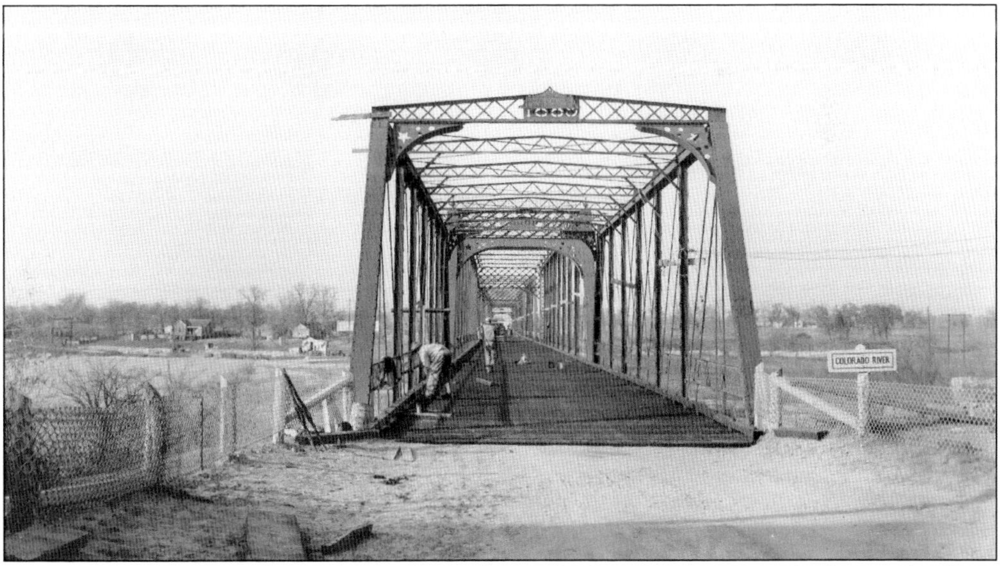


Construction of the original Montopolis Bridge in the late 1880s was watched very closely on both sides of the river. Travis County used $15,000 of questionable bond financing to build the bridge, and local newspaper coverage of the bridge's construction was critical.

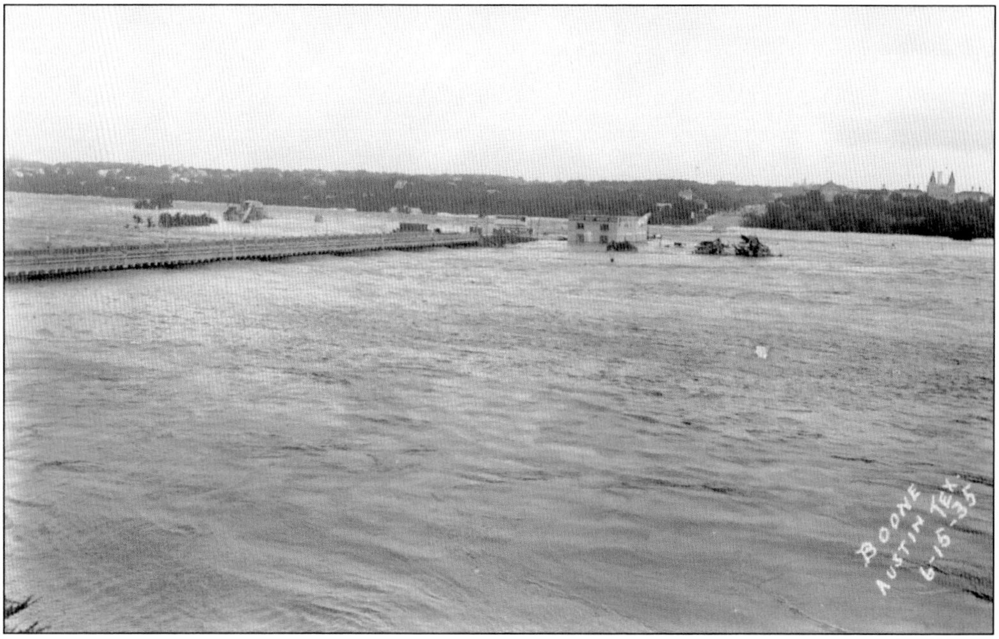


The 1935 flood that washed away the Montopolis Bridge wreaked havoc on bridges in Austin as well, as this photograph from June 15, 1935, shows.

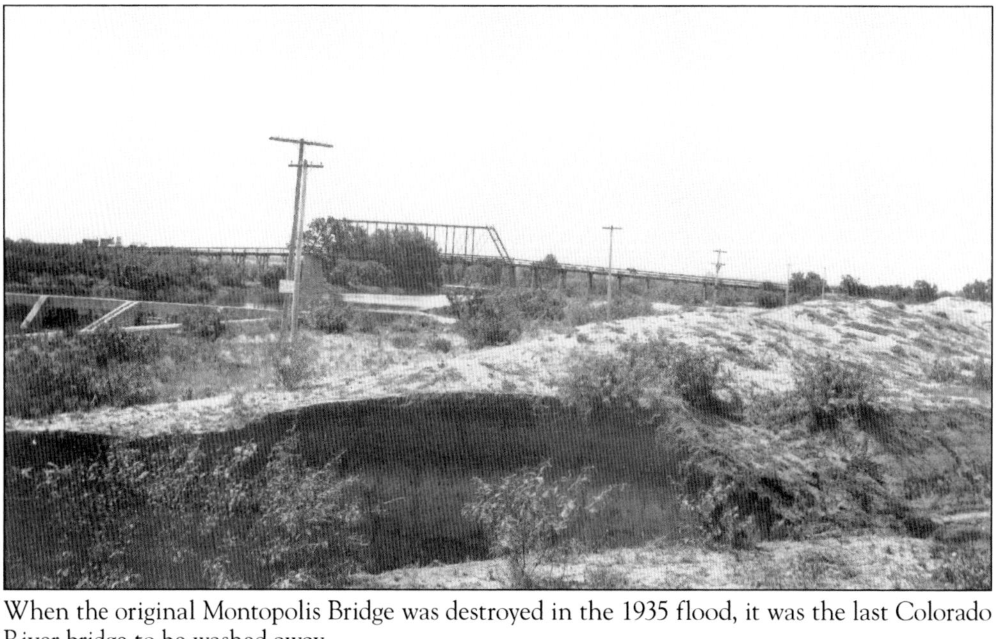

When the original Montopolis Bridge was destroyed in the 1935 flood, it was the last Colorado River bridge to be washed away.

# *Three*

# Migration and Poverty Island

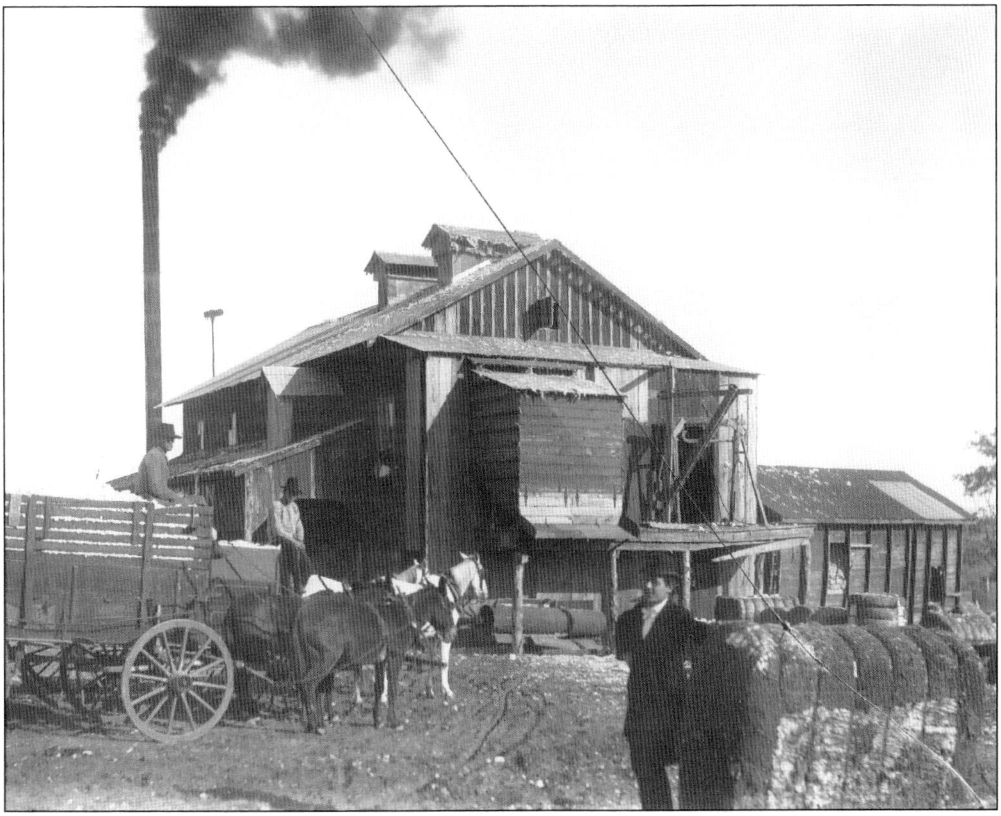

When Montopolis and Del Valle planters installed two cotton gins, like the one seen here, on their farms in the 1880s, it not only set the stage for an increase in agricultural production, but also for an increase in migration, both inward and outward.

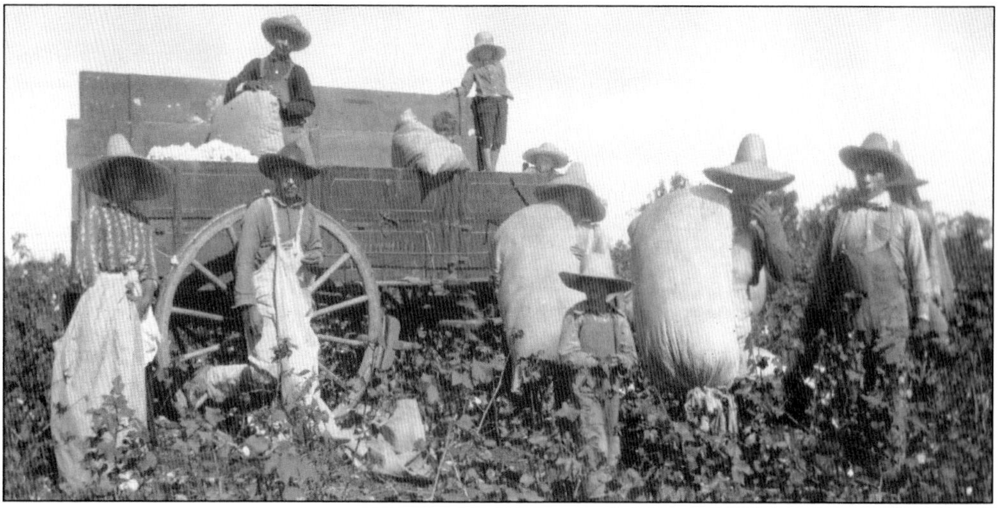

Once it became clear that Austin, not Montopolis, would be the region's metropolis, Euro-American settlers resolved themselves to develop the rural area as best they could. This meant the intensification of plantation agriculture. It also meant slavery and, after emancipation, sharecropping. While African Americans continued to predominate, by the 1920s, Mexican migration to rural areas such as Montopolis began to pick up steam, and black cotton workers increasingly found themselves working alongside Mexican farmhands.

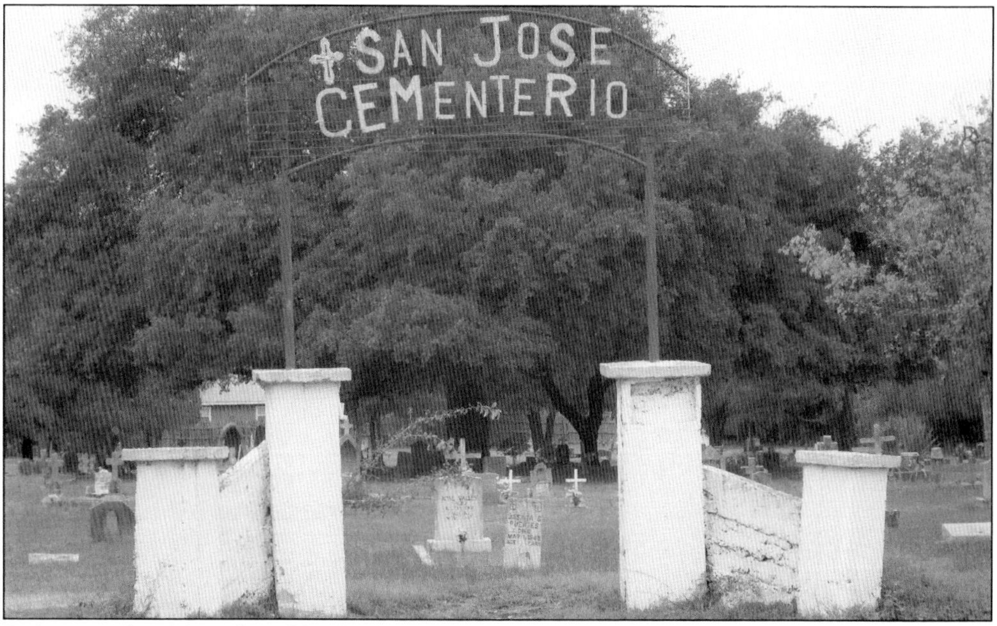


Embarrassed and humiliated by the fact that officials in rural Travis County forced Mexicans to bury their dead in indigent or African American cemeteries, various mutual aid societies began to organize and raise funds in the late 1910s and early 1920s for the platting and construction of Mexican cemeteries. The San Jose Cemetery, located along Montopolis Drive, is one of a series of Mexican cemeteries that began appearing at this time. The land for the San Jose Cemetery was donated by Lizzie Henry, an African American woman who died in 1980 and was buried at the Burdett Prairie Cemetery. Arturo Lehman and Phillipe Acosta were the cemetery's cofounders. (Courtesy of the author's collection.)

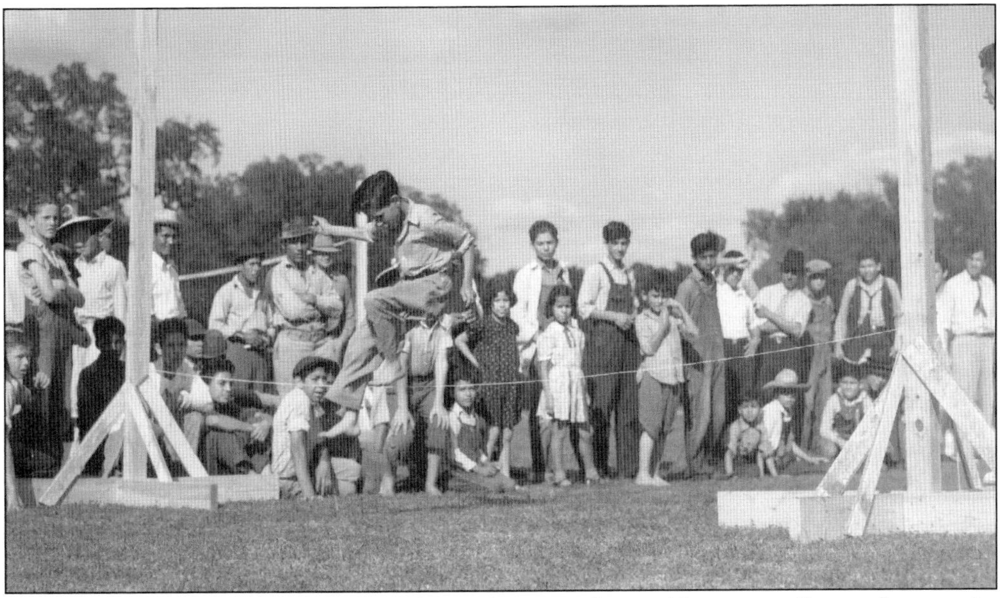

In the early 1930s, young Mexican residents of Montopolis would occasionally travel across the bridge to participate in recreational activities at Zaragosa Park, Austin's designated Mexican park. Established in 1931, the park's construction followed the city's segregationist establishment of the Rosewood Park for Negroes in 1930. This photograph is from January 9, 1934.

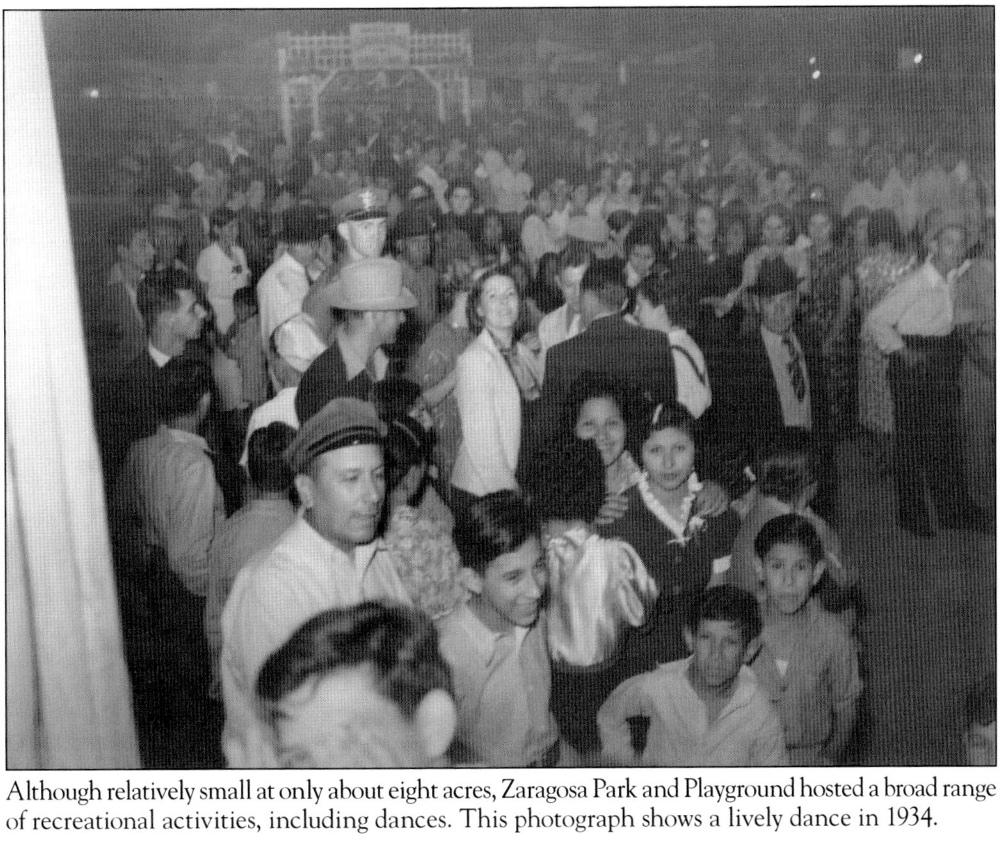

Although relatively small at only about eight acres, Zaragosa Park and Playground hosted a broad range of recreational activities, including dances. This photograph shows a lively dance in 1934.

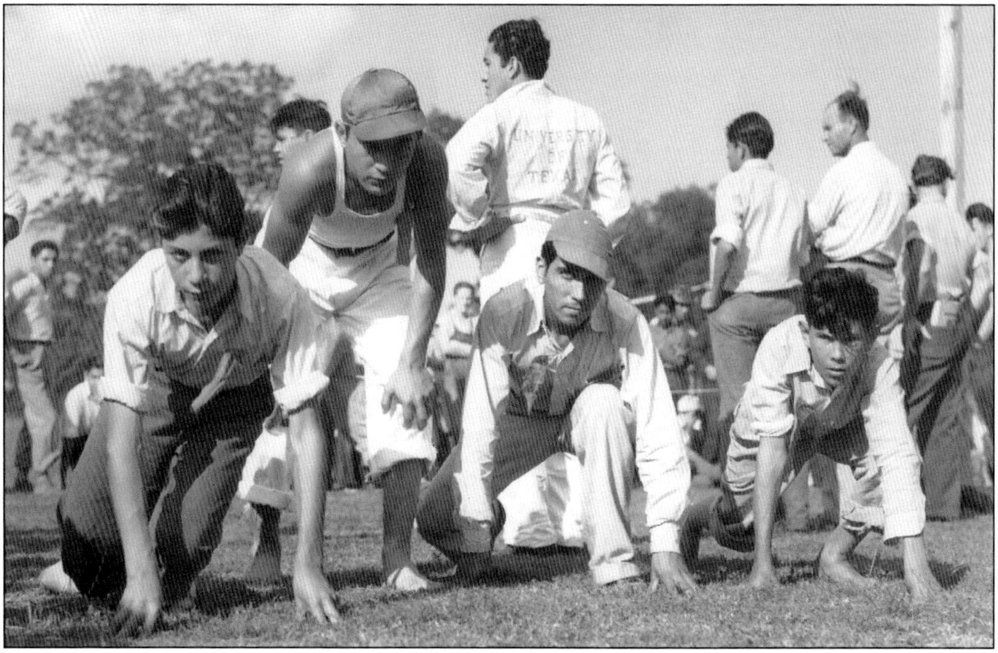

Lively athletic competitions were a common occurrence at Zaragosa Park in the 1930s. By the 1950s and 1960s, however, gang fights between Mexican gangs from East Austin and Montopolis began to replace these more collegial competitions.

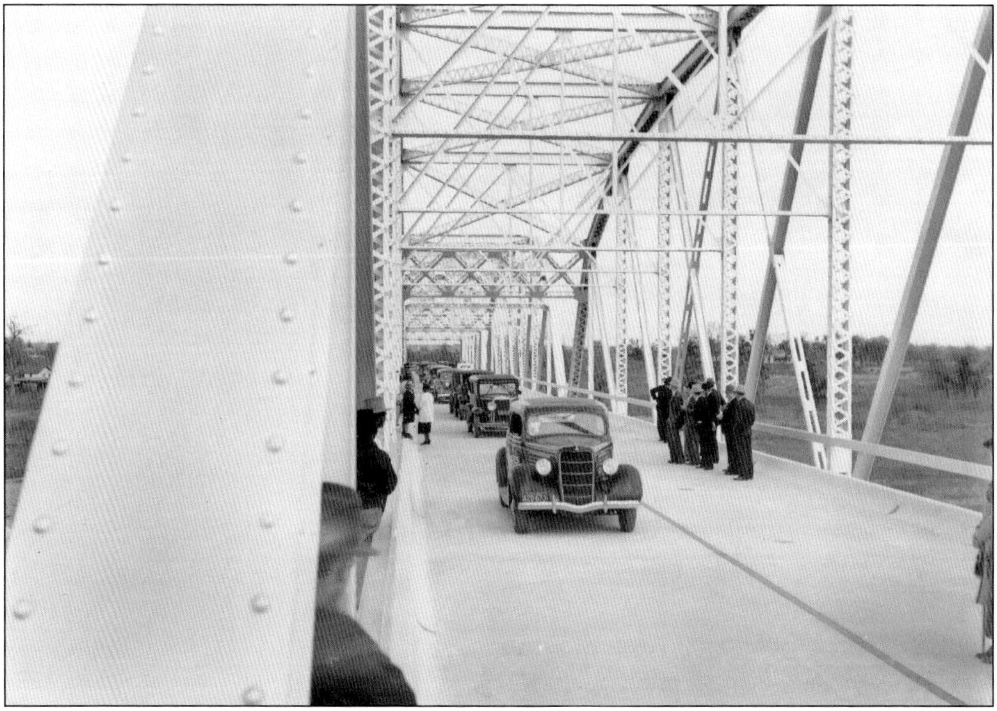

The 1935 destruction of the original Montopolis Bridge allowed the replacement bridge to be constructed with federal relief funding. In this photograph, the first cars drive across the new Montopolis Bridge, completed and dedicated in 1938.

This photograph shows the bronze plaque on the south side of the Montopolis Bridge commemorating its construction. The plaque reads, "Colorado River Bridge; Built in 1938 by the Texas Highway Department; United States Bureau of Public Roads; State Highway Commission: Robert Lee Bobbitt, Chairman; John Wood, Member; Harry Hines, Member; Julian Montgomery, Highway Engineer; Vincennes Steel Corp. Contractors." (Courtesy of the author's collection.)

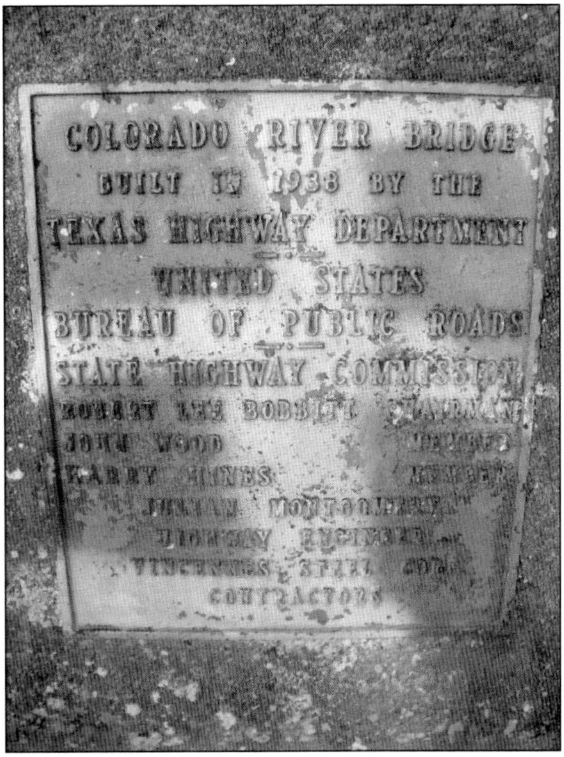


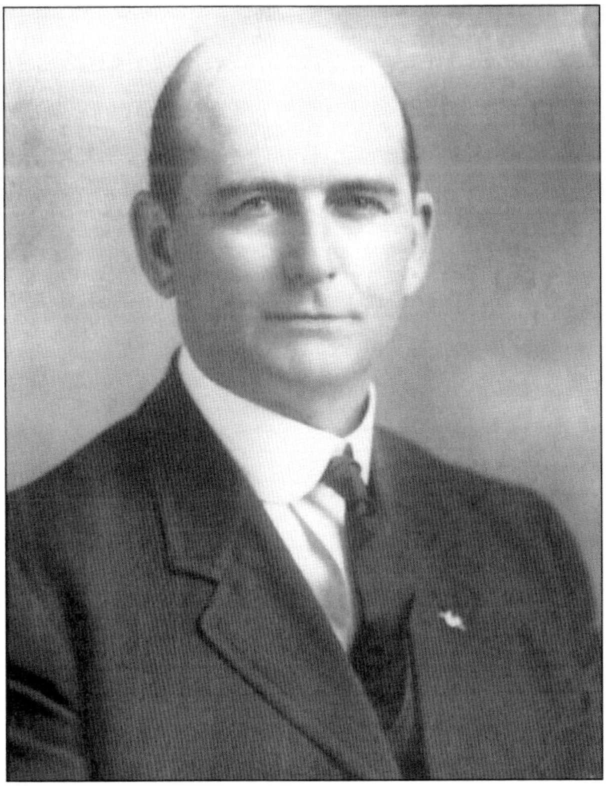

George S. Matthews (1867–1960) served as the Travis County sheriff from 1903 to 1920 and as the county judge from 1921 to 1948. He was first employed by Travis County in 1895 as the superintendent for a road-building crew and was intimately familiar with the original Montopolis Bridge. Immediately after the dedication ceremony for the new bridge in 1938, he burned the $14,000 in indebtedness bonds that were left over from the construction of the original bridge. (Courtesy of the Travis County Sheriff's Office.)

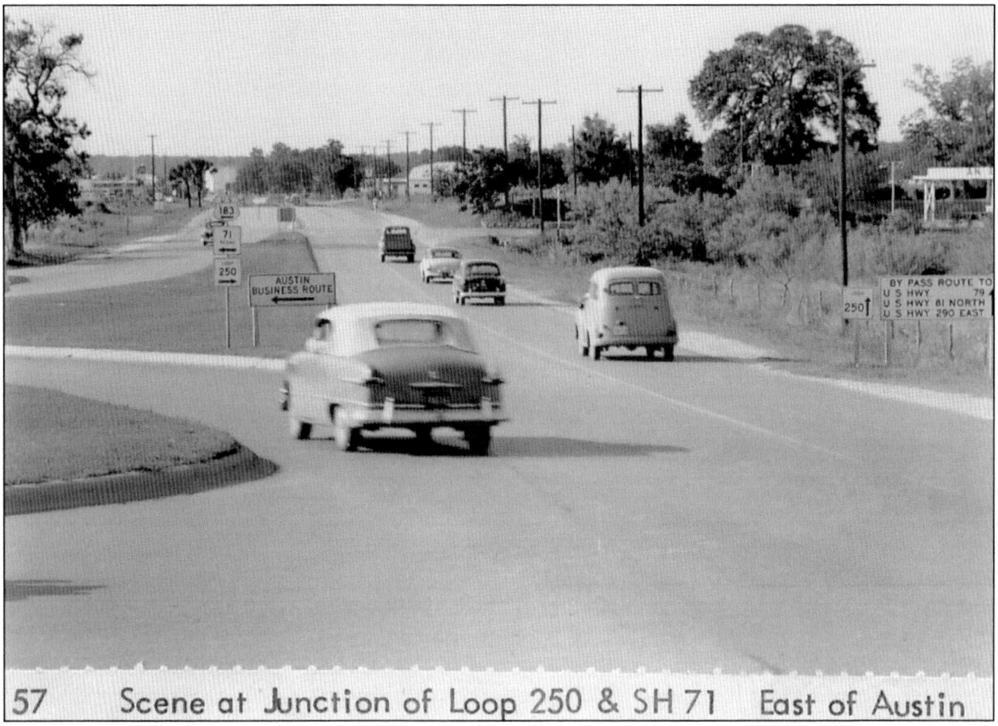


This is an early-1950s view of the north bank of the Colorado River just after crossing the Montopolis Bridge, at the intersection of First, Fifth, and Seventh Streets driving north. The Montopolis Drive-In was located to the right. (Courtesy of the Texas Department of Transportation.)

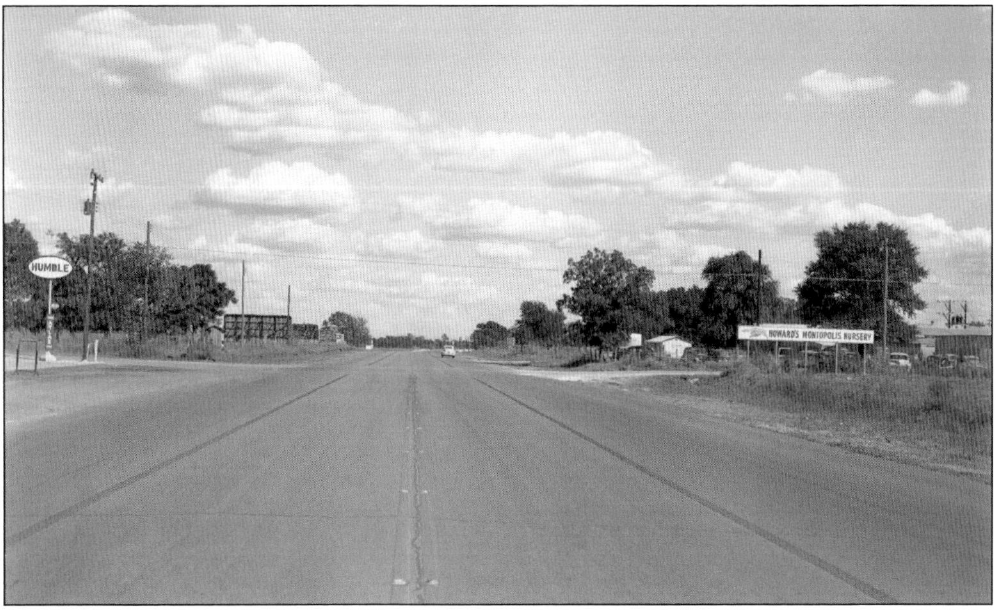


If one continued driving westward along Seventh Street toward Austin after crossing the Montopolis Bridge, they would encounter signs for a Humble gas station on the left and Howard's Montopolis Nursery on the right. The Howard family sold their Shady Lane property in 2004, but it continues in use as a nursery today.

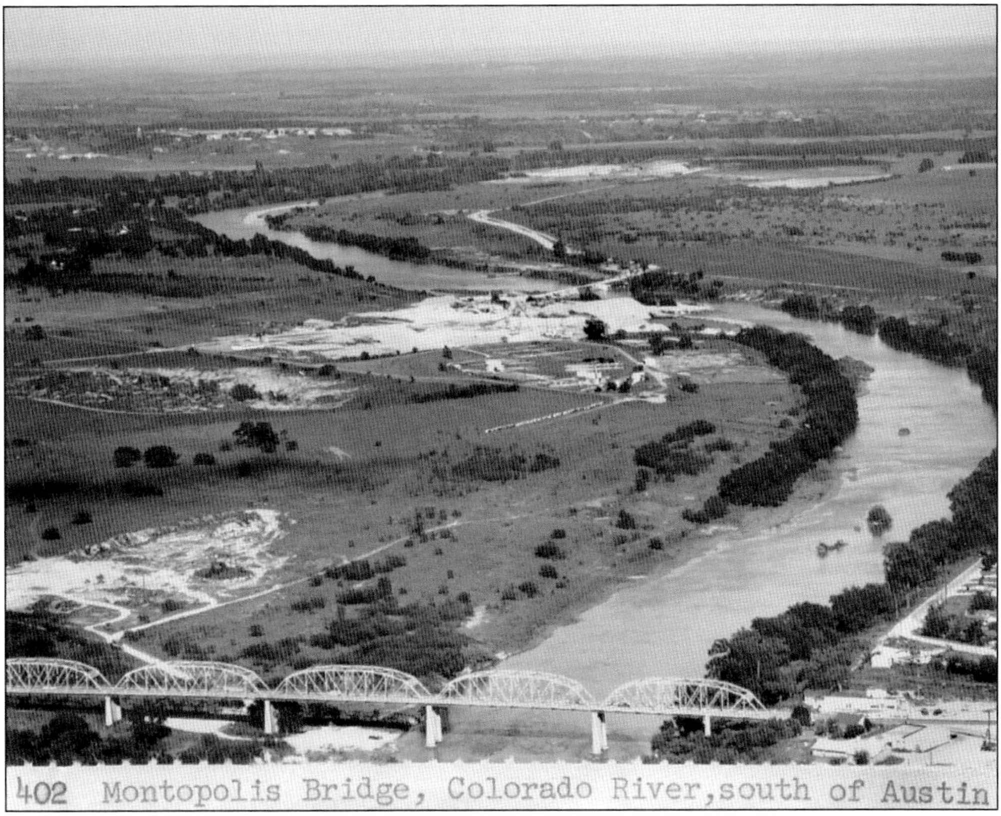


This 1959 Texas Highway Department photograph shows a good glimpse of the Montopolis Bridge, as well as the southeastern outskirts of Austin along the Colorado River. (Courtesy of the Texas Department of Transportation.)

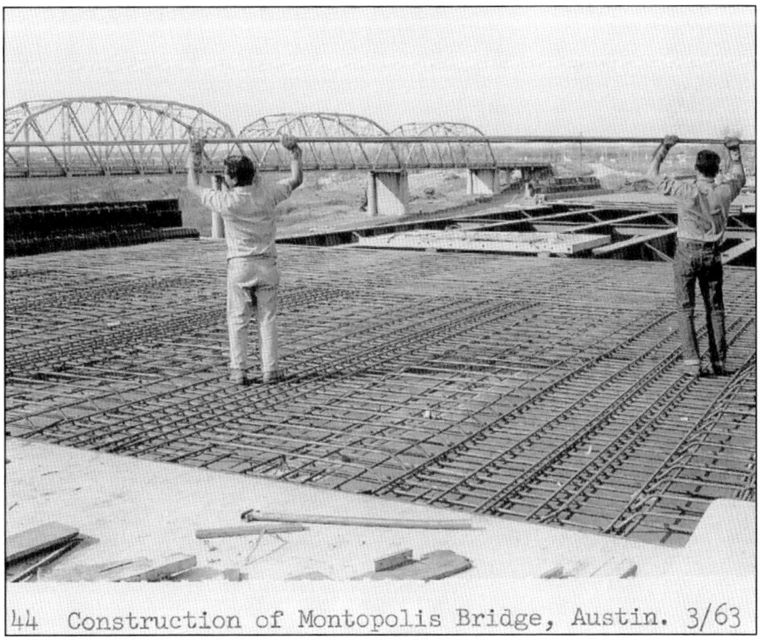


In 1963, the Texas Highway Department began construction of another span across the Colorado River in conjunction with the construction of Highway 183 and its conversion from Route 29 and Loop 250. (Courtesy of the Texas Department of Transportation.)

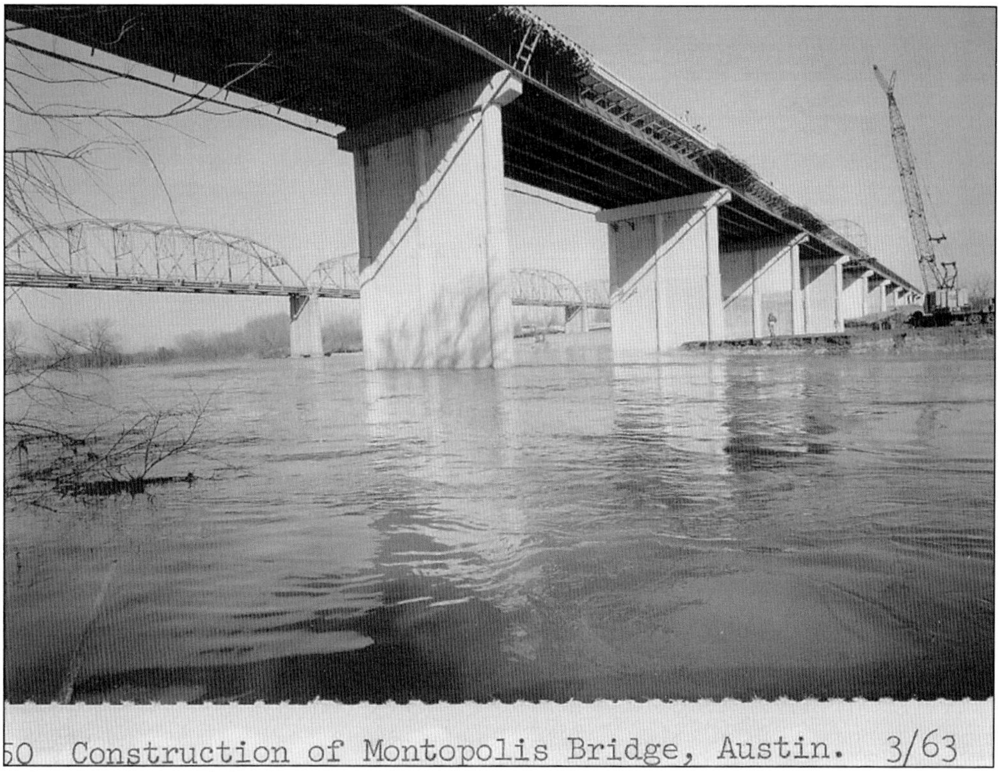


After completion of this bridge in the 1960s, another intermediate span was installed in the 1980s, which currently serves as the Colorado River crossing for motorists driving southbound on Route 183. The full freeway project was never realized, and three banks of four piers stand by themselves in the riverbank with no bridge going across them. (Courtesy of the Texas Department of Transportation.)

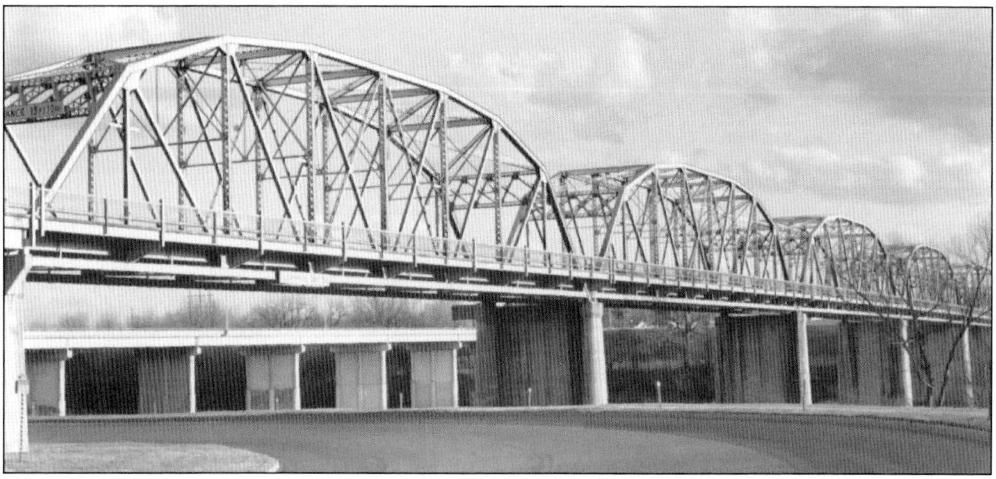

Although the Montopolis Bridge now serves traffic on Highway 183 (formerly Route 29), it was built to carry Route 71 over the Colorado River. Route 71 originated in downtown Austin along East First Street (now Cesar Chavez Street), paralleling the river for about a mile beyond the city limits before turning south to cross it. The route continued southeast towards the Gulf Coast through Bastrop, La Grange, Columbus, and El Campo. This photograph shows the bridge in February 1971.

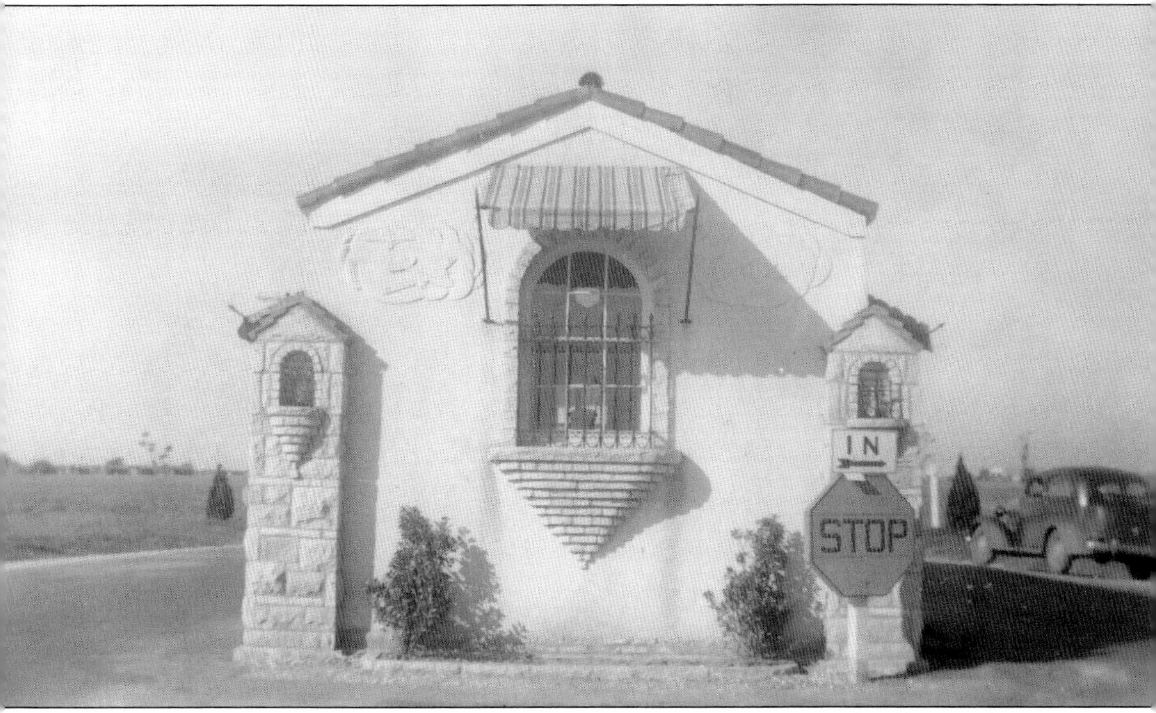


When the US government purchased most of the farming property in Del Valle in order to construct Del Valle Army Air Base, many residents of the area lost their jobs working on the farms and migrated into Montopolis, where they built homes and operated businesses that catered to the servicemen stationed in the area. This photograph of the main gate at the air base is from 1942, one year before it was renamed in honor of John August Earl Bergstrom, Austin's first casualty of World War II.

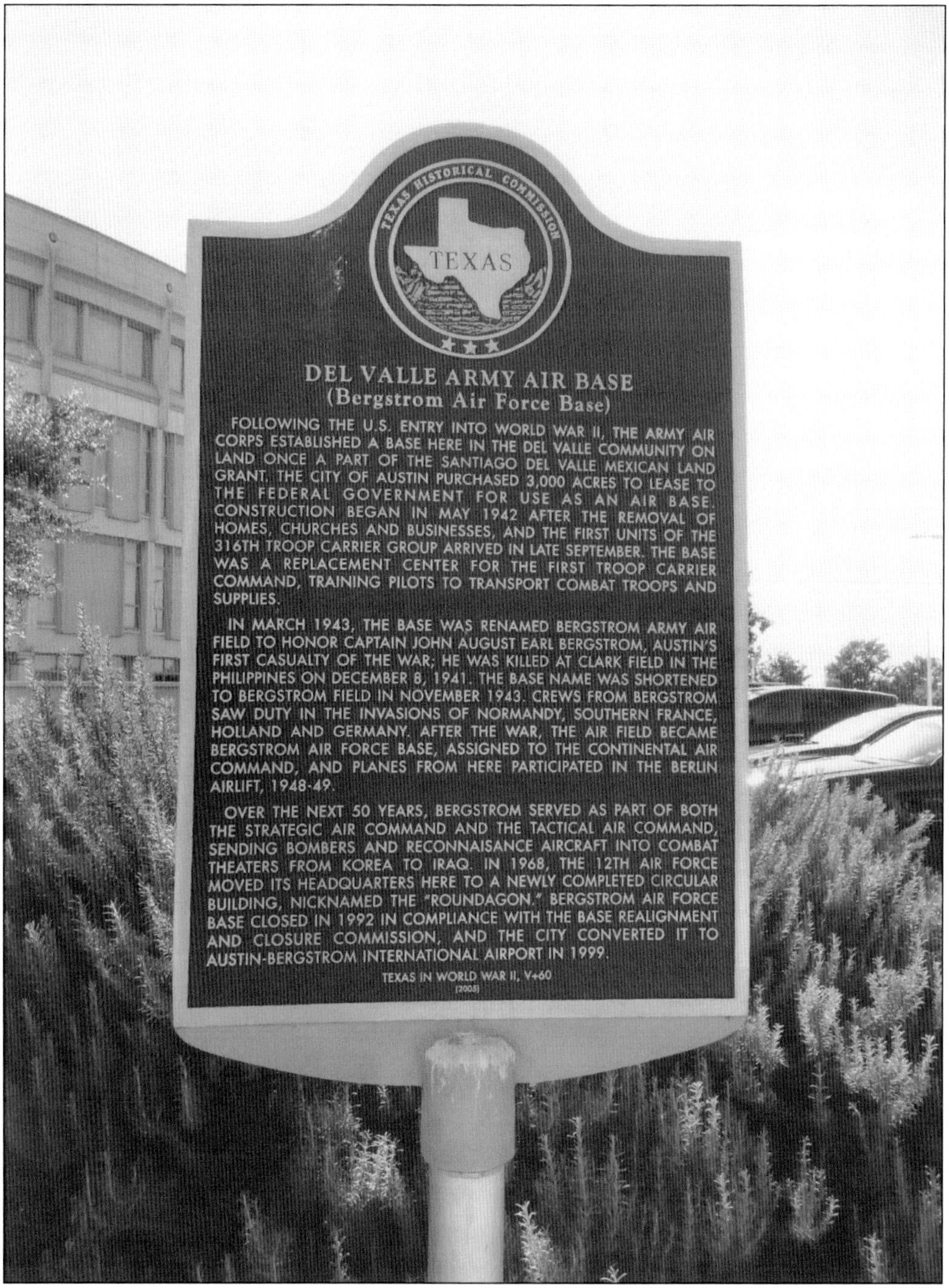


The City of Austin purchased 3,000 acres to lease to the federal government for use as an air base. Construction began in May 1942 after the removal of homes, churches, and businesses, and the first units of the 316th Troop Carrier Group arrived in late September. The base closed in 1992, and the city converted it to Austin-Bergstrom International Airport in 1999. (Courtesy of the author's collection.)

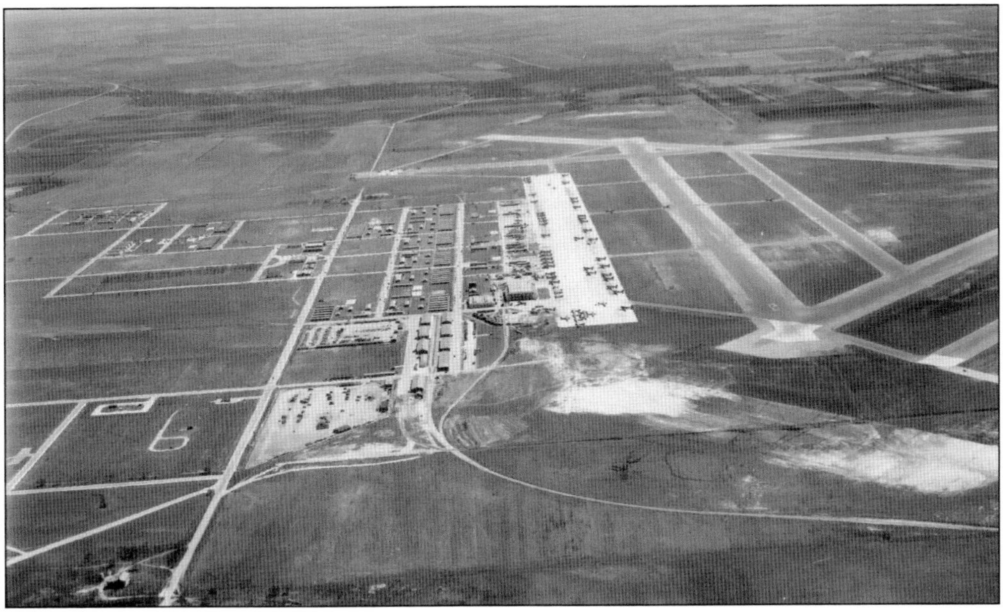

Bergstrom Army Air Field is seen here around 1943. It was originally known as the Del Valle Army Air Base. The surrounding farmland and farm structures demonstrate the base's rural origins.

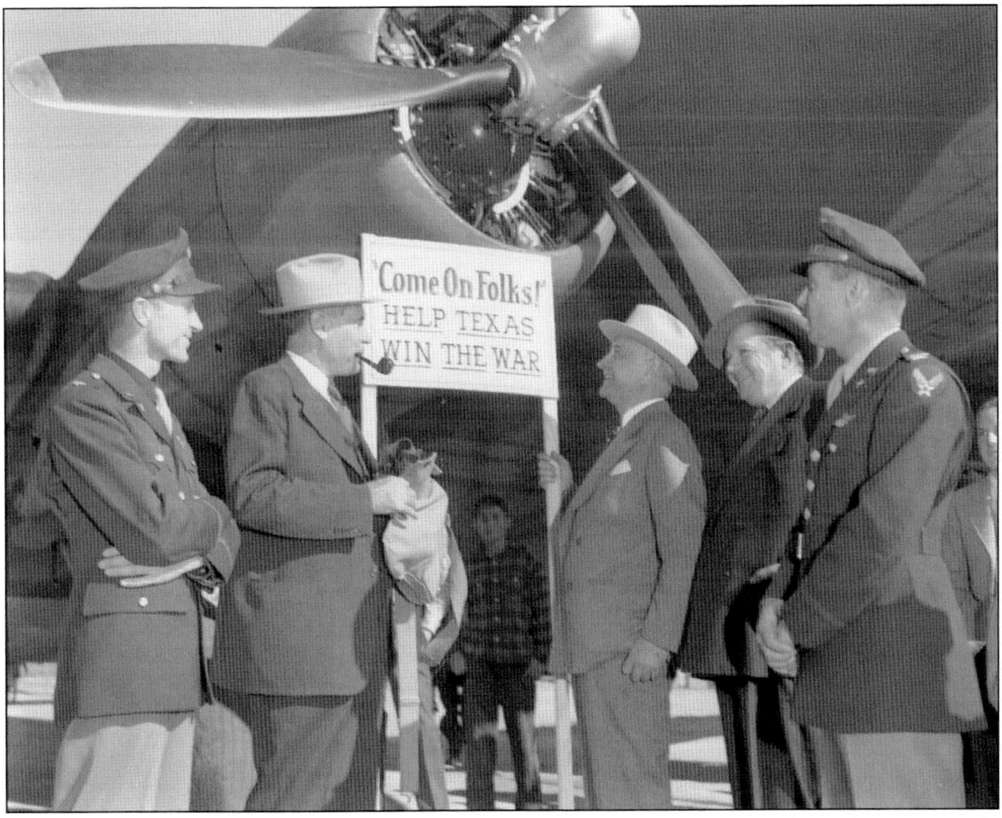



Gov. Coke Stevenson visited Del Valle Army Air Field in January 1942 and urged Texans to do their part to help win the war.

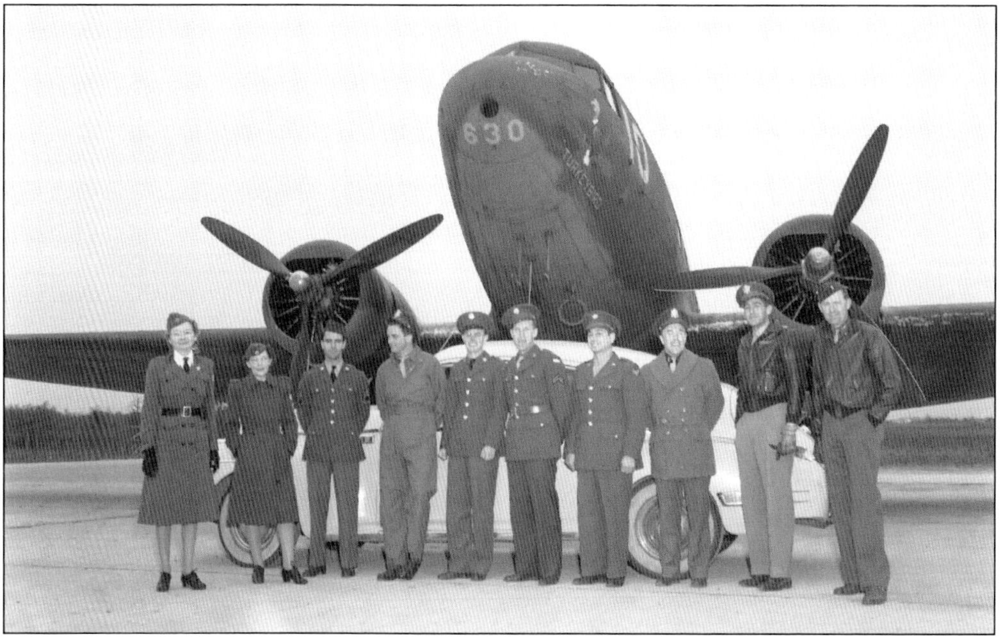


This photograph from January 6, 1943, shows soldiers, both men and women, standing in front of an automobile and an airplane named *Turkey Bird*.

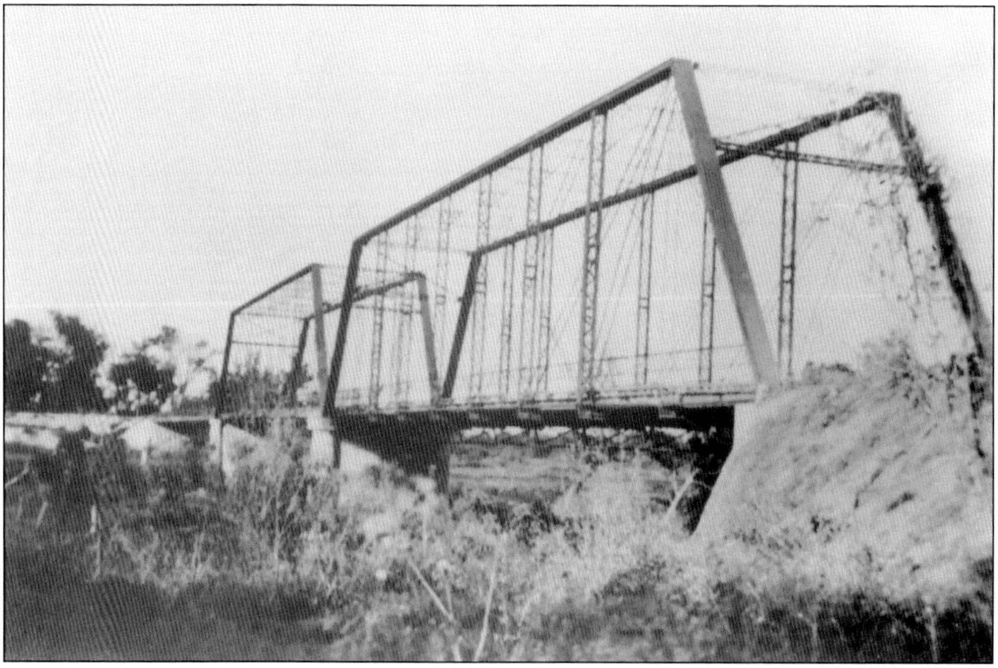

Moore's Crossing was another important community in southeastern Travis County that interacted heavily with Del Valle and Montopolis. The community is named for John B. Moore, who settled the area in the early 1900s and established a store. The area was also famous for its iron bridge, which was similar in form to the original Montopolis Bridge. Originally called the Onion Creek Bridge, the Moore's Crossing Bridge is now located at Richard Moya Park and serves as a pedestrian bridge.

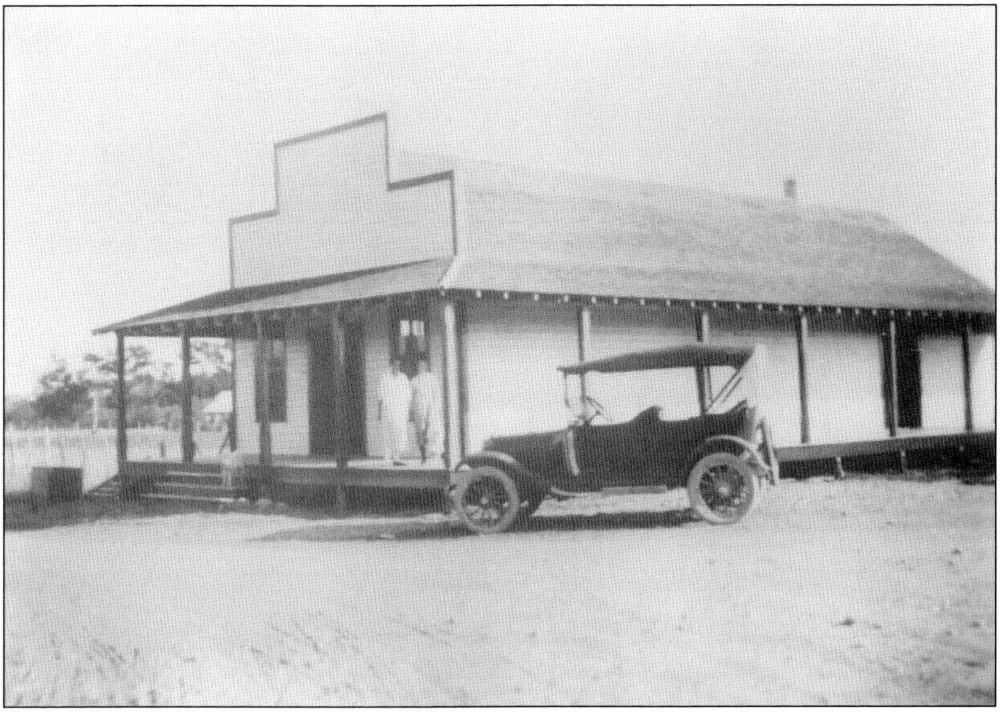

The Moore's Crossing General Store served an important segment of the agricultural population of southeastern Travis County: those who were located too far from the Givens General Store.

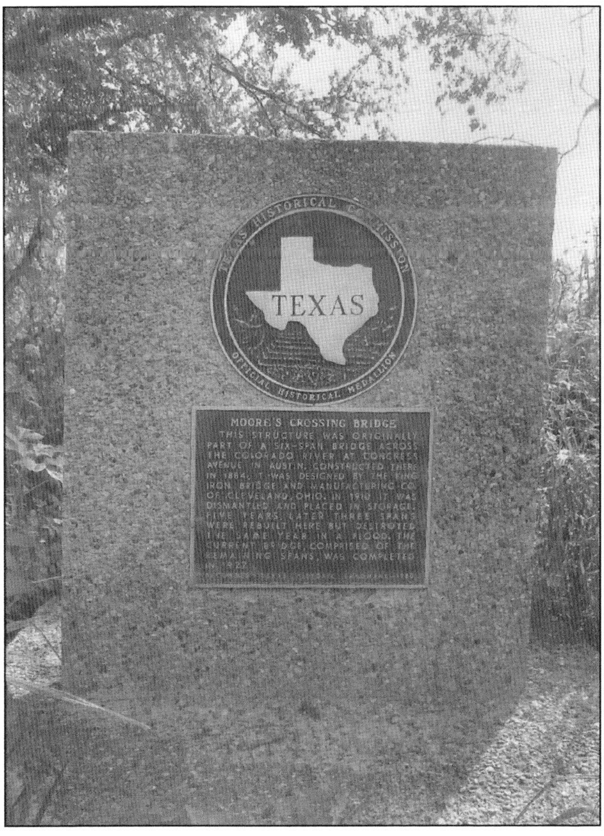


This historical marker commemorating the Moore's Crossing Bridge was installed in 1980. The Moore's Crossing Historic District was added to the National Register of Historic Places in 1996. (Courtesy of the author's collection.)

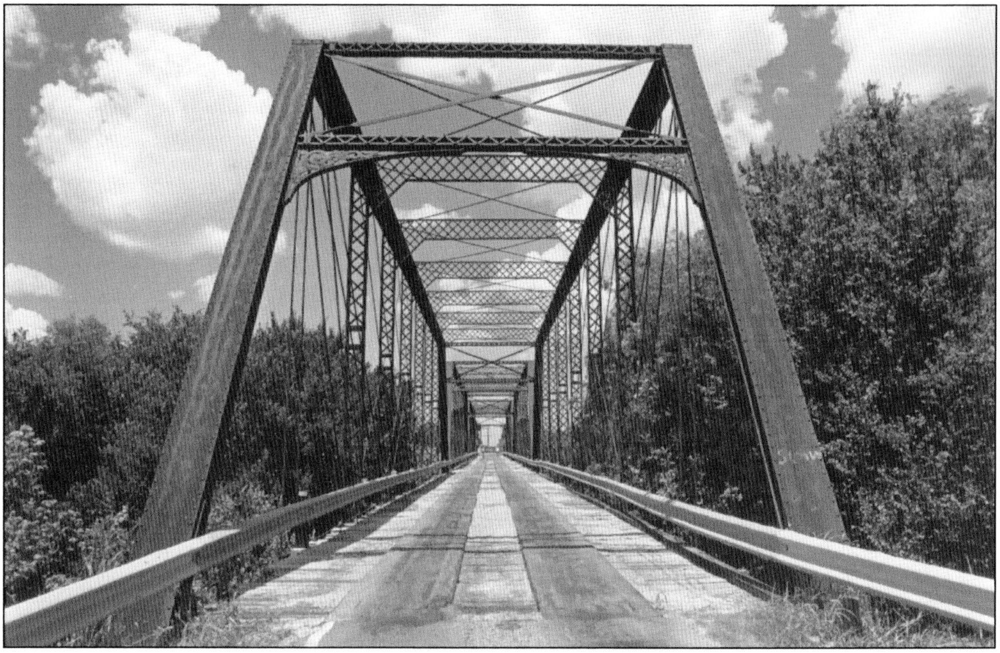

The original Moore's Crossing Bridge was constructed in 1915 and was built using three of six spans from the 1884 Congress Avenue Bridge, which had been placed in storage in 1910. The bridge did not last long; it was washed away within months. The current bridge, located at Richard Moya Park, was constructed in 1922 using the remaining three spans from the Congress Avenue Bridge.

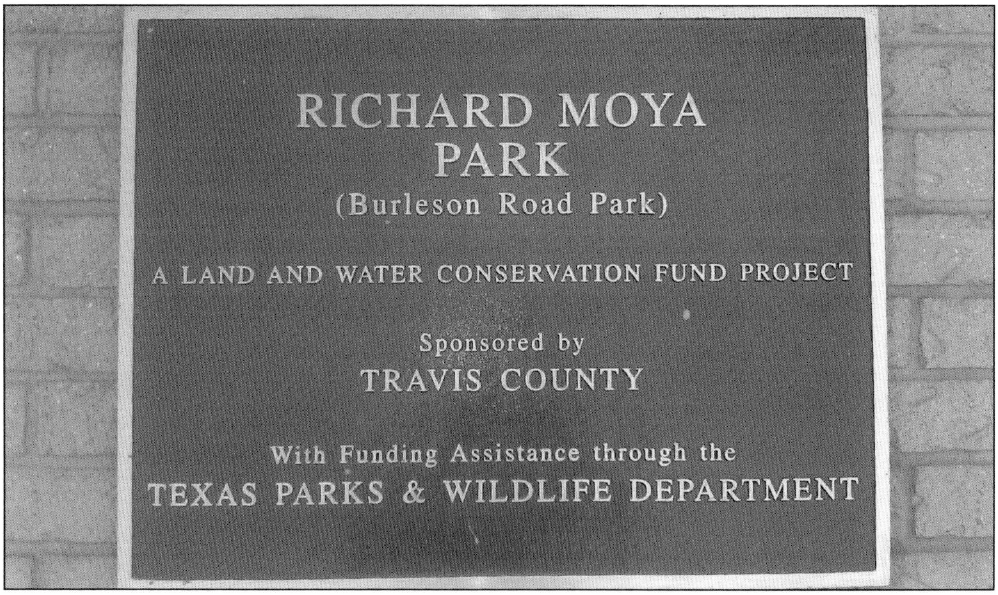


Richard Moya Park is named in honor of the first Mexican American elected to the Travis County Commissioners Court from Precinct 4, which represents the southeastern quadrant of the county. First elected in 1970, Moya went on to serve four full terms, or 16 years, and he remains civically active in the Austin community. The park is located along the lower reaches of Onion Creek and has been impacted by heavy flooding on numerous occasions, most recently in 2013. (Courtesy of the author's collection.)

The Michalk Grocery continues in operation today and served as the favorite refreshment location for the author's son, who learned to ride his bicycle at Richard Moya Park and across the Moore's Crossing Bridge. (Courtesy of the author's collection.)

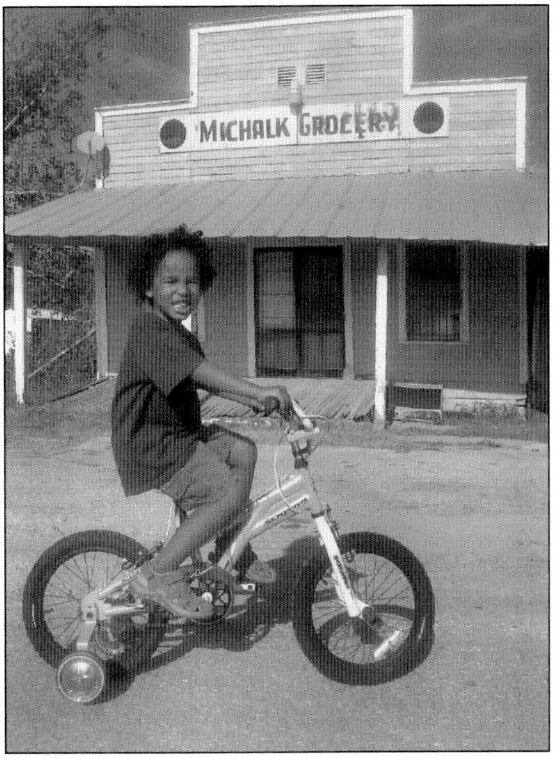


The 2013 Onion Creek flood devastated the southeastern portion of Travis County, much of which now sits within the Austin city limits. Several people died as a result of the flood, and hundreds of families lost their homes. As this photograph shows, previous Onion Creek floods were just as devastating.

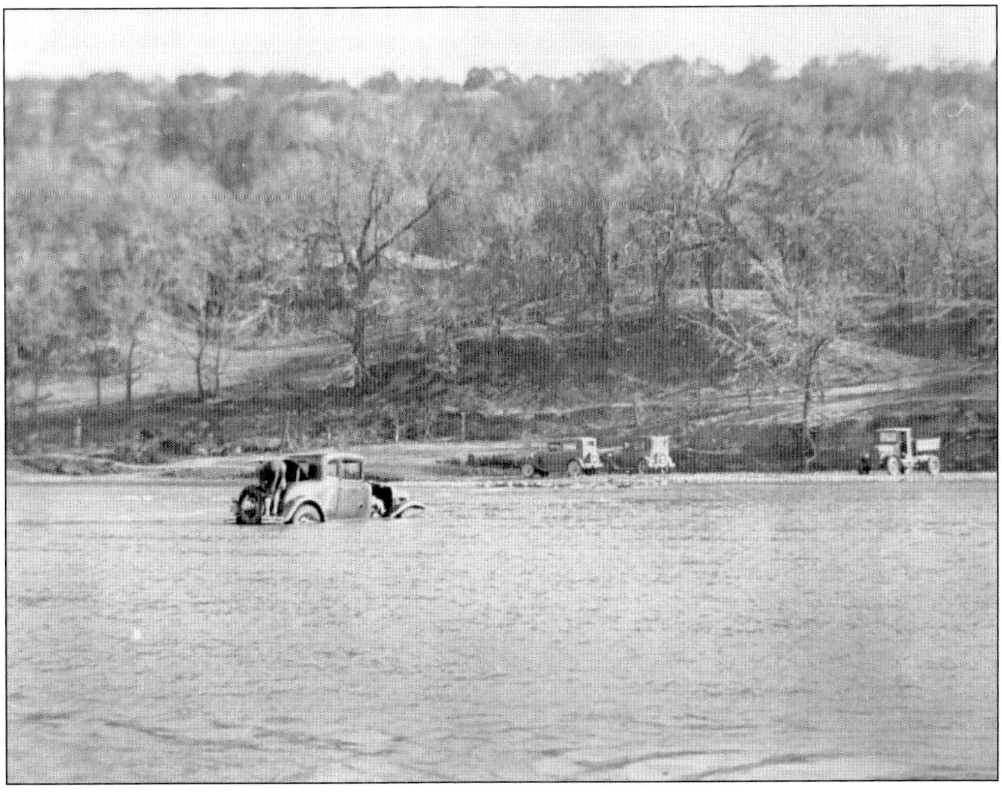

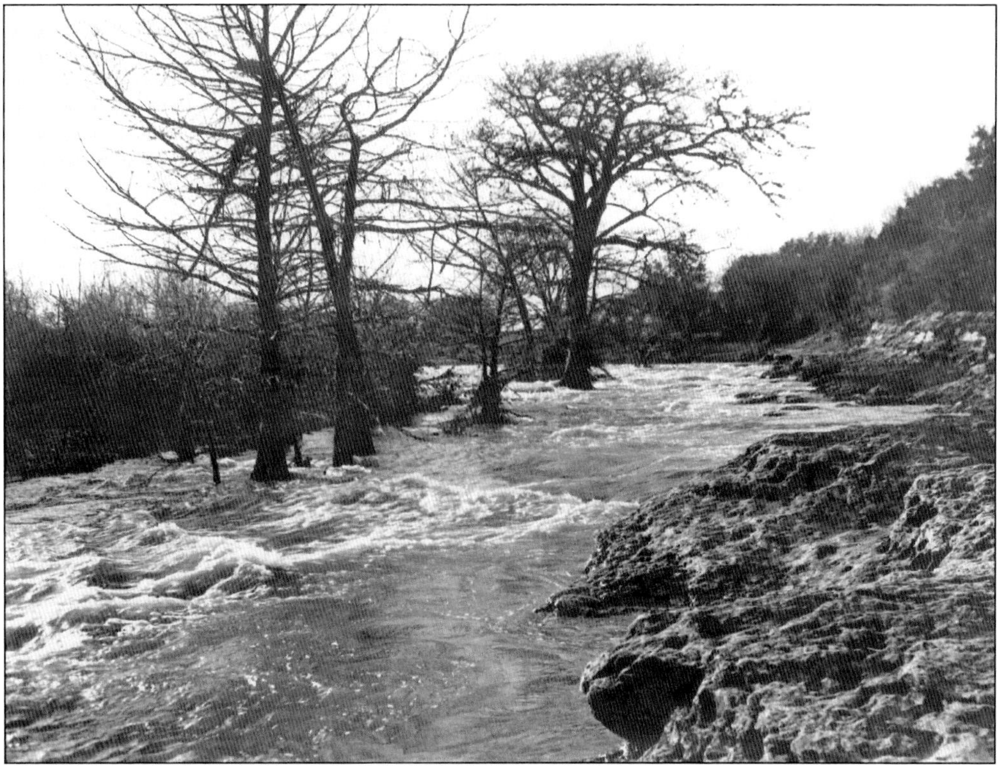

Above is a photograph from February 1, 1934, that shows Onion Creek flooding at Del Valle. The creek is seen below under a highway bridge on January 27, 1938.

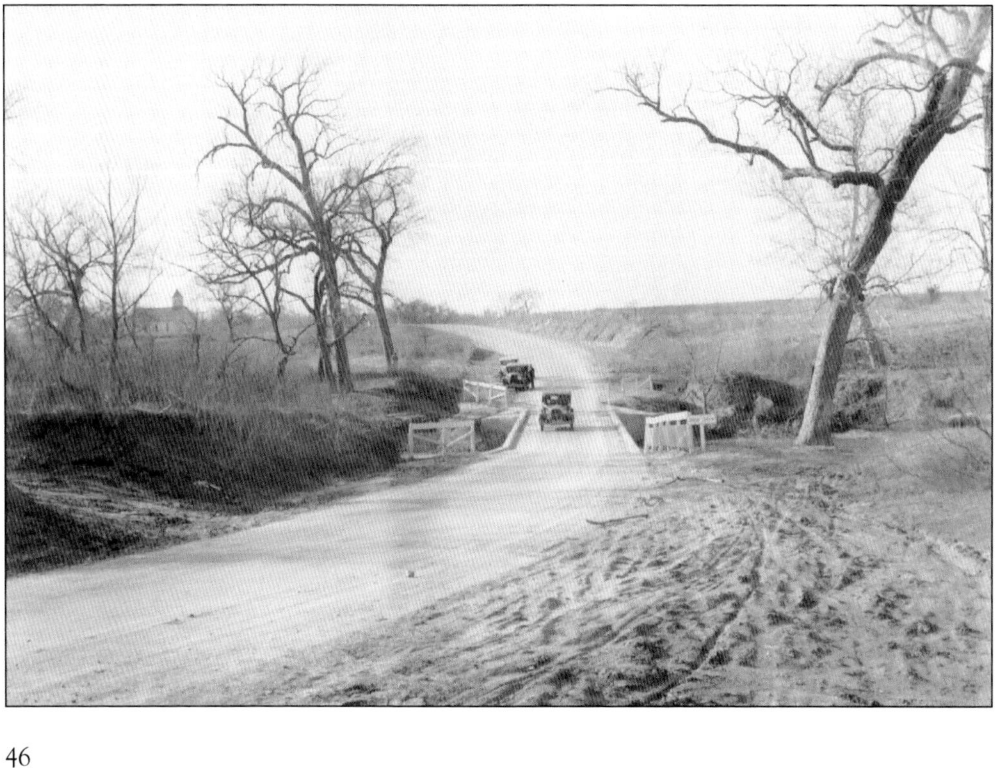

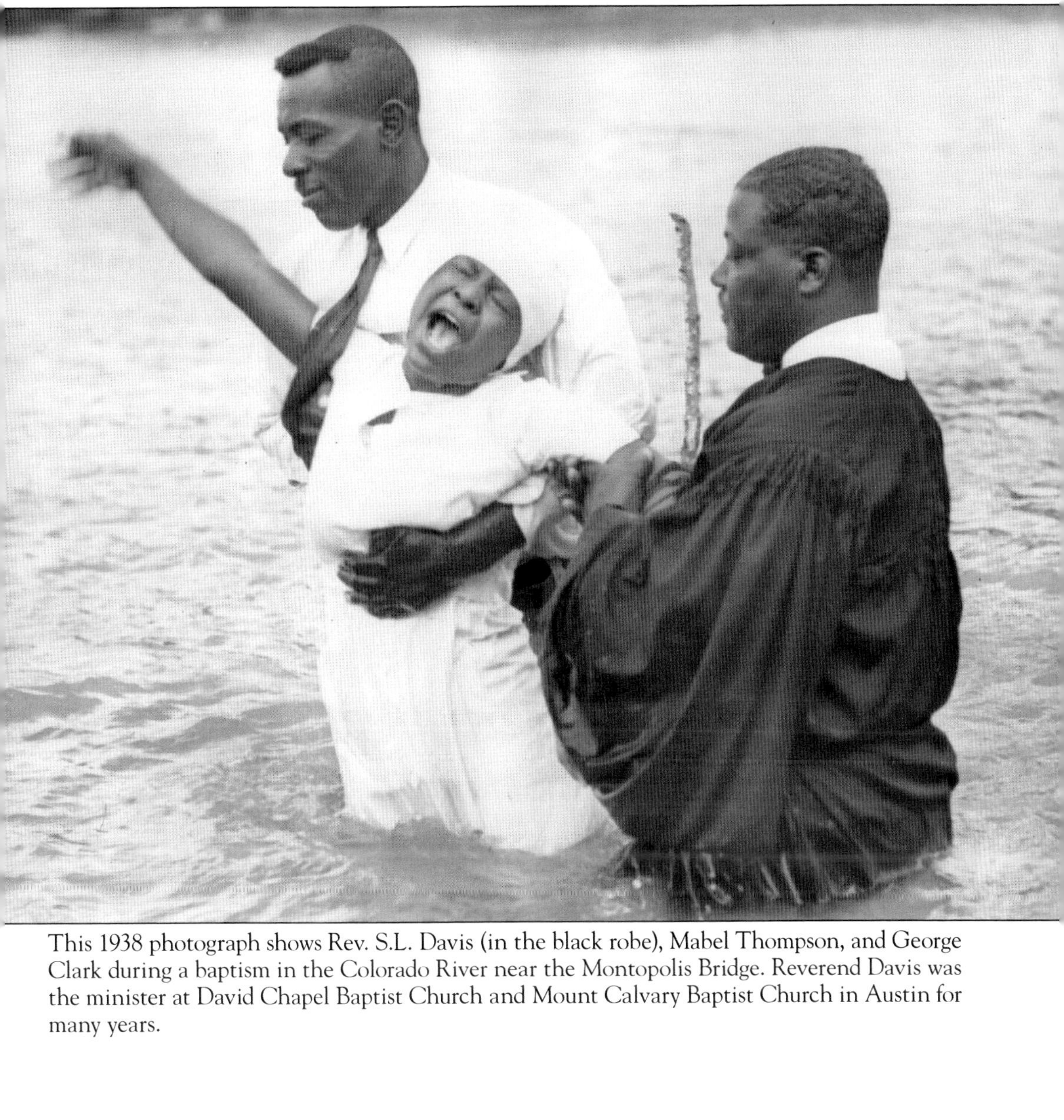

This 1938 photograph shows Rev. S.L. Davis (in the black robe), Mabel Thompson, and George Clark during a baptism in the Colorado River near the Montopolis Bridge. Reverend Davis was the minister at David Chapel Baptist Church and Mount Calvary Baptist Church in Austin for many years.

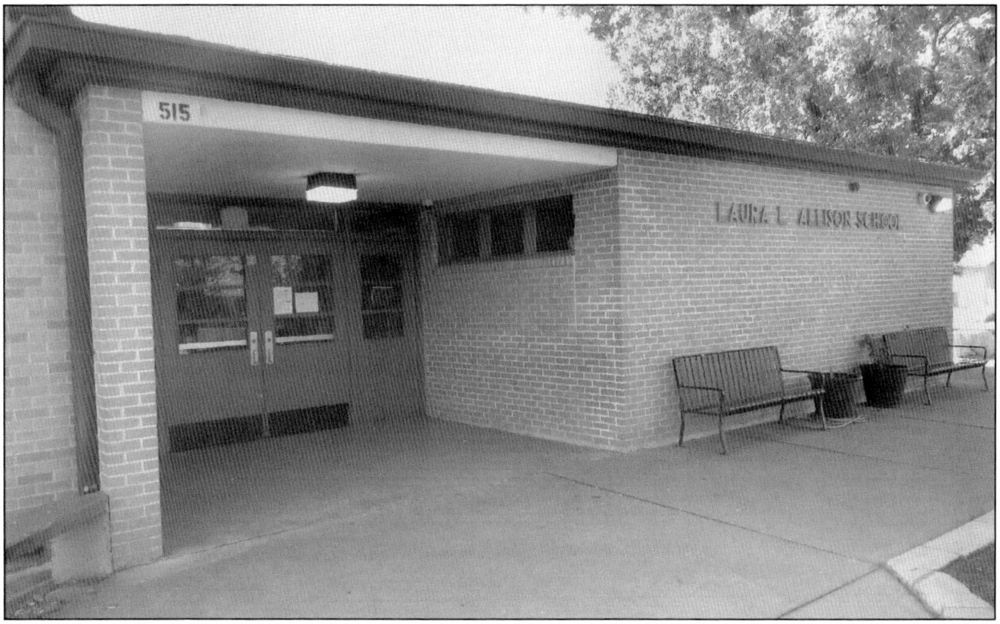


Montopolis Elementary School was a county school under the Colorado School District until 1952, when the City of Austin started annexing Montopolis. Allison Elementary School is named for Laura Louticia Allison, an Austin schoolteacher from 1892 to 1942 who spent the last 34 of her teaching years at John B. Winn Elementary School. Allison was also instrumental in the establishment of the state teacher retirement system. The school named in her honor was built in 1955 and played an important role in building community in the early years after the annexation of Montopolis, a function it continues to fulfill.

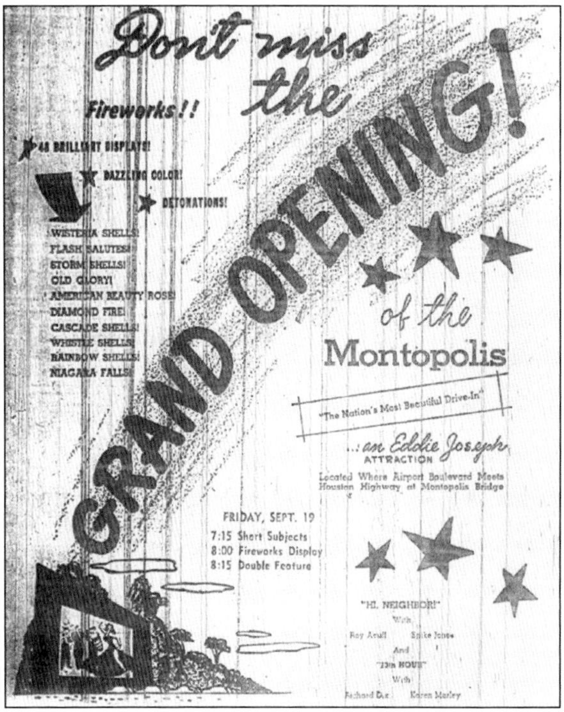


The Montopolis Drive-In billed itself as "The Nation's Most Beautiful Drive-In" and opened for business on Friday, September 19, 1947. The theater had an 850-car capacity, as well as seating for 500 patrons who preferred to view the movies from outside their cars. The proprietor for the drive-in was Eddie Joseph, who also owned other Austin drive-ins at the time. The theater was located just north of the Montopolis Bridge on Airport Boulevard.

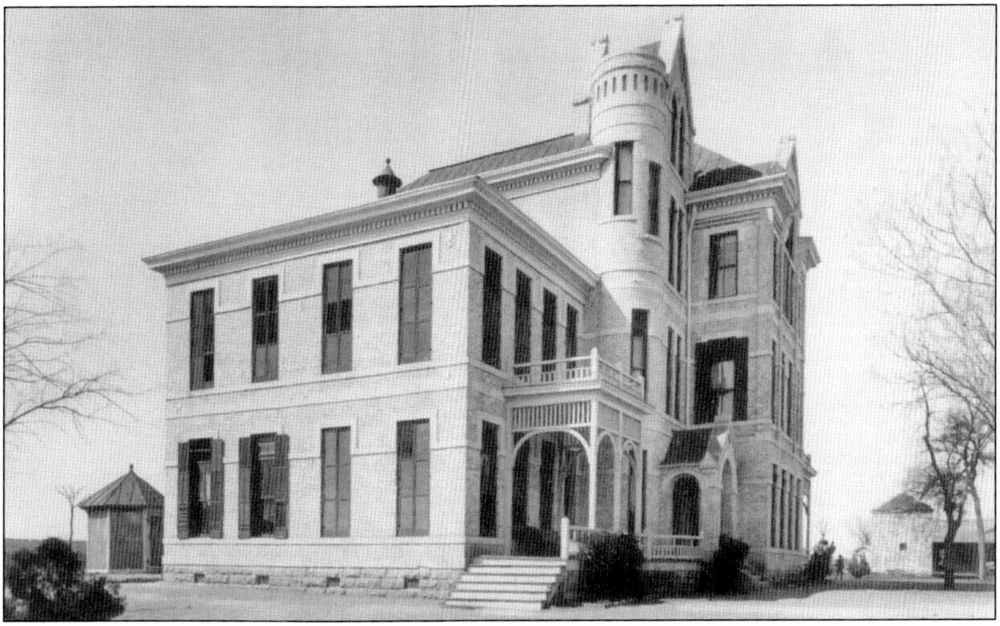

Founded in 1887, the Texas Blind, Deaf, and Orphan School was originally located on Bull Creek Road between Thirty-eighth and Forty-fifth Streets. After the Montopolis Drive-In, located at 601 Airport Boulevard, closed in 1959, the school moved to that location. The new residential campus accommodated over 1,200 students and served as the segregated counterpart to the Texas schools for the deaf and blind. In 1965, the state institutes for the blind and deaf desegregated, and the Montopolis institute became the east campus of the Texas School for the Deaf. The State of Texas sold the property to the City of Austin in 1999.

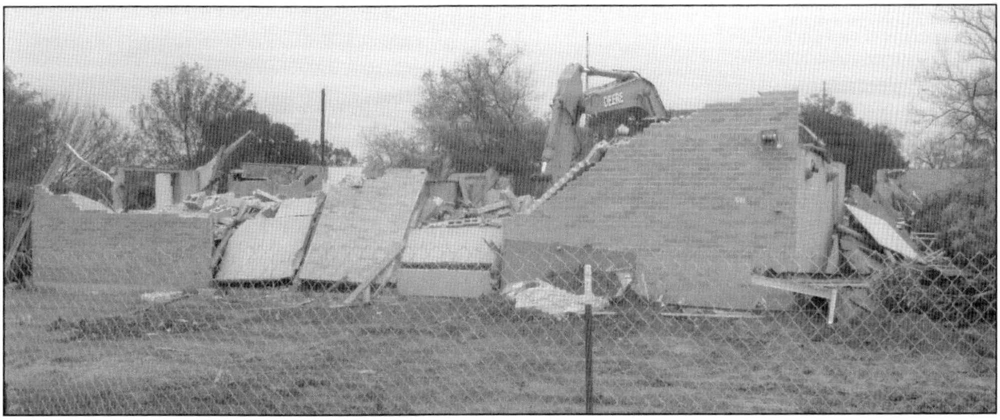

After acquiring the property from the State of Texas, the City of Austin and Travis County placed the Austin/Travis County Health and Human Services Department in some of the buildings there. By 2008, the city had decided to also relocate its new dog shelter to the site, and it was faced with a decision about what to do with the most important remaining historic structures at the school: a gymnasium and an auditorium that had also served as the school's chapel and administrative headquarters. The auditorium was named for J.C. McAdams, a local African American leader and superintendent at the school from 1951 until its integration in 1965. Regrettably, by late 2009, the Austin City Council decided against adaptive reuse and voted to demolish the historic school buildings and "green build" a new dog shelter on the site, an unfortunate example of "greenwashing." (Courtesy of the author's collection.)

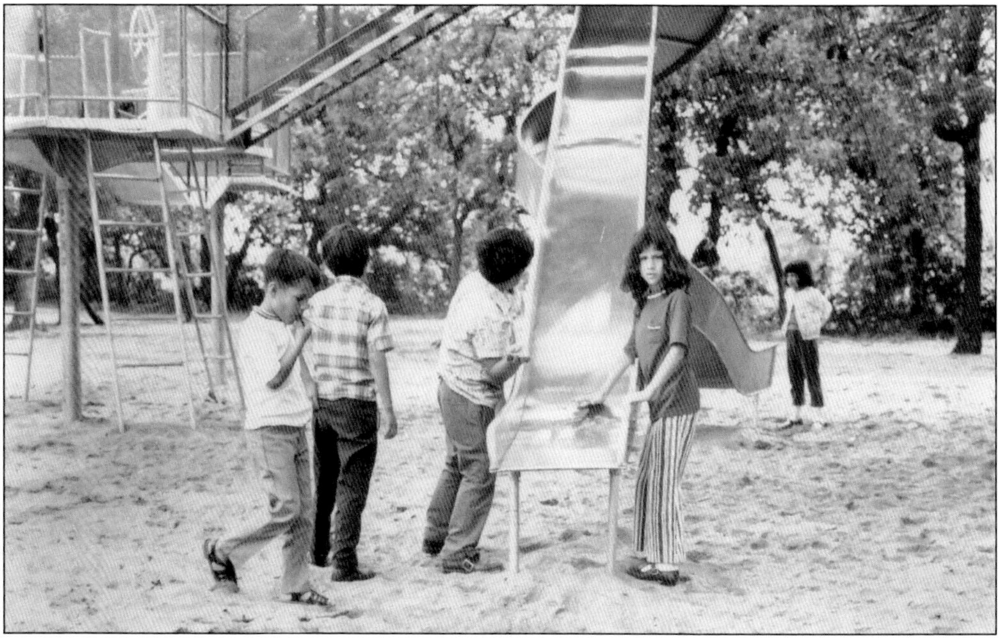

Civitan Neighborhood Park was installed in the mid-1960s next to Allison Elementary School, largely thanks to the early advocacy of Montopolis priest Fr. Fred Underwood of Dolores Parish, who went on to play an important advocacy role in the neighborhood throughout the 1960s, 1970s, and 1980s.

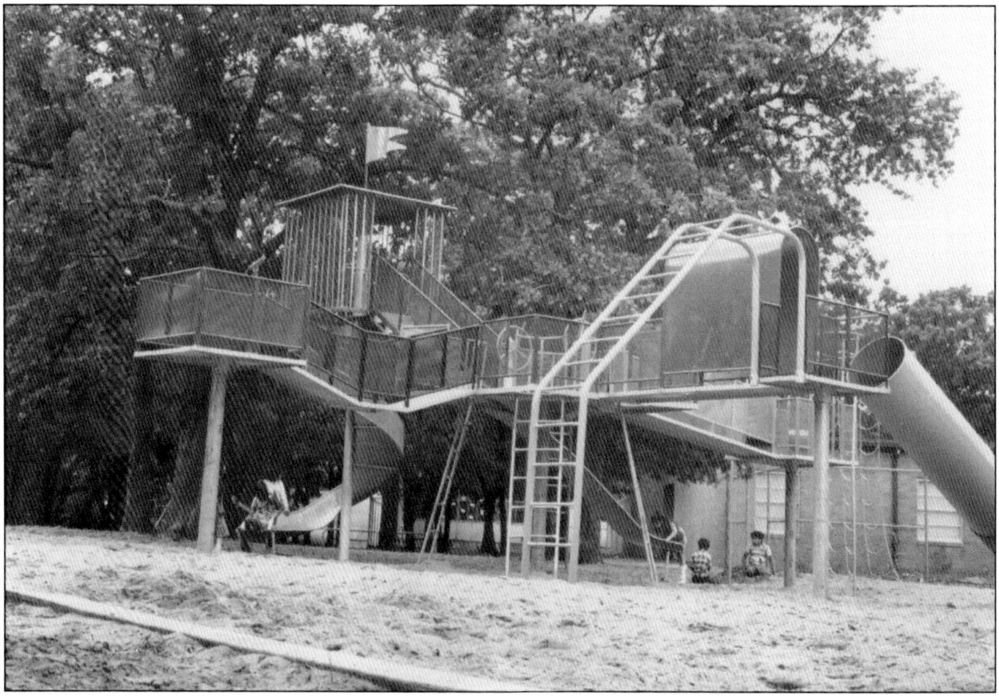

Regrettably, African American children were initially not able to use the facilities at Civitan Park because the park was segregated. As a result of civil rights advocacy at the local and national level, including by St. Edward's Baptist Church, this began to change by the end of the 1960s.

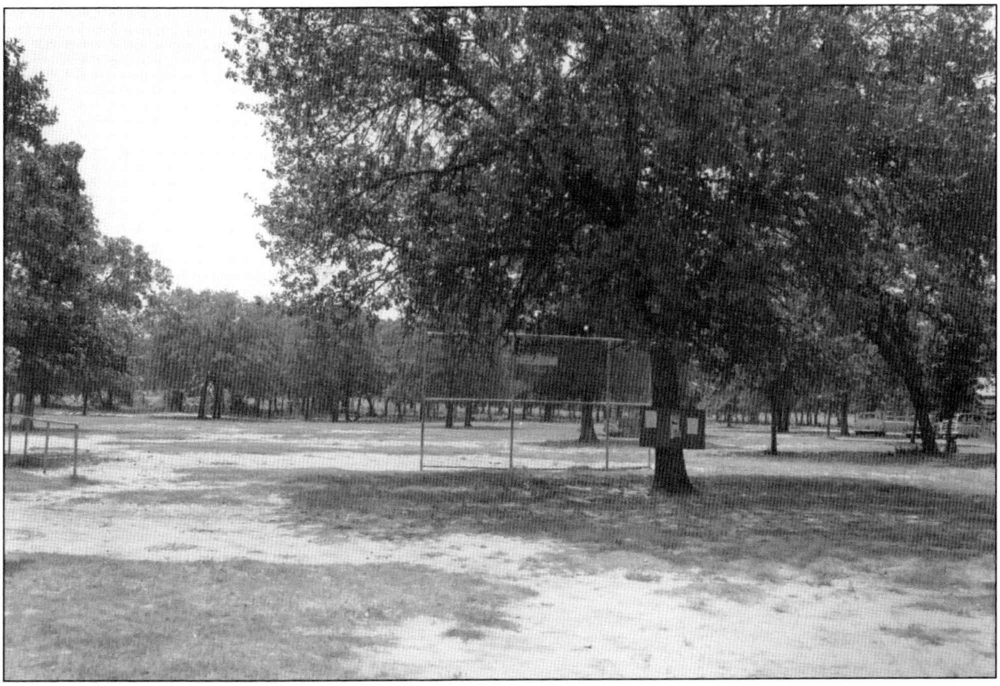
Civitan Park also included baseball fields and tennis courts.

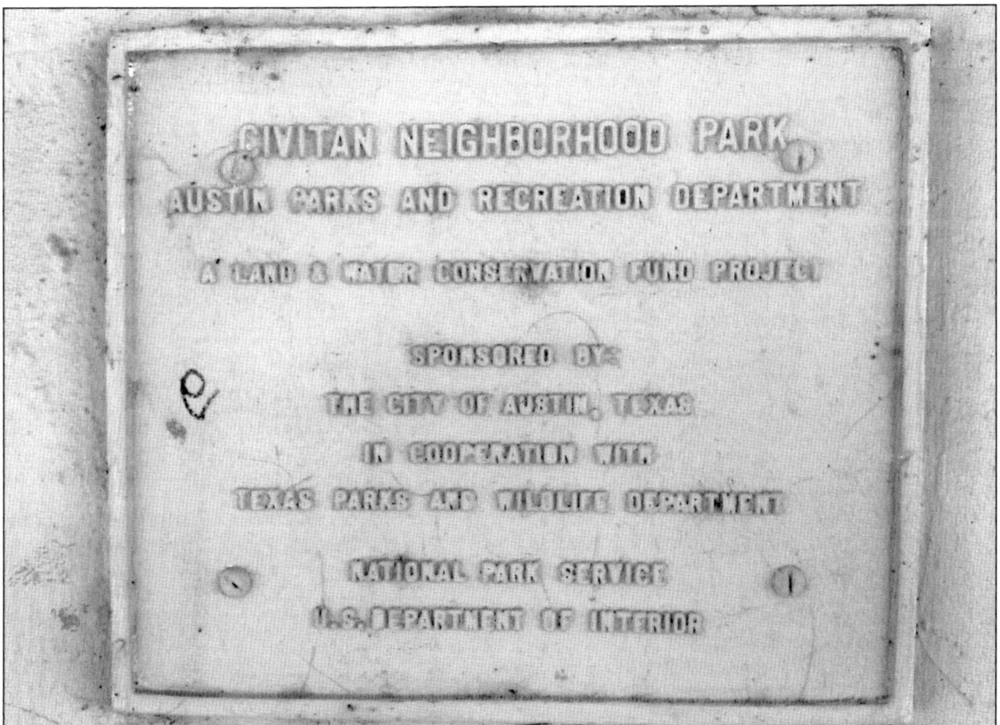

The construction of Civitan Neighborhood Park was a joint venture between the City of Austin, the Texas Parks and Wildlife Department, and the National Park Service's Land and Water Conservation Group. (Courtesy of the author's collection.)

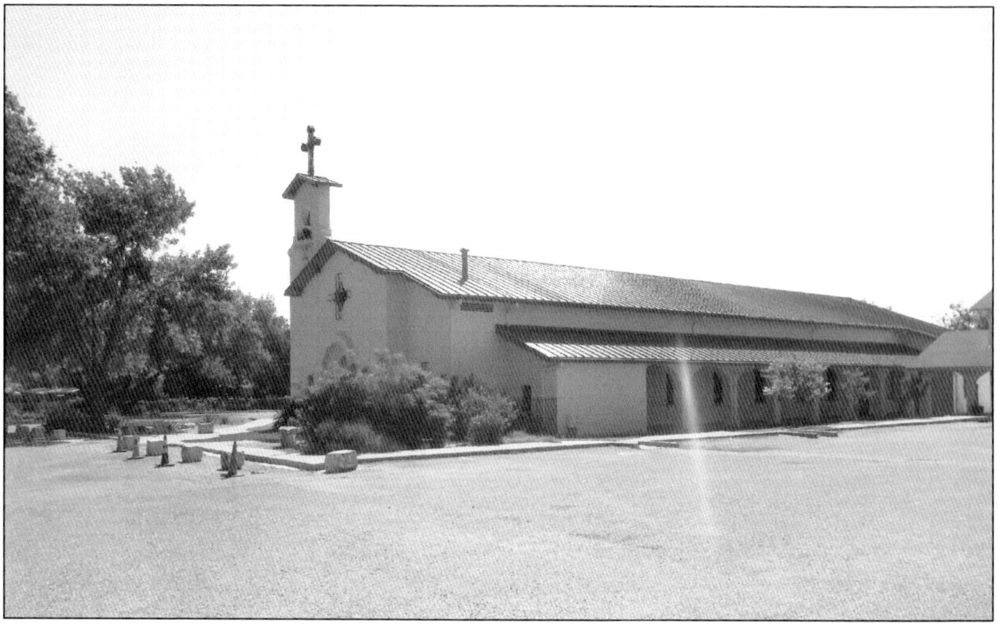

Founded by the Fathers of the Holy Cross Congregation, Dolores Parish began in the 1930s as a Mexican mission named Mission Nuestra Señora La Luz (usually just shortened to La Luz) when Montopolis was still a rural farming area. Fr. Alfred Mendez was appointed as the first pastor in 1940 and oversaw the completion of the original church in 1946. The present church, located farther south than the original, was completed in 1952, the same year the name was changed to Nuestra Señora de Siete Dolores, or "Our Lady of the Seven Sorrows." (Courtesy of the author's collection.)

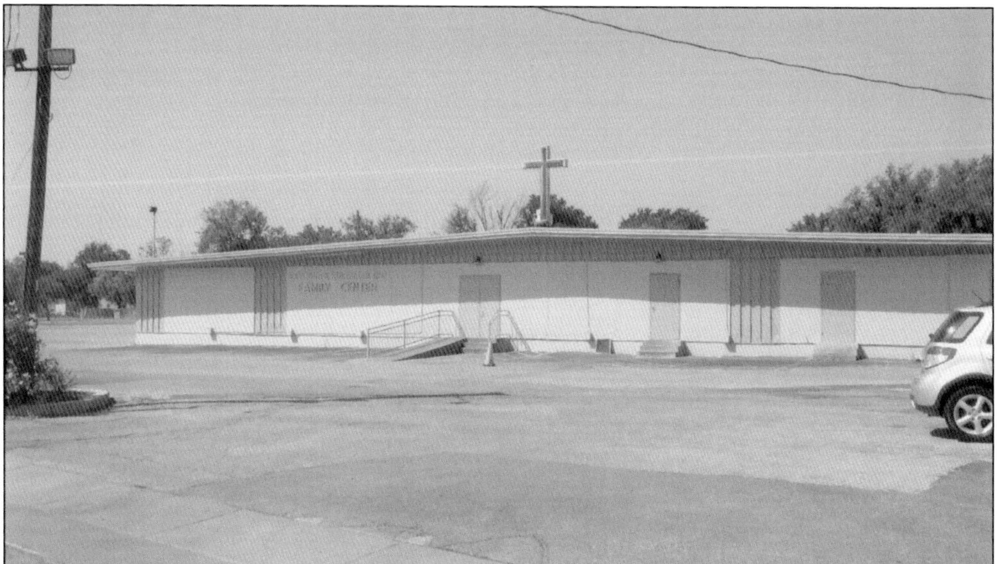

By 1954, Dolores Parish had established a church school, and most of the teachers were missionaries from Sacred Heart in San Antonio. Most of the children were from Montopolis or Bergstrom Air Force Base and were assigned to the Colorado School District. (Courtesy of the author's collection.)

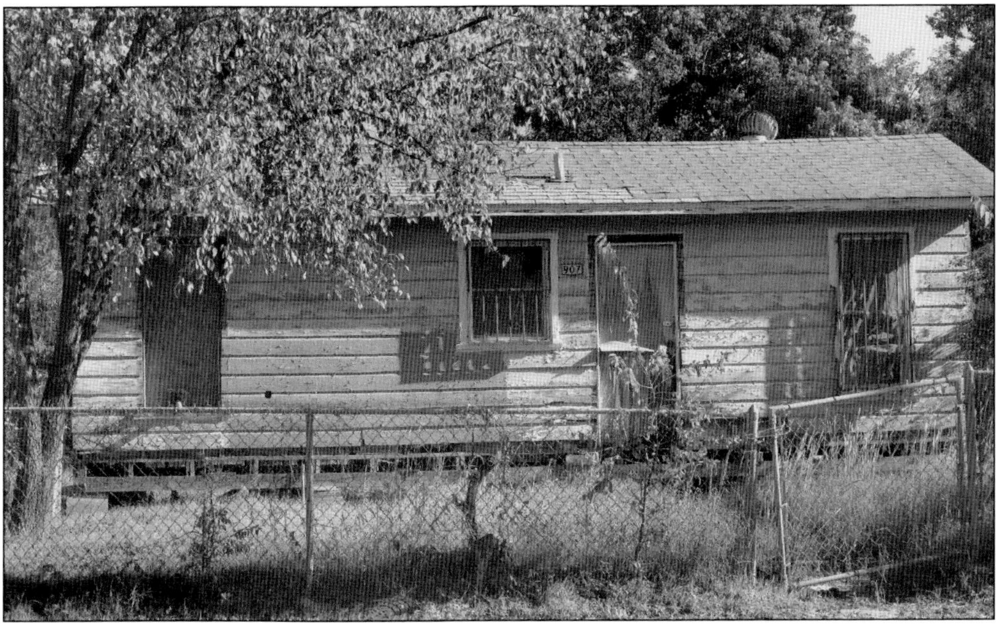


In 1956, there were approximately 2,000 people living in Montopolis, but the area was neglected by city officials and was not growing economically. Housing prices in Montopolis were the lowest in the area, which led to an influx of mostly unemployed Mexican and African Americans. Most of the residents of the neighborhood were living in crudely built shacks and hovels, recalled Rev. James Connelly, Congregatio a Sancta Cruce (CSC), who took over the leadership of Dolores Church in 1957. (Courtesy of the author's collection.)

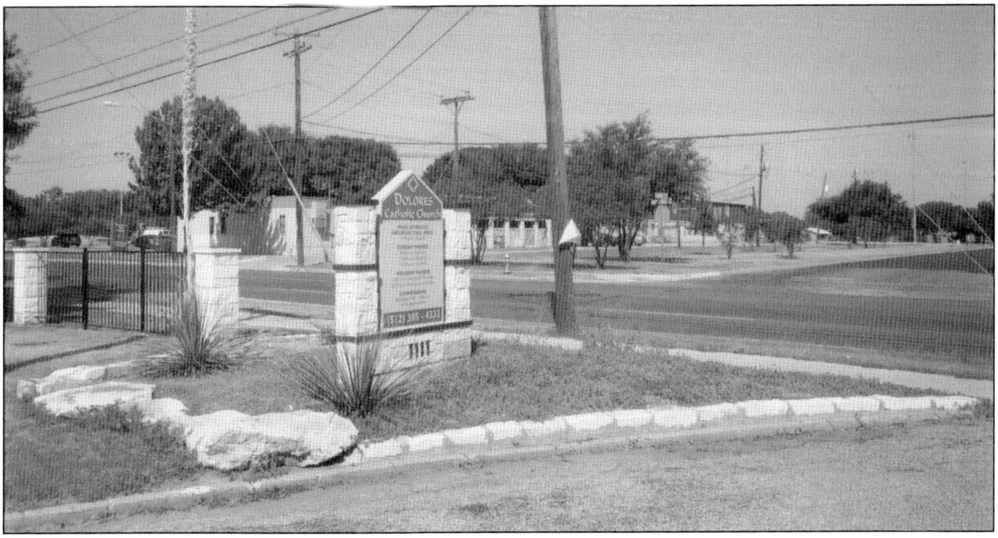


The late 1950s and early 1960s is remembered by longtime Montopolis residents as an era of rampant juvenile delinquency and ethnic youth gangs. Robberies, knifings, and assaults were common occurrences, as Montopolis deteriorated into a classic suburban barrio. Montopolis gangs not only engaged in violent confrontations with East Austin gangs from north of the river, but also with gangs from as far away as San Antonio and Corpus Christi. Things began to change when Father Connelly was replaced at Dolores Parish by an energetic young priest from the Midwest named Rev. Fred Underwood, CSC. (Courtesy of the author's collection.)

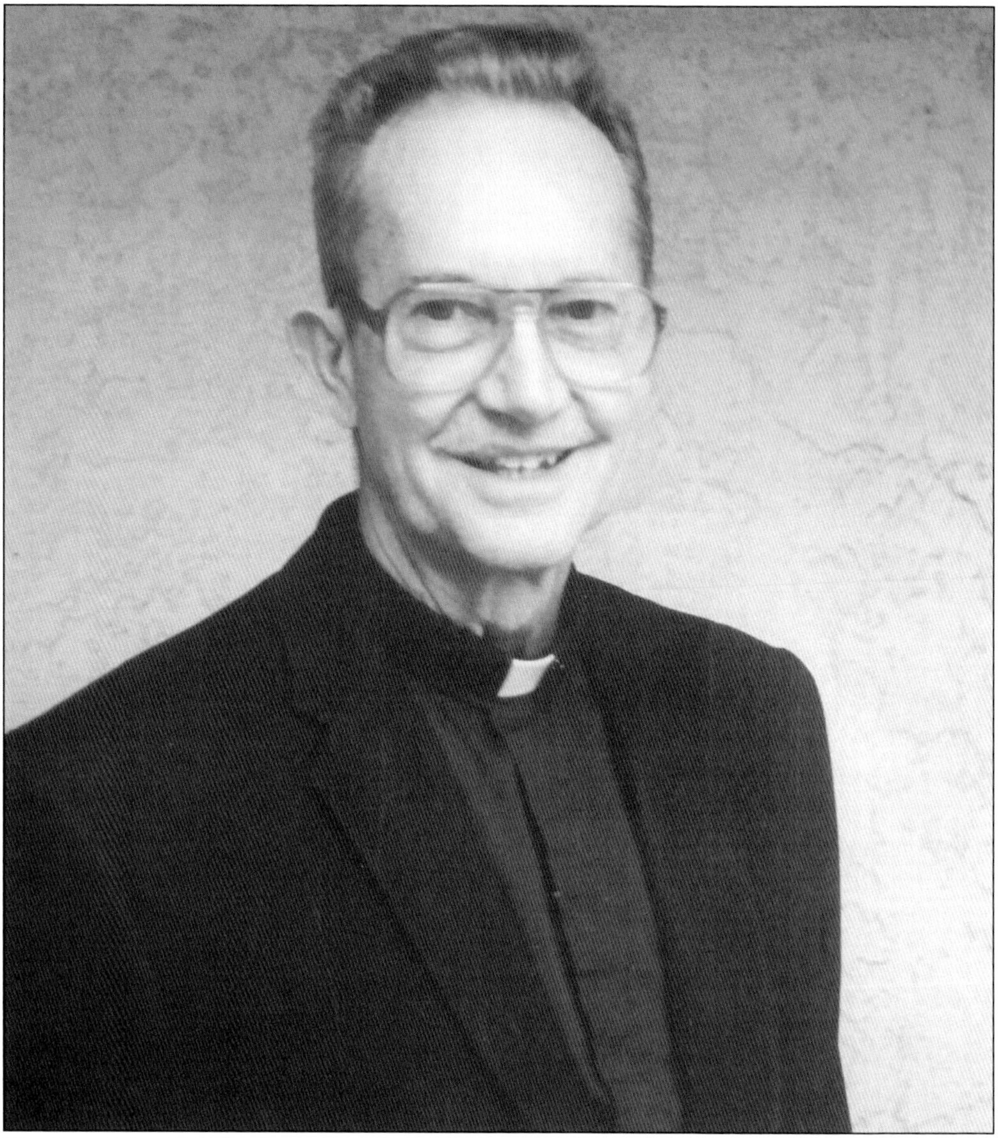

The Rev. O. Fred Underwood, CSC, (July 23, 1923–February 25, 2000) became pastor of Dolores Church in 1962 and was instrumental in addressing the neighborhood's longstanding educational, infrastructure, crime, and housing needs. After spending several weeks studying and assessing the needs of the community, Underwood concluded that one of the most important steps in rehabilitating the area would be the establishment of a community center. In 1963, he applied for financial aid to establish the center from the City of Austin and was coldly refused. Undaunted, Underwood utilized his extensive experience in the construction industry and built the community center anyway, with the assistance of parishioners and a $75,000 loan he was able to obtain during construction. The Montopolis Community Center was finished in May 1964. After the completion of the center, Underwood applied for operating funds from the Austin Parks and Recreation Department and was again rebuffed. Once Pres. Lyndon Johnson's War on Poverty initiatives began to gather momentum in the mid-1960s, Father Underwood bypassed local officials and obtained federal funding directly. Father Underwood's can-do spirit and dedication to service have left a powerful legacy in Montopolis. (Courtesy of San Jose Church.)

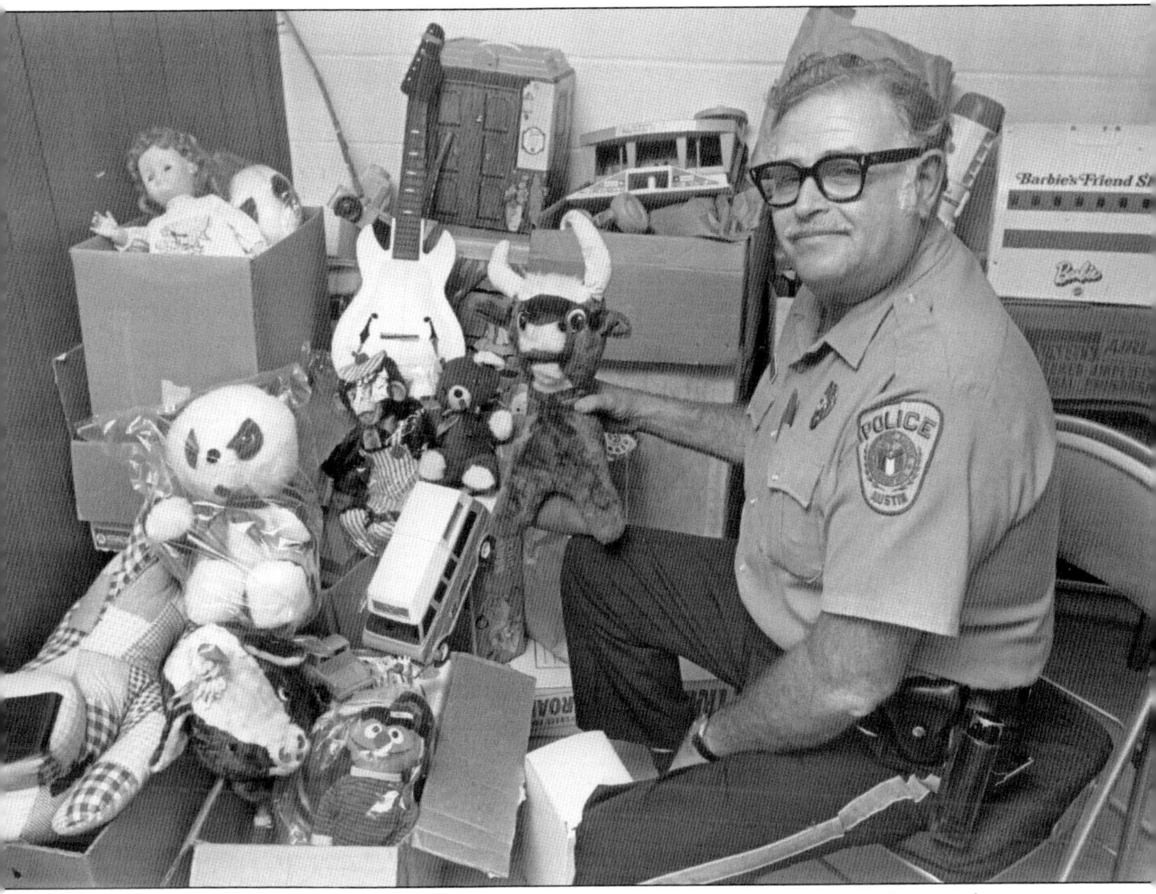


One of the first projects initiated by the Montopolis Community Center in 1965 was a daycare program, which was, and still remains, a pressing need in the neighborhood. Funding for the program was provided by the federal Office of Economic Opportunity, with staff supplied by Head Start. In 1968, Father Underwood, with the help of a $68,000 grant from the US Department of Labor, established the Montopolis Youth Corps, which explicitly targeted gang members and drug offenders in the community. The teenagers drafted into the program were initially motivated to attend the training by the promise of a salary for attending the sessions. It was eventually agreed that the participants would be paid $1.25 per hour and that all participants would check their guns at the community center door, come to the training sessions sober, and agree to not sell drugs on church property. After some initial growing pains, the program proved to be a sterling success; 82 percent of the youths in the first program were rehabilitated and placed in jobs. Gang activity ceased, and crime in Montopolis dropped by over 80 percent, one of the most precipitous crime reductions in the history of Austin. Impressed, the Department of Labor funded subsequent training sessions, which were just as successful, and eventually asked Dolores Parish to expand the program to the rest of Austin. This photograph shows Mike Porfiro at the Montopolis Community Center in the 1970s.

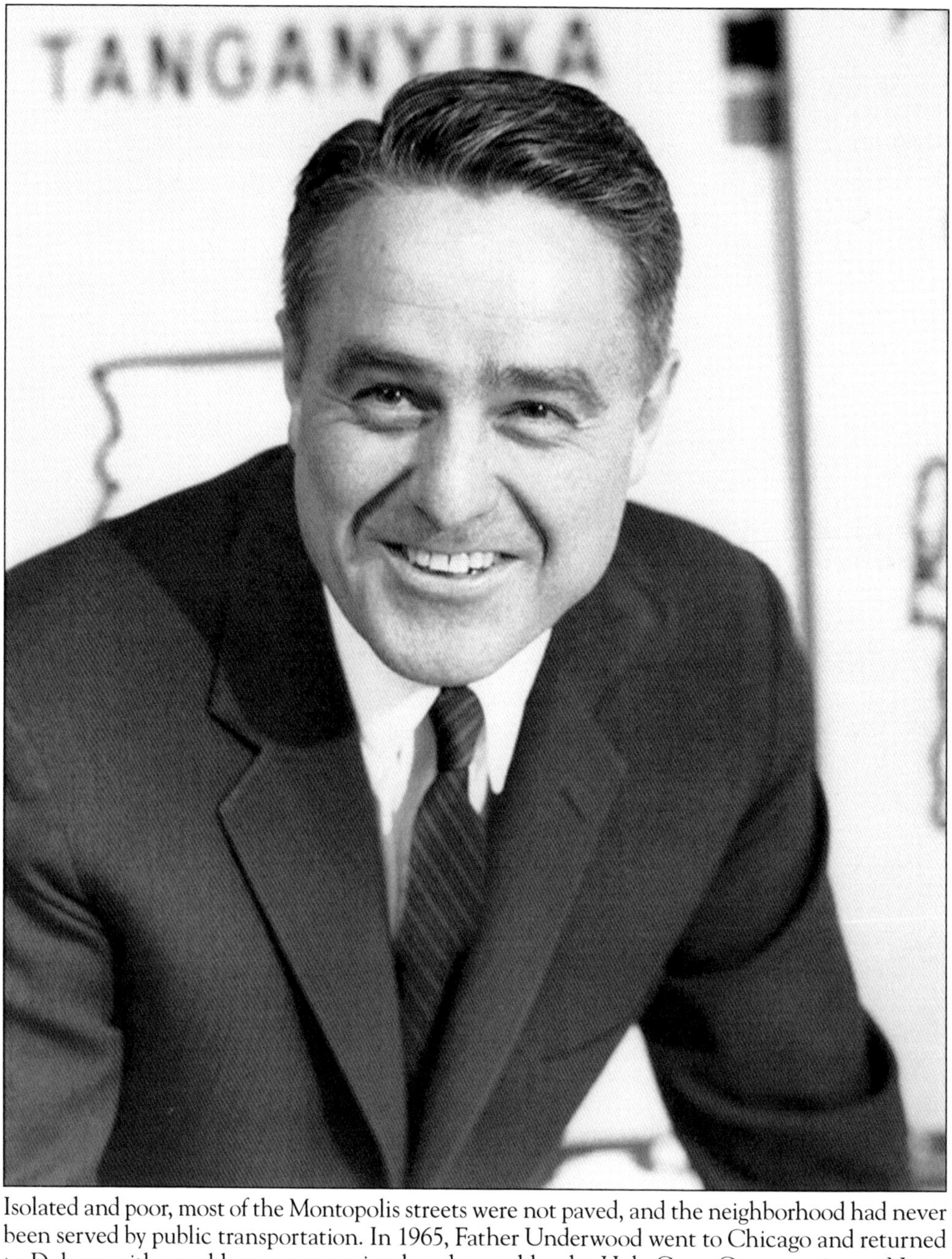


Isolated and poor, most of the Montopolis streets were not paved, and the neighborhood had never been served by public transportation. In 1965, Father Underwood went to Chicago and returned to Dolores with an old army evacuation bus donated by the Holy Cross Congregation at Notre Dame, where he had been ordained as a priest in 1956. A bus system known as "Poverty Island Transportation" (PIT) was organized, which not only gave Montopolis residents the chance to visit health and welfare clinics, but also allowed them to seek work outside of the neighborhood. The bus system was the first of its kind in the nation to be allotted funds from the Office of Economic Opportunity (OEO). The OEO's national director, Sargent Shriver, seen here, a close friend of Father Underwood, took one of the first rides on the bus in February 1966. (Courtesy of the John F. Kennedy Presidential Library and Museum.)

One of Father Underwood's many accomplishments was the 1969 establishment of the Montopolis Community School at the community center. Until 1972, it was known as the Dolores Parochial School. It served children of all backgrounds and income levels and played a significant role in reducing juvenile delinquency in Montopolis.

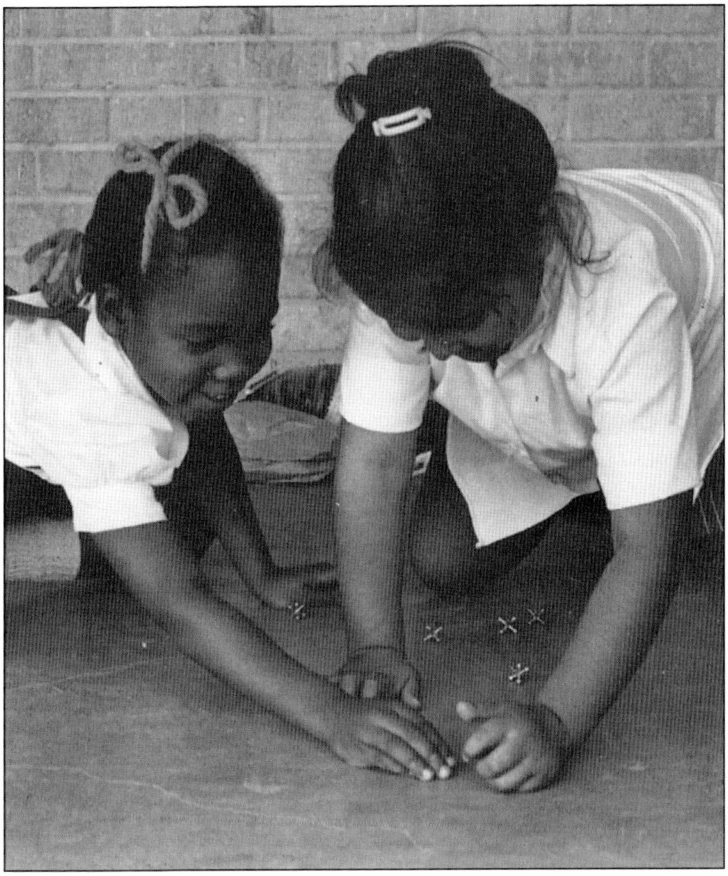

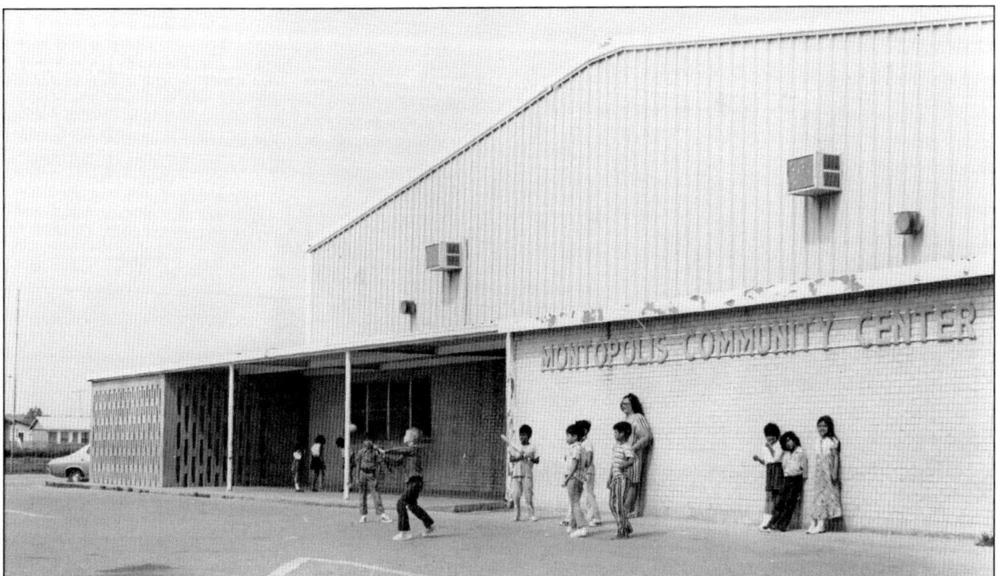


In this photograph, teacher's aide Mary Perez supervises as second graders from the Montopolis Community School take recess in front of their school building.

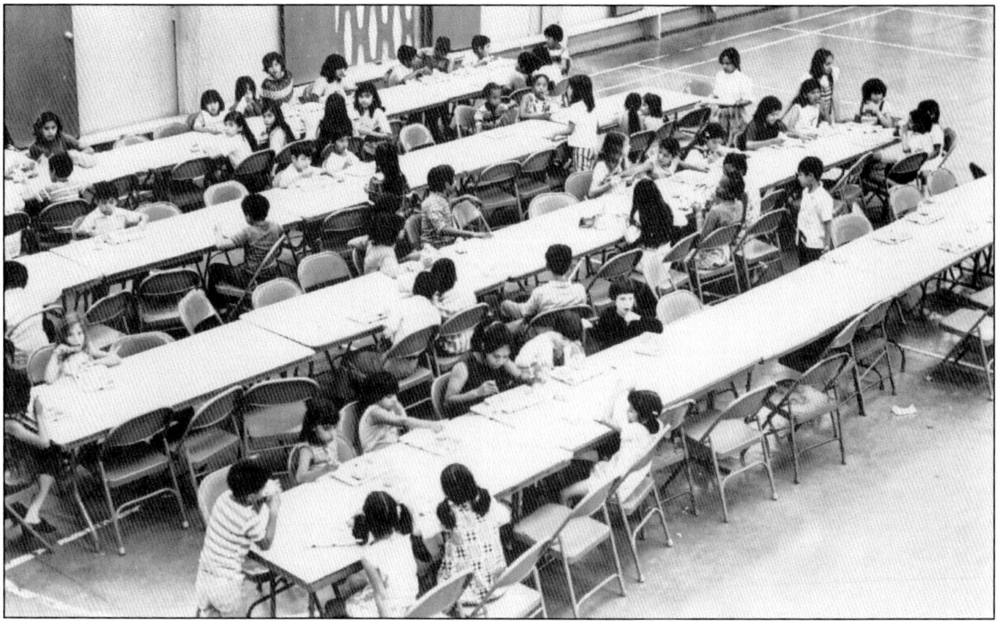

Schoolchildren ate their lunch in the community center gymnasium, as seen here.

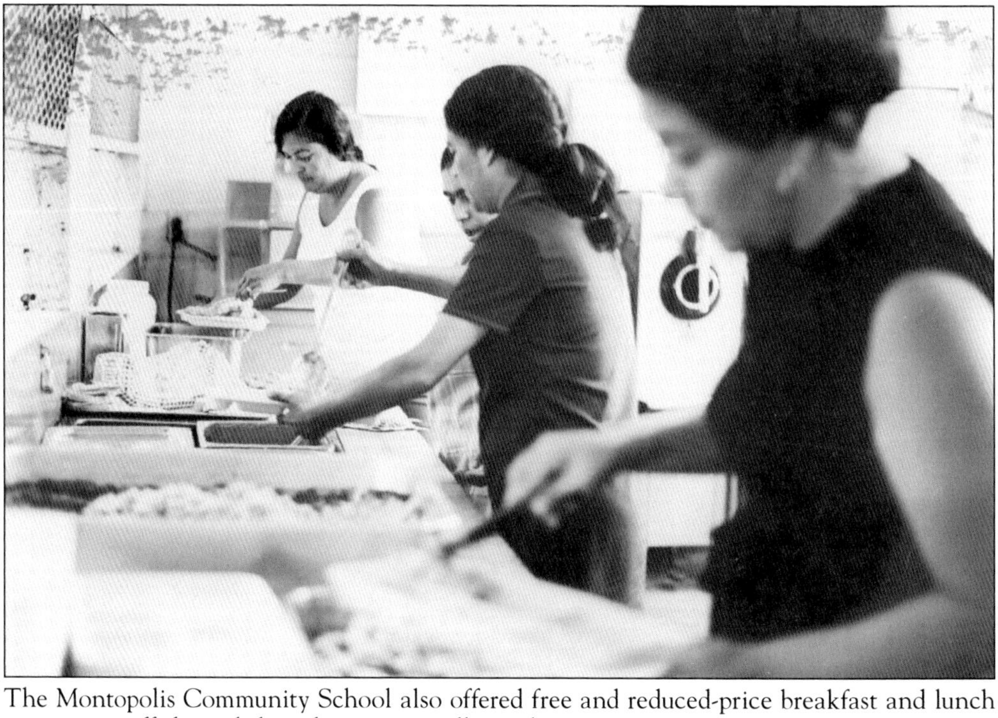

The Montopolis Community School also offered free and reduced-price breakfast and lunch programs, staffed mostly by volunteers, usually mothers.

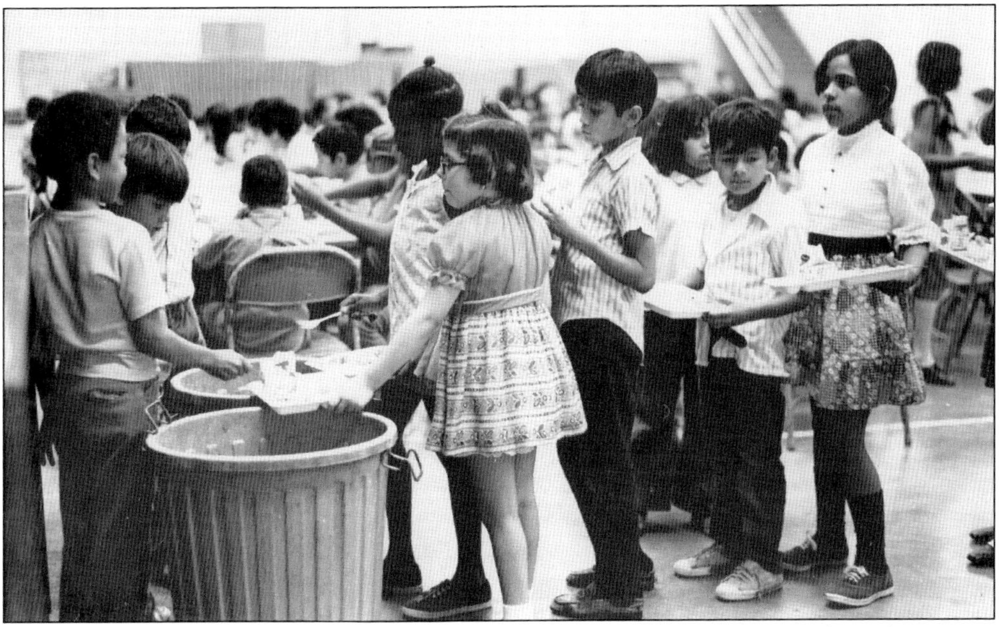

Tray inspection committees help dispose of food waste as children line up at the garbage cans. All food on a tray had to be eaten before going for seconds.

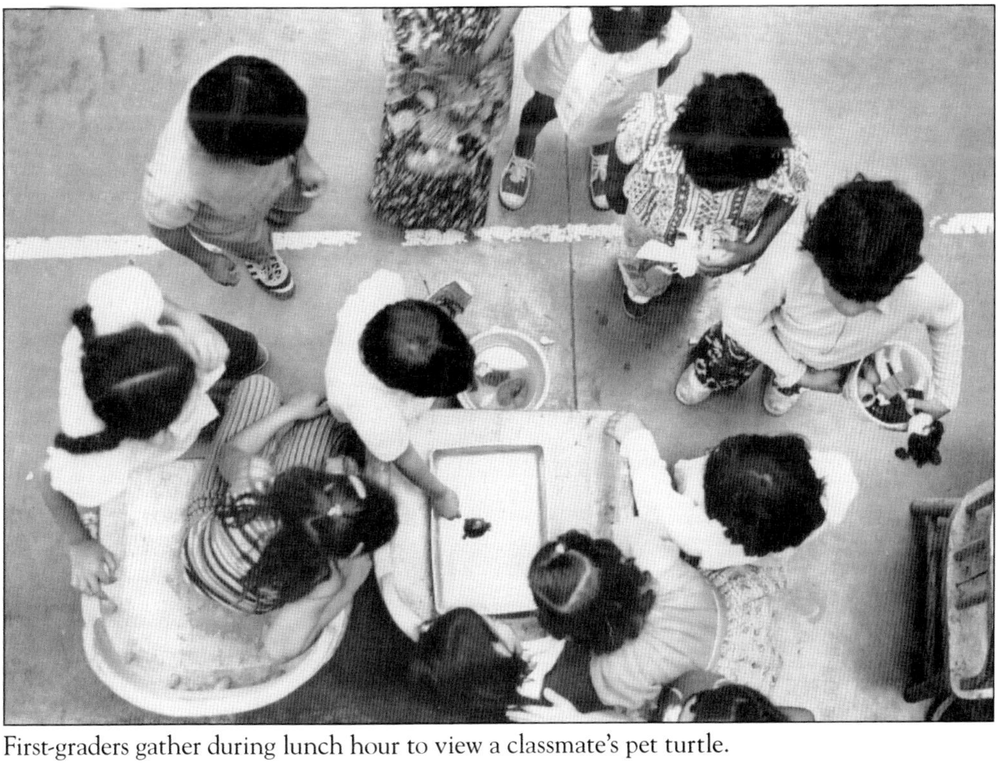

First-graders gather during lunch hour to view a classmate's pet turtle.

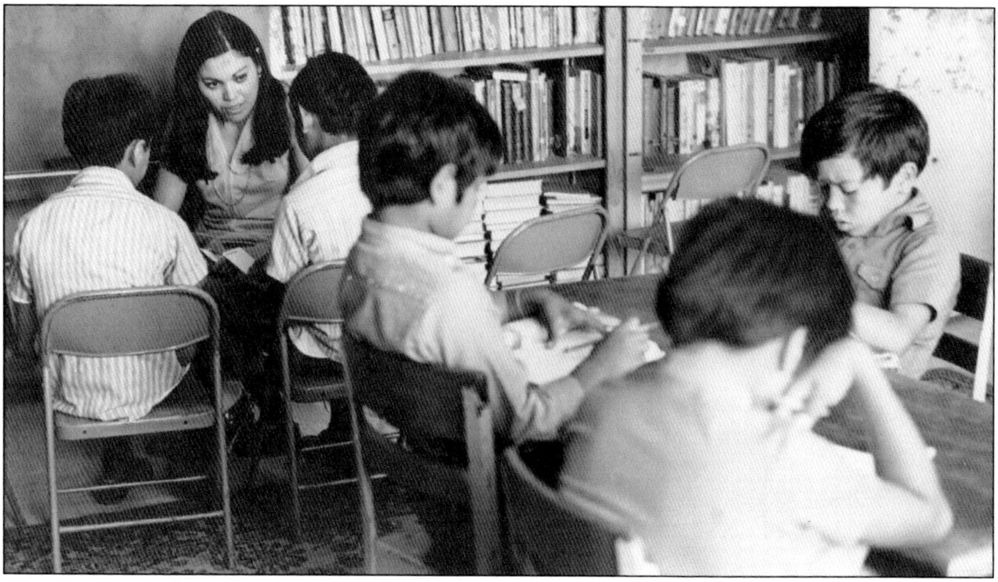

Olga Ramos works with a small group of remedial reading students for a short, intensive session while the other students pursue independent reading activities.

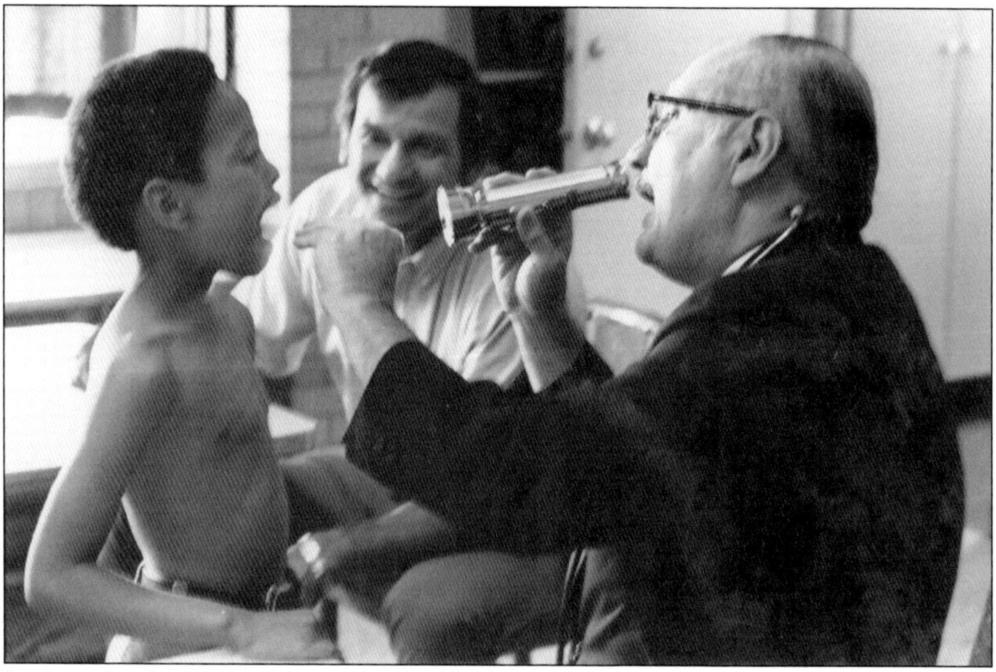

By the mid-to-late 1960s, Father Underwood had started to refer to Montopolis as "Poverty Island." The Model Cities Program and other War on Poverty initiatives played a major role in reducing poverty, building housing, and educating children in Montopolis in the 1960s. Father Underwood was creatively effective in bypassing city and county officials, who kept giving him the cold shoulder regarding his rehabilitation initiatives. Instead, he made direct appeals to federal officials such as Sargent Shriver. In this photograph, Dr. Todaro examines Michael Moore, one of about 40 youngsters from the Montopolis Community School who were able to attend the Rene Ramirez summer camp, located at a ranch 16 miles south of Austin, thanks to War on Poverty funding.

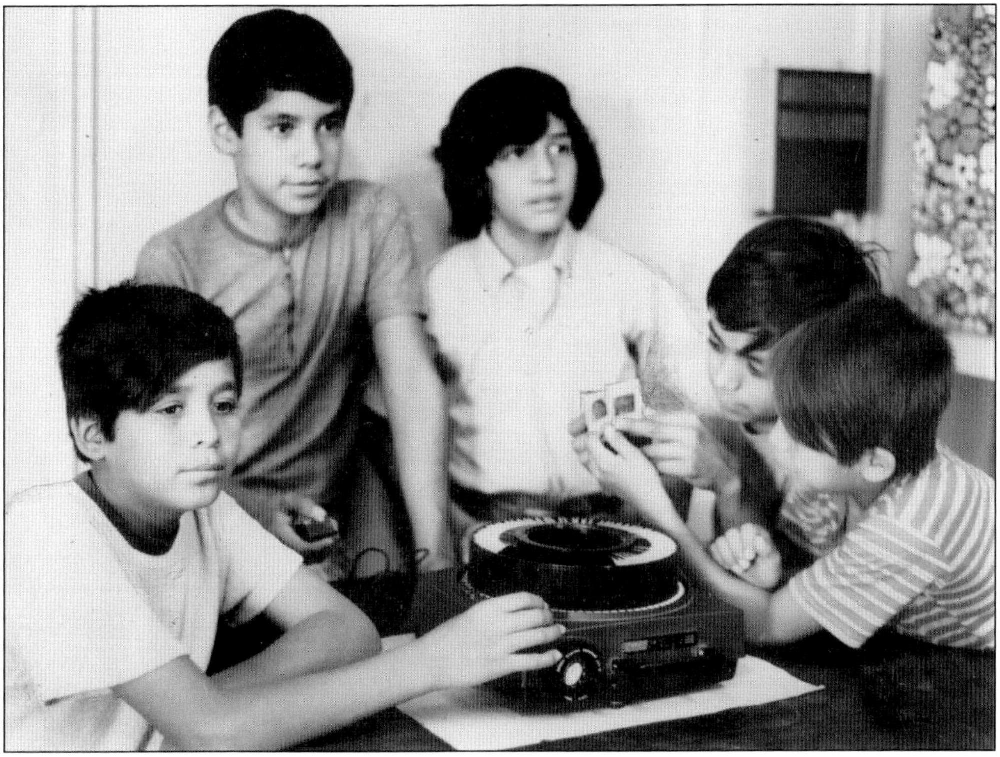

Here, a group of sixth-graders rehearses a slide show presentation.

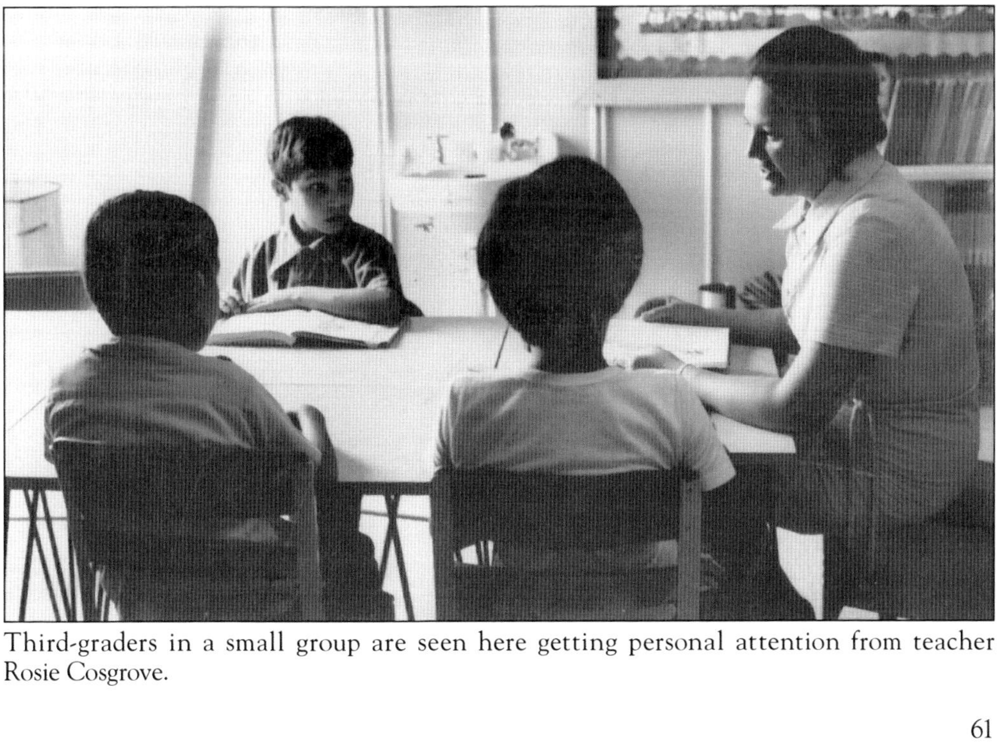

Third-graders in a small group are seen here getting personal attention from teacher Rosie Cosgrove.

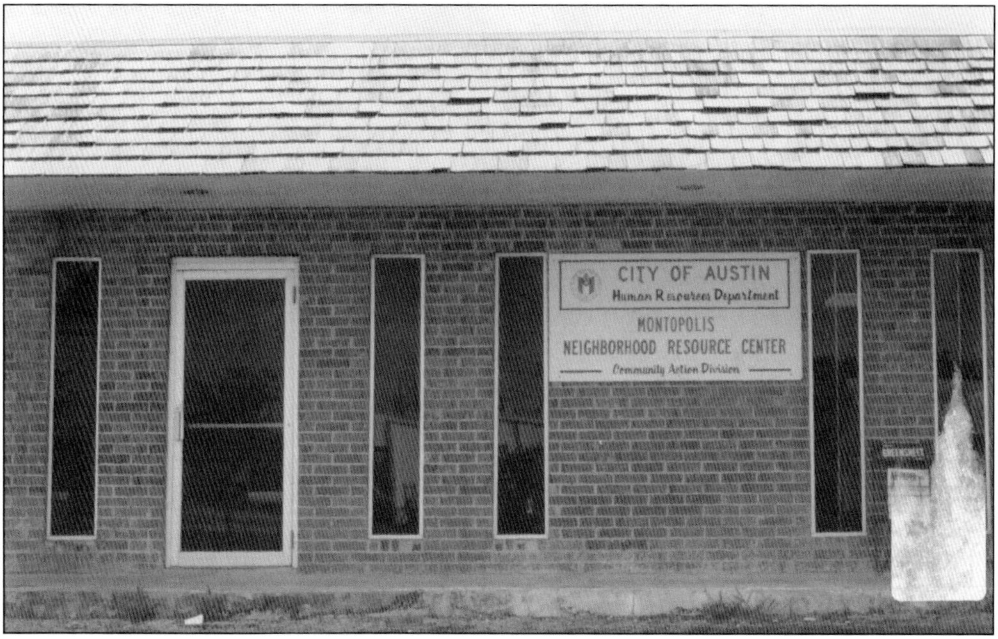


The City of Austin opened the Montopolis Neighborhood Center in the 1970s. The center is primarily utilized to house the neighborhood's Women, Infants, and Children (WIC) program. The Montopolis Community Center was absorbed by the city's parks and recreation department at about the same time and is now known as the Montopolis Recreation Center. In 2012, Austin voters approved bond funding for the construction of a new Montopolis Recreation Center, which will replace the current historic structure built by Father Underwood.

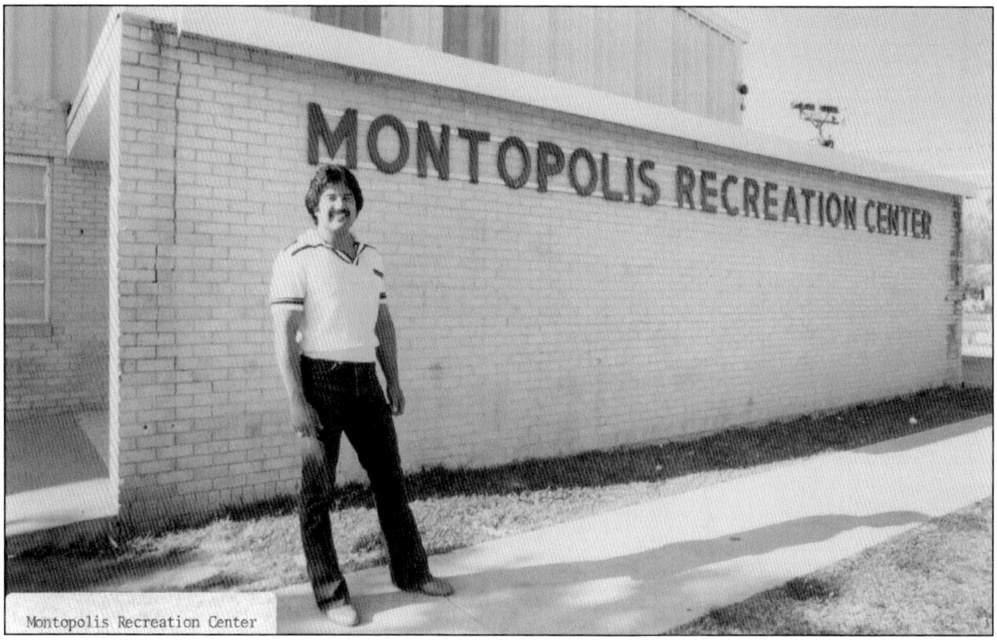


Jesus Olivares stands in front of the Montopolis Recreation Center in the 1970s. The Austin Parks and Recreation Department acquired the community center from the nonprofit organization started by Dolores Church using funds from the federal Model Cities Program in the early 1970s.

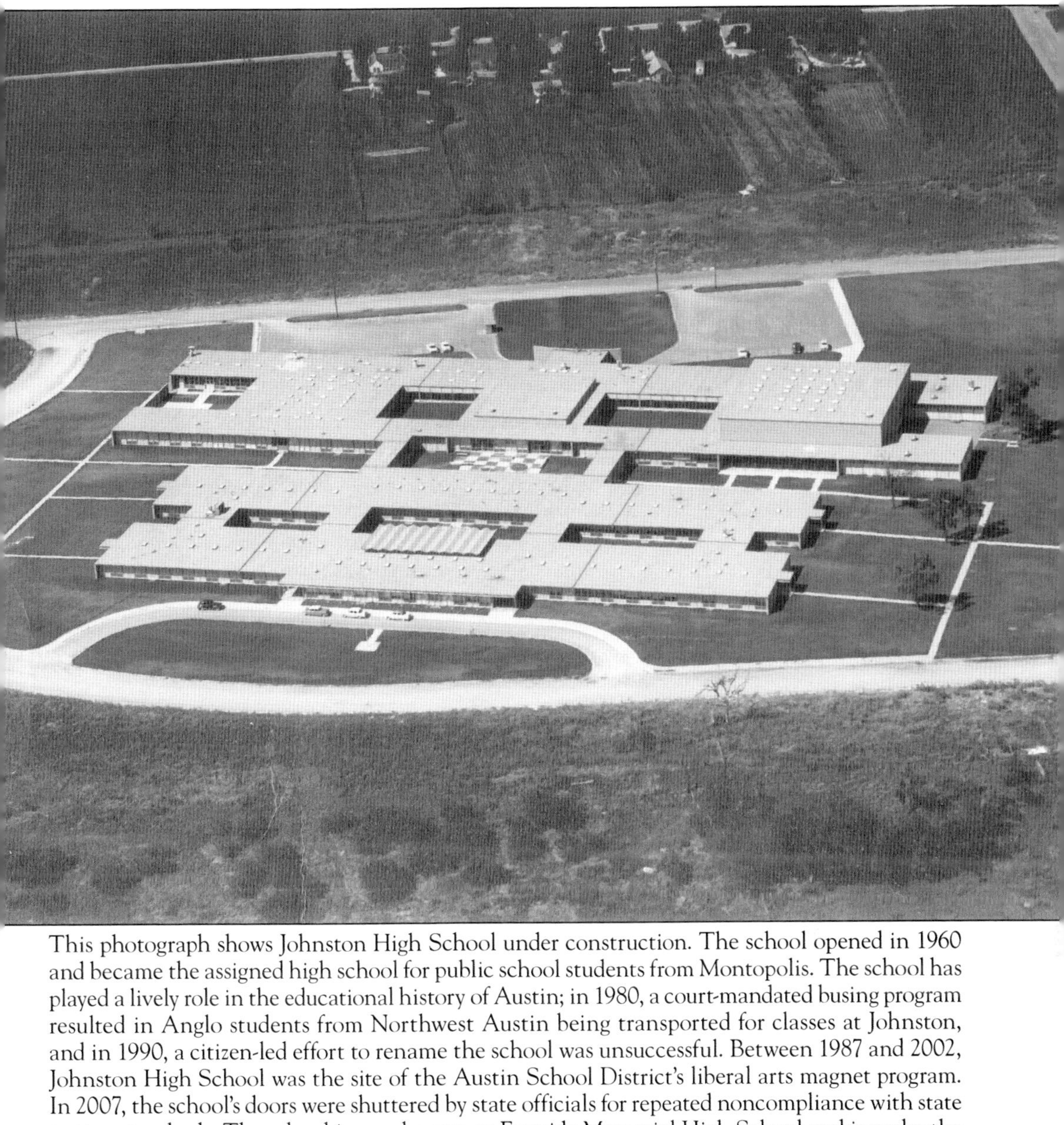

This photograph shows Johnston High School under construction. The school opened in 1960 and became the assigned high school for public school students from Montopolis. The school has played a lively role in the educational history of Austin; in 1980, a court-mandated busing program resulted in Anglo students from Northwest Austin being transported for classes at Johnston, and in 1990, a citizen-led effort to rename the school was unsuccessful. Between 1987 and 2002, Johnston High School was the site of the Austin School District's liberal arts magnet program. In 2007, the school's doors were shuttered by state officials for repeated noncompliance with state testing standards. The school is now known as Eastside Memorial High School and is under the management of Johns Hopkins University's American Institute for Research.

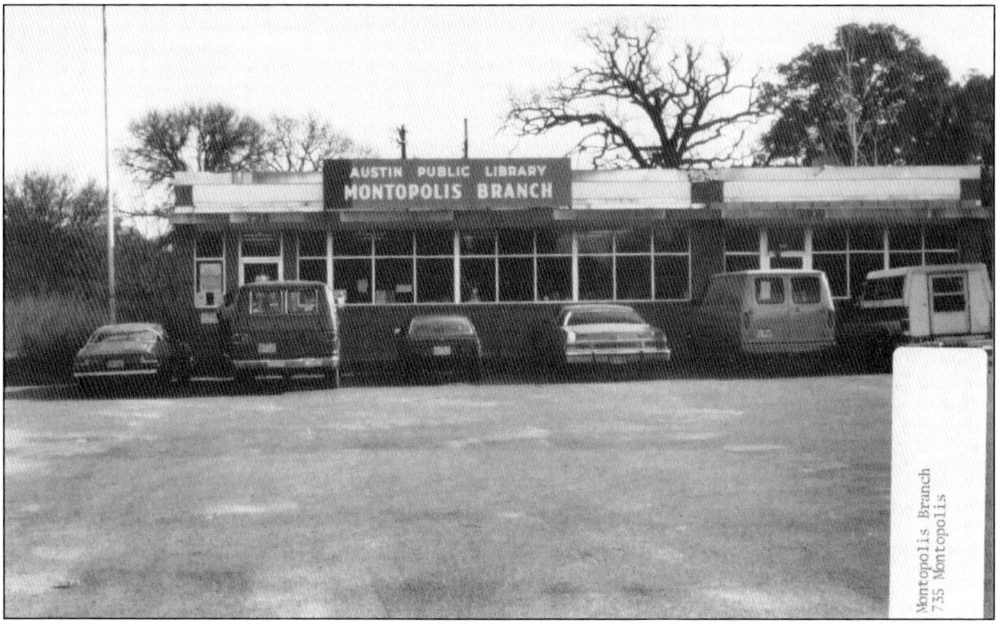


Upon its annexation by the City of Austin, Montopolis was served by a public library bookmobile between 1952 and 1968. Because of high bookmobile usage, city officials authorized the installation of a permanent Montopolis library branch in 1968 at 735 Montopolis Drive. The Montopolis Branch was the first library in the Austin Public Library system to shelve juvenile and adult nonfiction books together. Ironically, the branch was closed in 1983 due to low circulation.

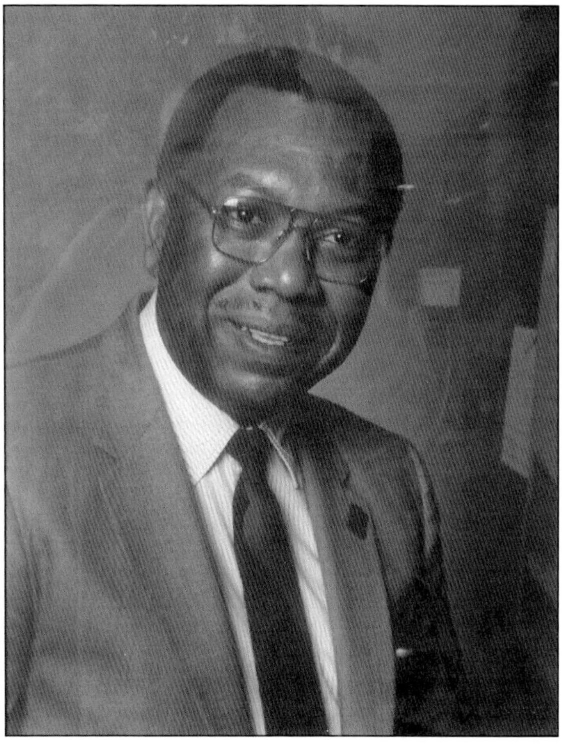

The first manager of the Montopolis Branch was Clifton Griffin, a native of the neighborhood, who at the time was a student at Huston-Tillotson College. After graduating with his bachelor of arts degree in 1970, Griffin accepted a position as manager of the Carver Branch in East Austin, which was considered for closure due to low circulation at the time. Griffin increased circulation by developing the most extensive black history collection in central Texas. He received *NOKOA*'s Community Servant of the Decade award in 1994 and the *Villager*'s Austin Living Legend award in 1995. (Courtesy of the Carver Branch of the Austin Public Library.)

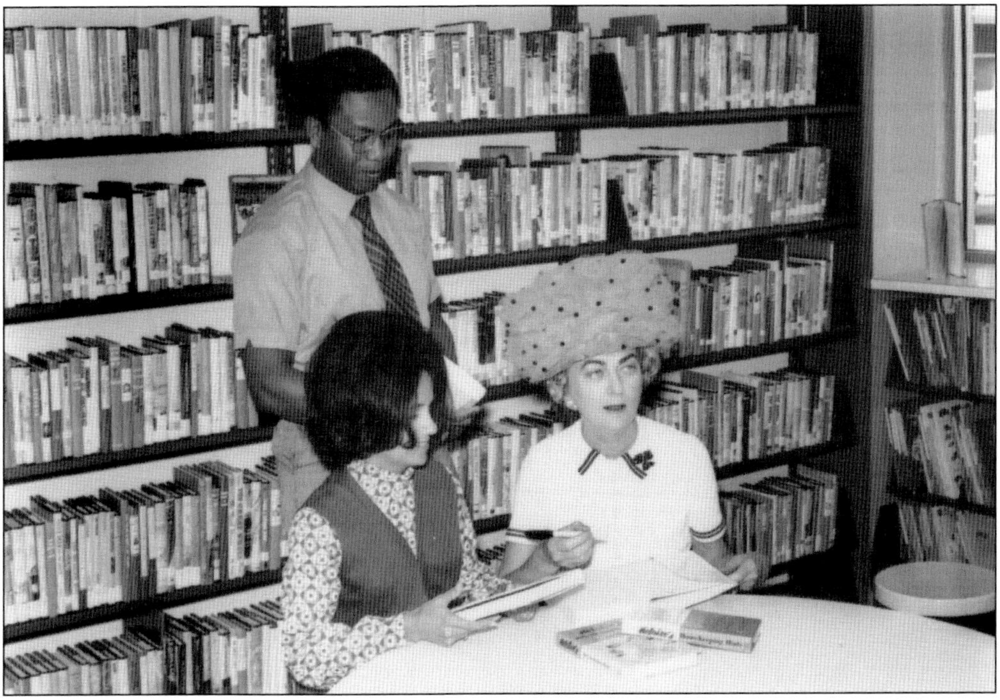

In the late 1960s, the "Hints from Heloise" newspaper column was quite popular, and during a stopover in Austin, Heloise Bowles Cruise paid a visit to the Montopolis community. From left to right are Alice Sanchez, Clifton Griffin, and Cruise.

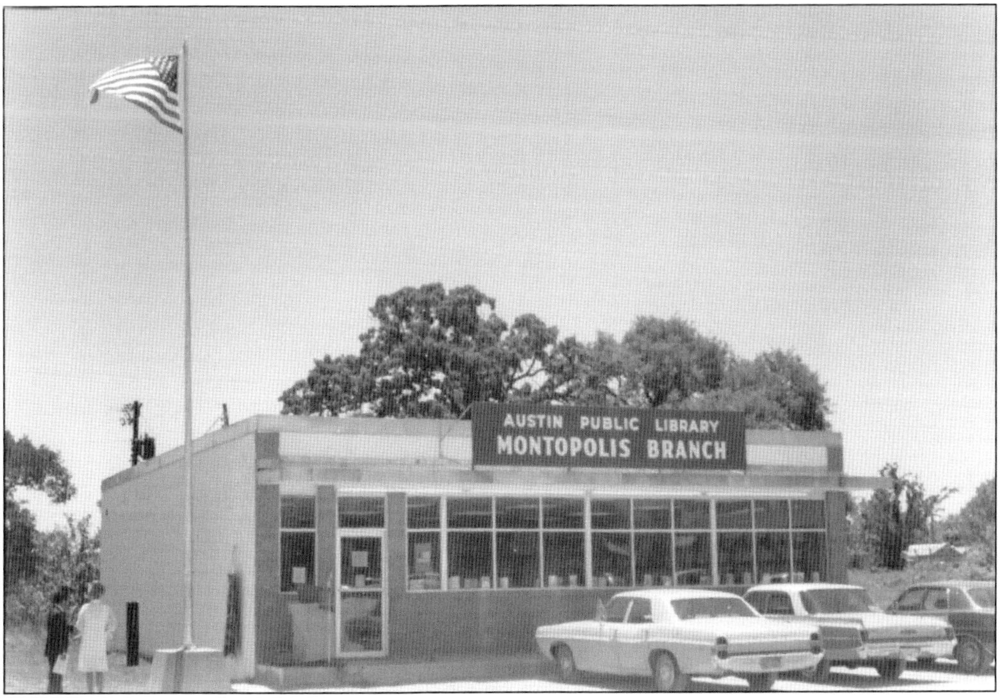


The flagpole inauguration at the Montopolis Branch of the Austin Public Library is seen here on July 4, 1971.

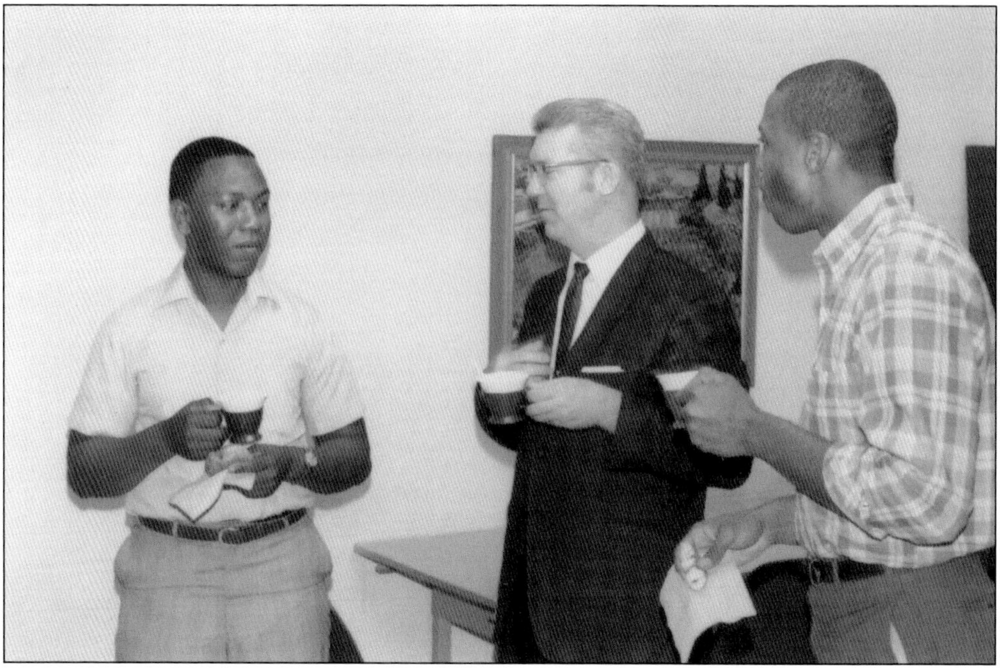

When Clifton Griffin left Montopolis in order to take over the Carver Branch, his friends and coworkers threw him a farewell party. Here, Griffin is on the left and David Earl Holt is in the center.

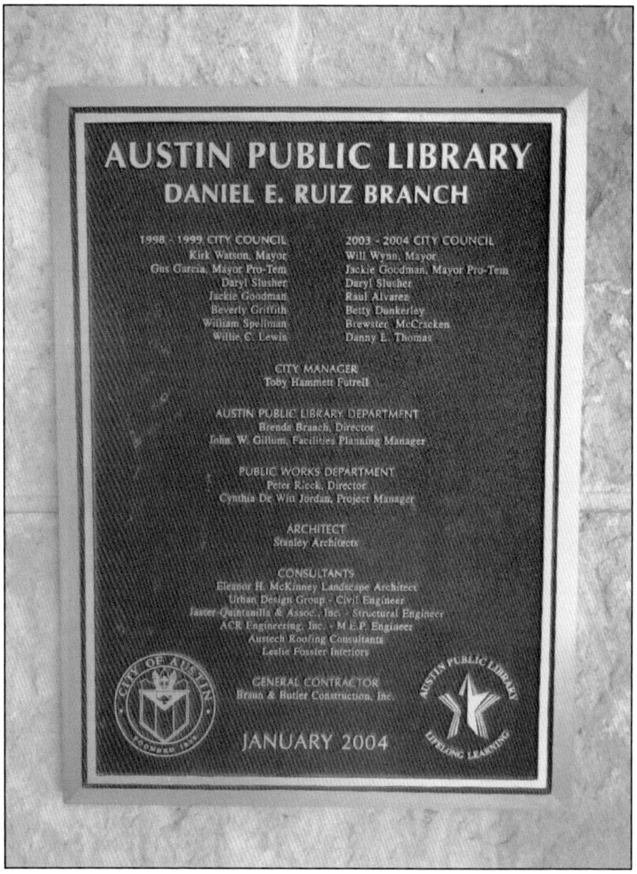


In 2004, the Daniel E. Ruiz Branch of Austin Public Library opened, and the Montopolis neighborhood was once again served by a permanent library. Ruiz was an Austin native who worked as a grassroots community organizer in the 1970s to help elect some of Austin's first Hispanics to local office. (Courtesy of the author's collection.)

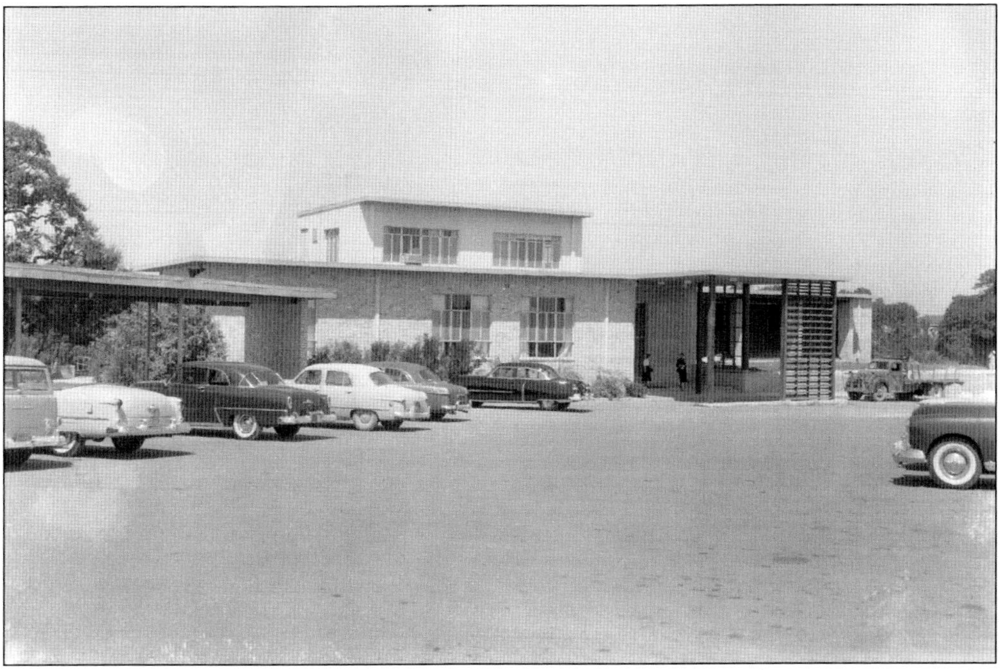

Between 1949 and 1984, the Austin Country Club was located off Riverside Drive in Montopolis. It was here that local golf icon Harvey Penick (1904–1995) taught many future PGA and LPGA professionals such as Ben Crenshaw, Tom Kite, Sandra Palmer, and Judy Kimball, all of whom would go on to win major championships. Penick, Crenshaw, and Kite are all members of the World Golf Hall of Fame. This 1953 photograph depicts the exterior entrance and parking lot on the east end of Felix Avenue. For most of its existence, the golf club was segregated.

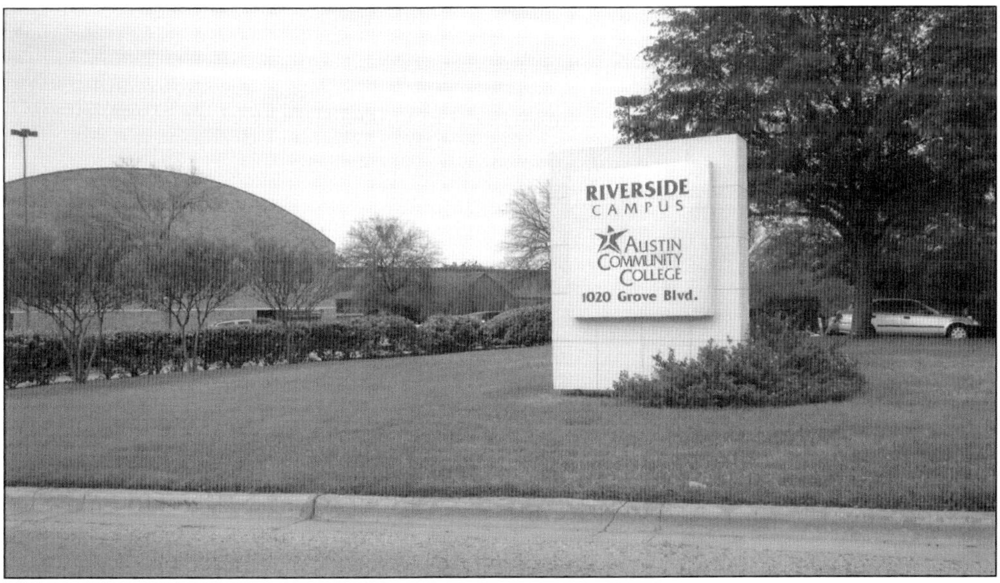


When the Austin Country Club relocated, Austin Community College acquired the property and built its third campus at the site. The Riverside Campus opened on September 1, 1984, and houses some of the college's most important vocational programs. (Courtesy of the author's collection.)

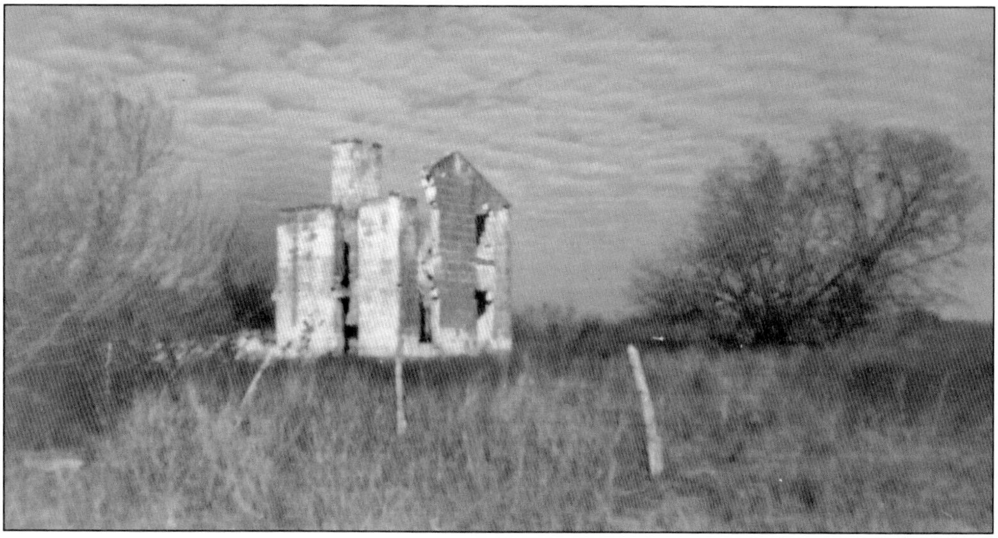

After distinguishing himself during various intrigues in the Texas revolutionary and Republican periods, Thomas Freeman McKinney (1801–1873) built a large estate on the Santiago Del Valle grant near Montopolis in 1850 in order to devote himself to trading and stock raising. He built a limestone house, a gristmill, and a quarter horse track and lived the life of a country gentleman until the Civil War and indebtedness caused him to lose his slaves and go bankrupt. This 1976 photograph shows the ruins of the "big house" at McKinney's ranch.

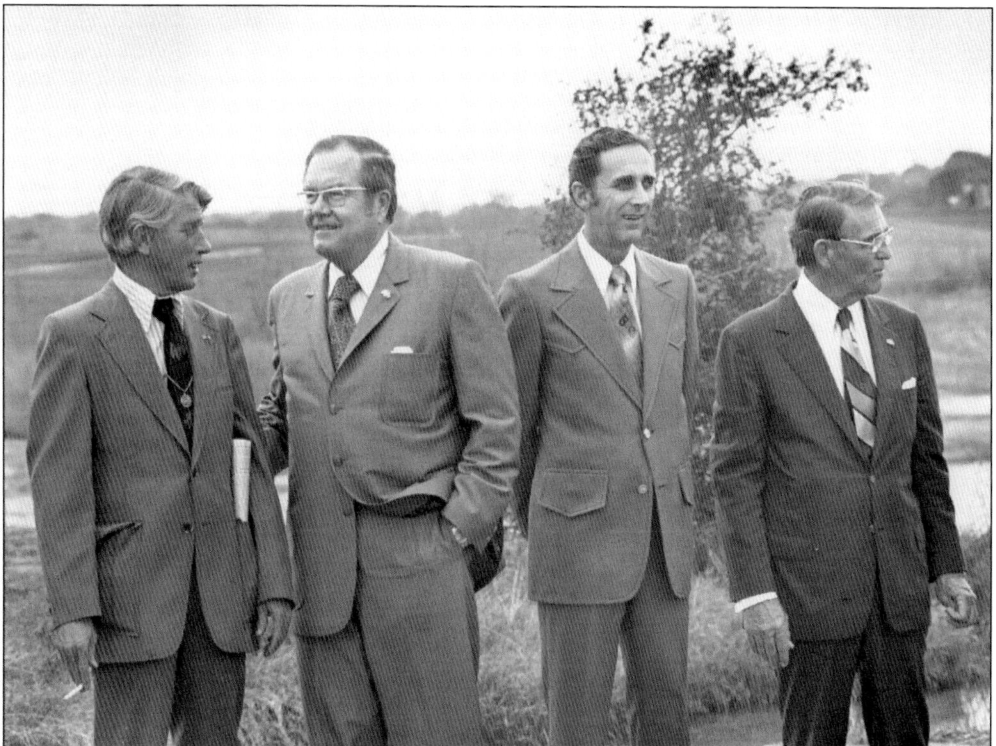

Thomas F. McKinney's ranch became a state park in 1976. This photograph from the dedication ceremony on April 14, 1976, shows Gov. Dolph Briscoe (second from left).

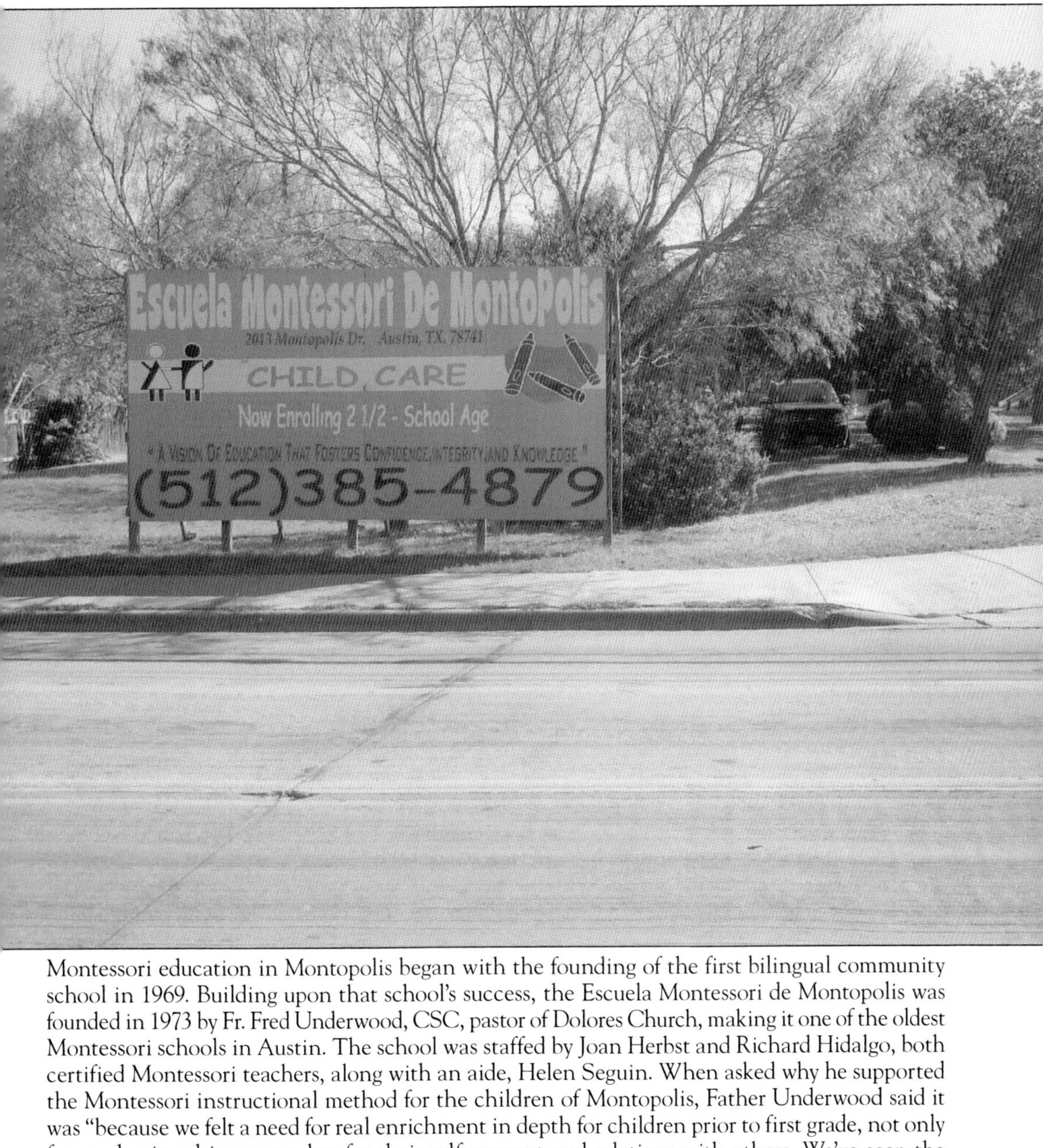


Montessori education in Montopolis began with the founding of the first bilingual community school in 1969. Building upon that school's success, the Escuela Montessori de Montopolis was founded in 1973 by Fr. Fred Underwood, CSC, pastor of Dolores Church, making it one of the oldest Montessori schools in Austin. The school was staffed by Joan Herbst and Richard Hidalgo, both certified Montessori teachers, along with an aide, Helen Seguin. When asked why he supported the Montessori instructional method for the children of Montopolis, Father Underwood said it was "because we felt a need for real enrichment in depth for children prior to first grade, not only for academic achievement, but for their self-concept and relations with others. We've seen the children in Montessori develop more quickly and positively, showing a respect for the materials, an ability to function on their own without constant supervision, and a better self image." The school's personnel and educational philosophy have changed, but it continues in operation today. The name *Montessori* is not a trademark and can be applied to schools that do not in fact use the method or fully certified teachers. (Courtesy of the author's collection.)

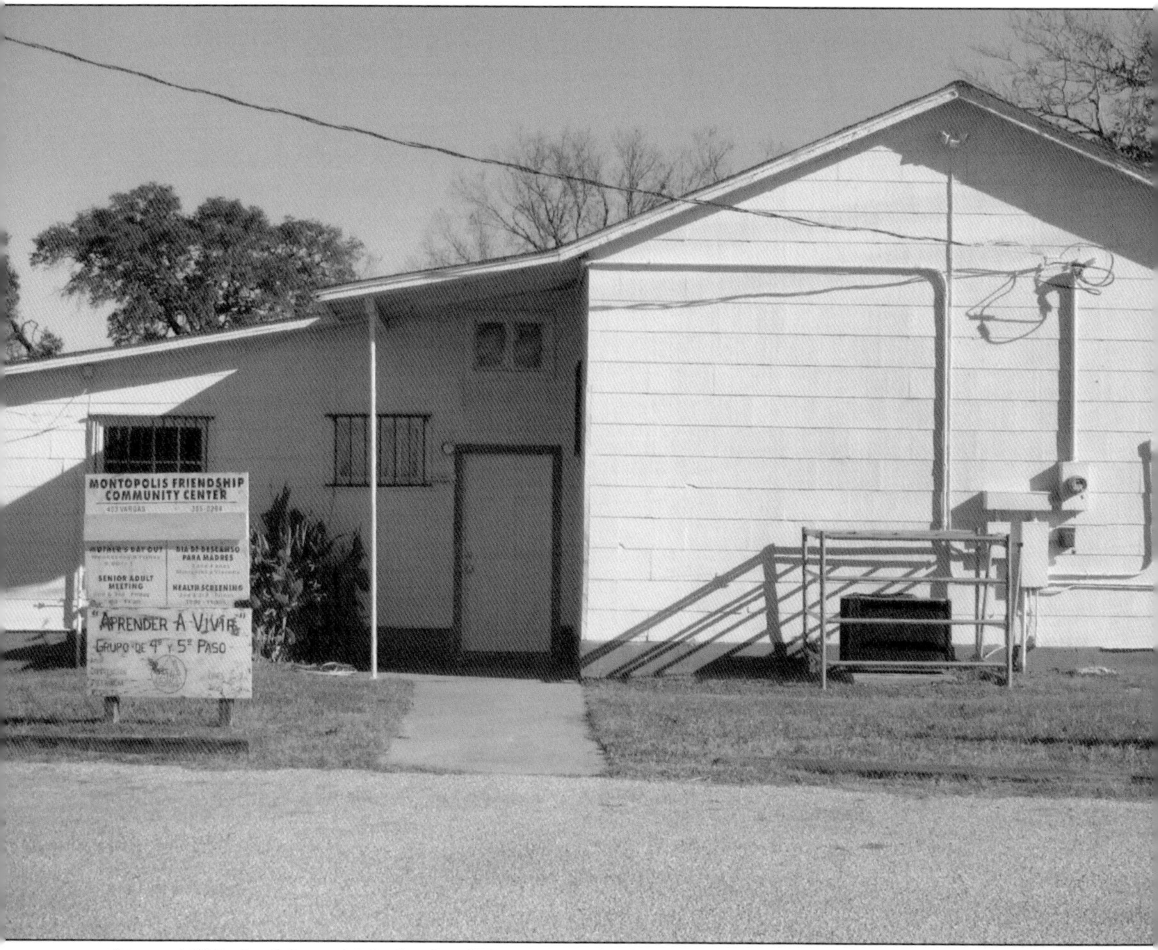


Since 1957, the United Methodist Women, with the support of Methodist churches, individual donors, and other funding sources, have operated the Montopolis Friendship Community Center out of a former school building on Vargas Road. The center furnishes drop-in daycare twice per week (it also once served as a local Head Start center) and operates a store that sells used clothing and household goods. The person most associated with the establishment of the center is Velma Miles, the wife of Austin's longtime, controversial police chief Bob Miles. By the early 1970s, African American activists such as Velma Roberts and Austin NAACP chair Volma Overton, as well as Chicano activist groups such as the Brown Berets, were actively calling for Miles's ouster as police chief for his support of segregation and his lack of attention to police brutality incidents in Montopolis and other parts of East Austin. (Courtesy of the author's collection.)

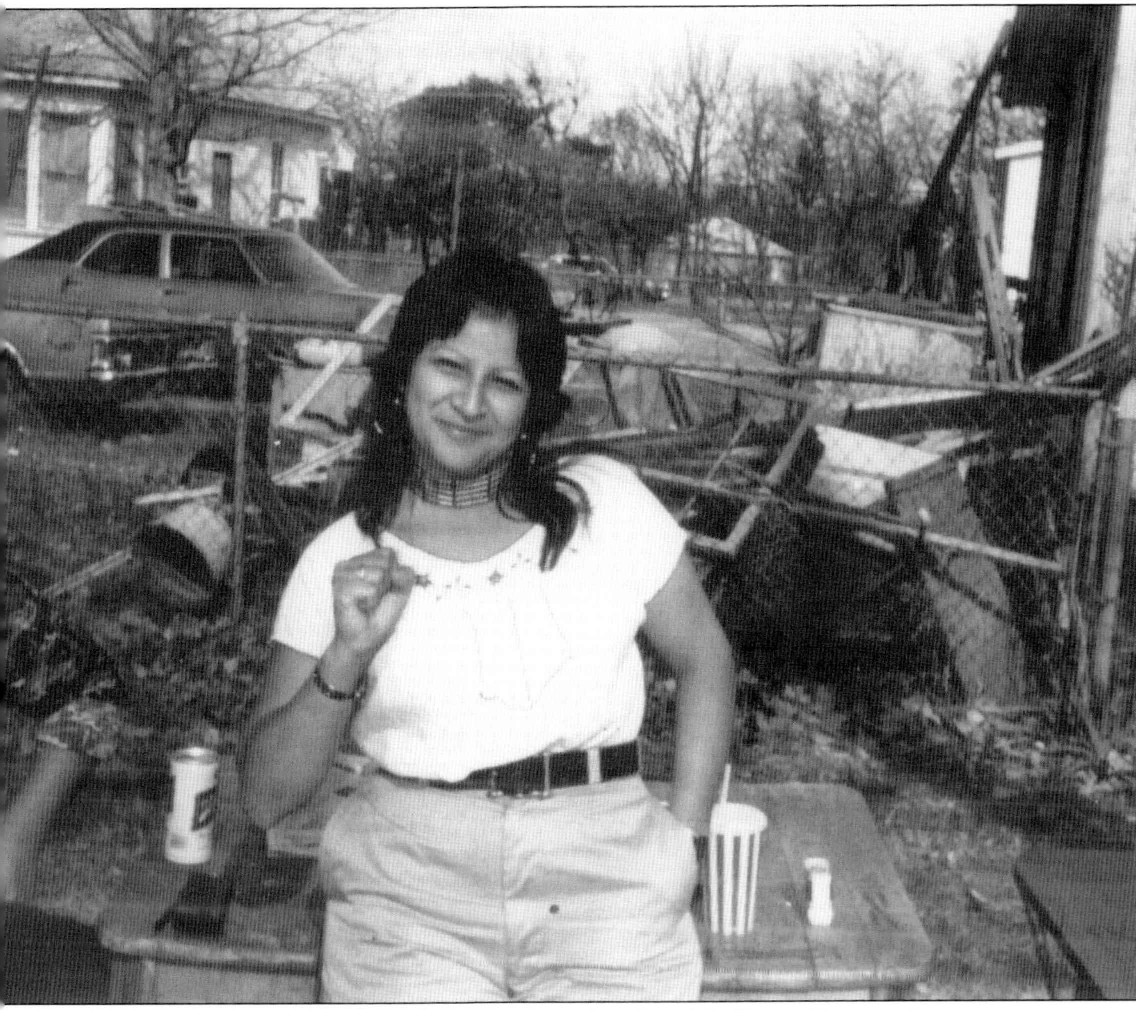

East Austin icon Susana Renteria Almanza was a cofounder of the Brown Berets and went on to found People Organized in Defense of the Earth and her Resources (PODER) in the early 1990s. In this 1979 photograph, she is seen at a Brown Berets barbecue fundraiser at El Centro, located on East First Street.

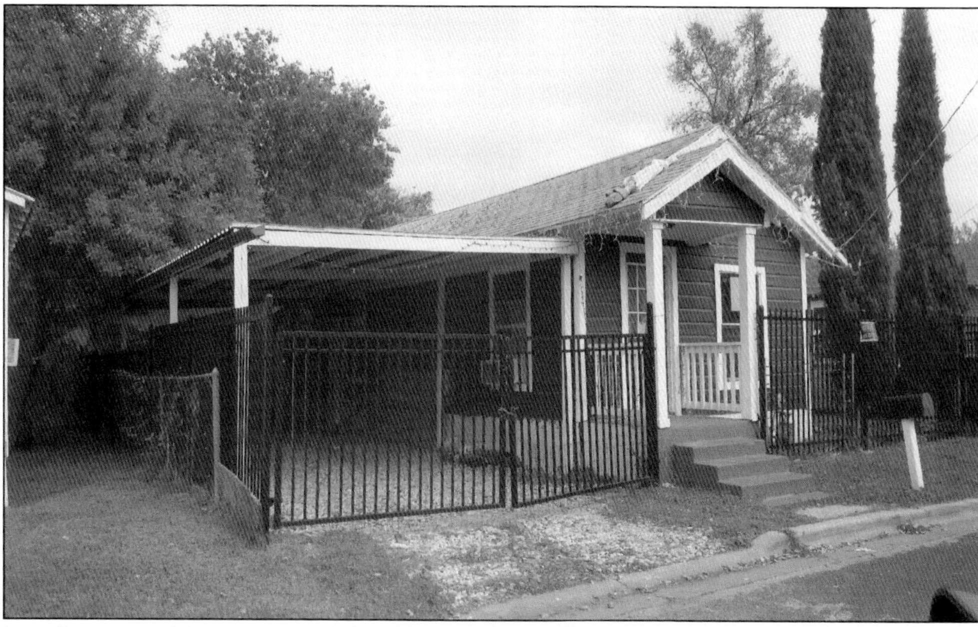

East Austin neighborhoods, including Montopolis, are facing increasing gentrification pressures. However, because it has not yet faced the gentrification pressures of East Austin's 78702 zip code, Montopolis still contains some of Austin's most interesting examples of vernacular architecture, particularly "shotgun homes" such as this. (Courtesy of the author's collection.)

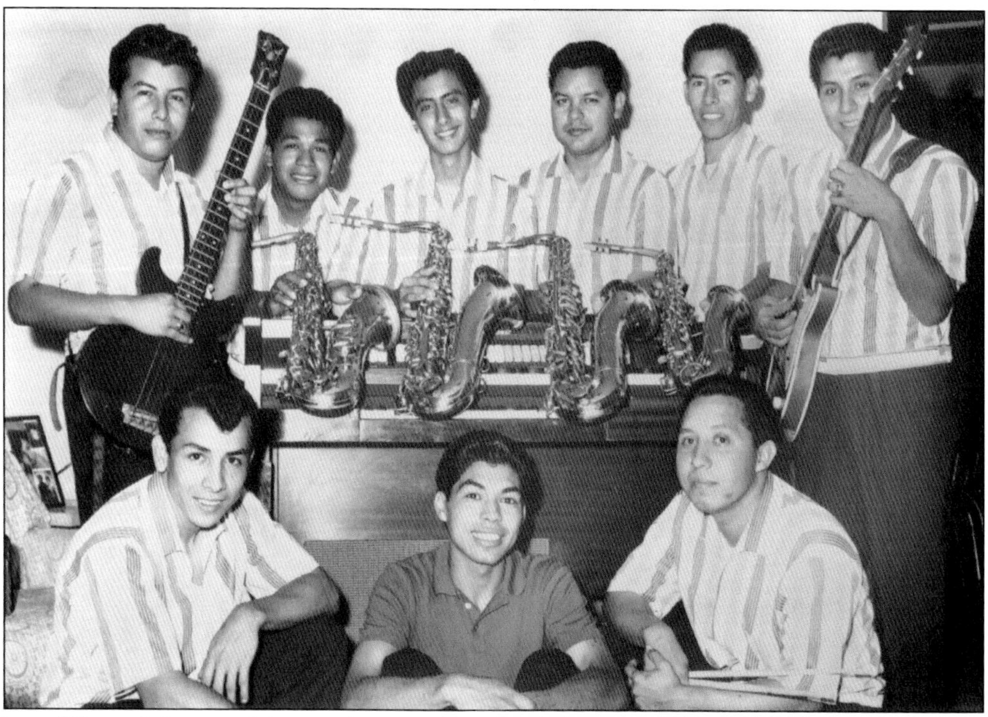

Lupe "Shorty" Ortiz is a Montopolis icon whose band Shorty and the Corvettes entertained fans for over 40 years. Now known as Mariachi Corbetas, Ortiz's band, which includes his son and grandson, continues to perform at venues all over Texas and Louisiana.

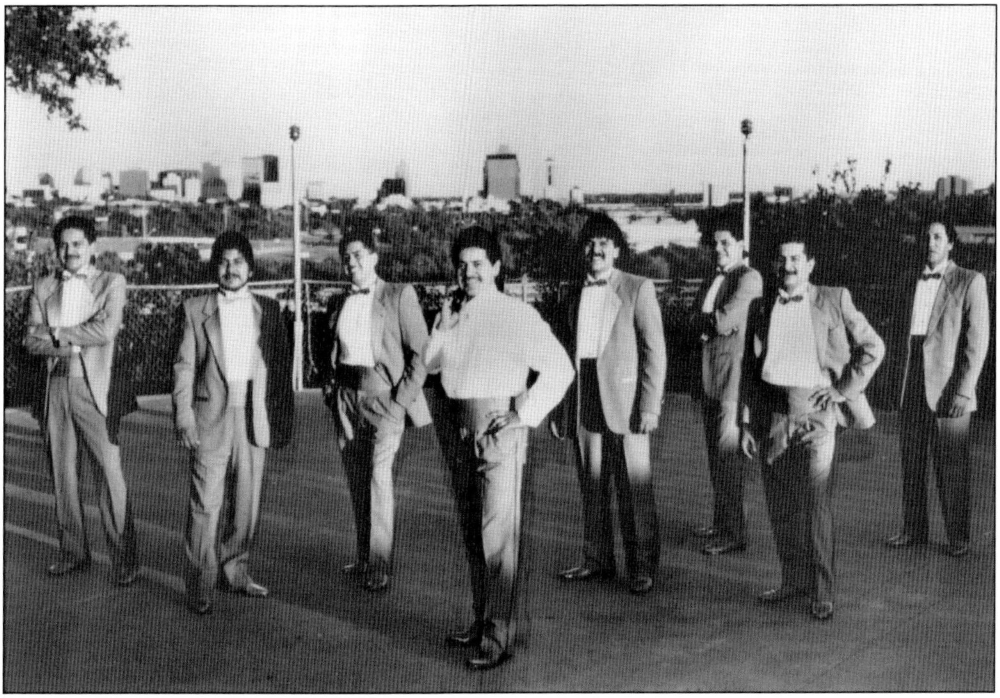

Another band with strong Montopolis ties is Yayo Castillo y Rumores, whose discography and revolving family membership reads like a who's who of modern central Texas Tejano music history.

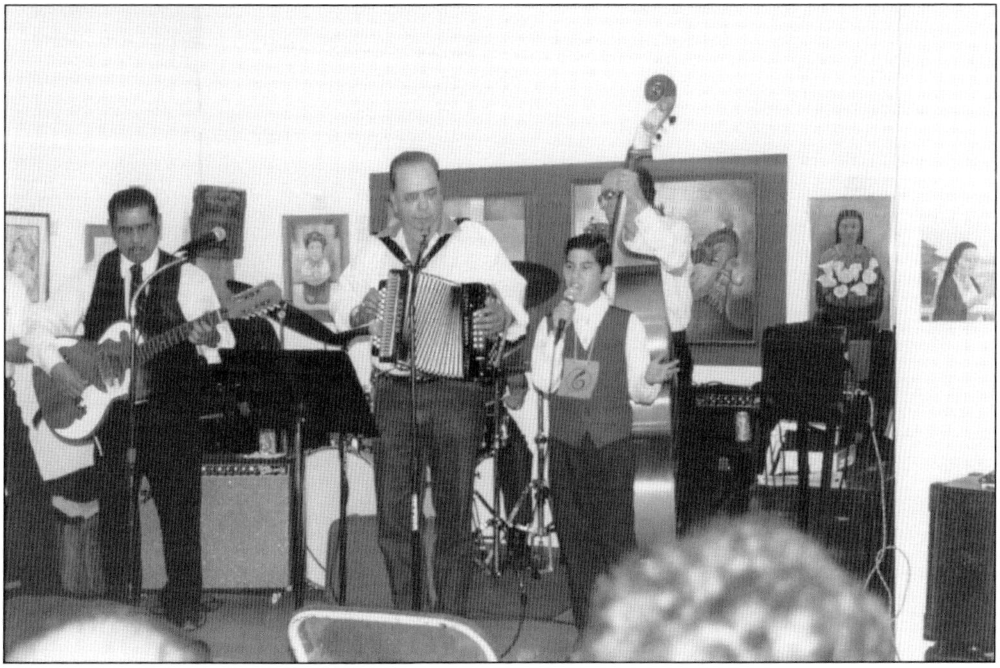

Johnny Degollado, also known as the "Montopolis Kid," is the dean of Austin area conjunto accordionists and bandleaders. Inducted into the Tejano Music Hall of Fame in 1986, Degollado started his band at age 15 in 1952 in Montopolis, where he continues to reside. The pavilion at the Fiesta Gardens Stage is named in his honor. (Courtesy of the Mexic-Arte Museum.)

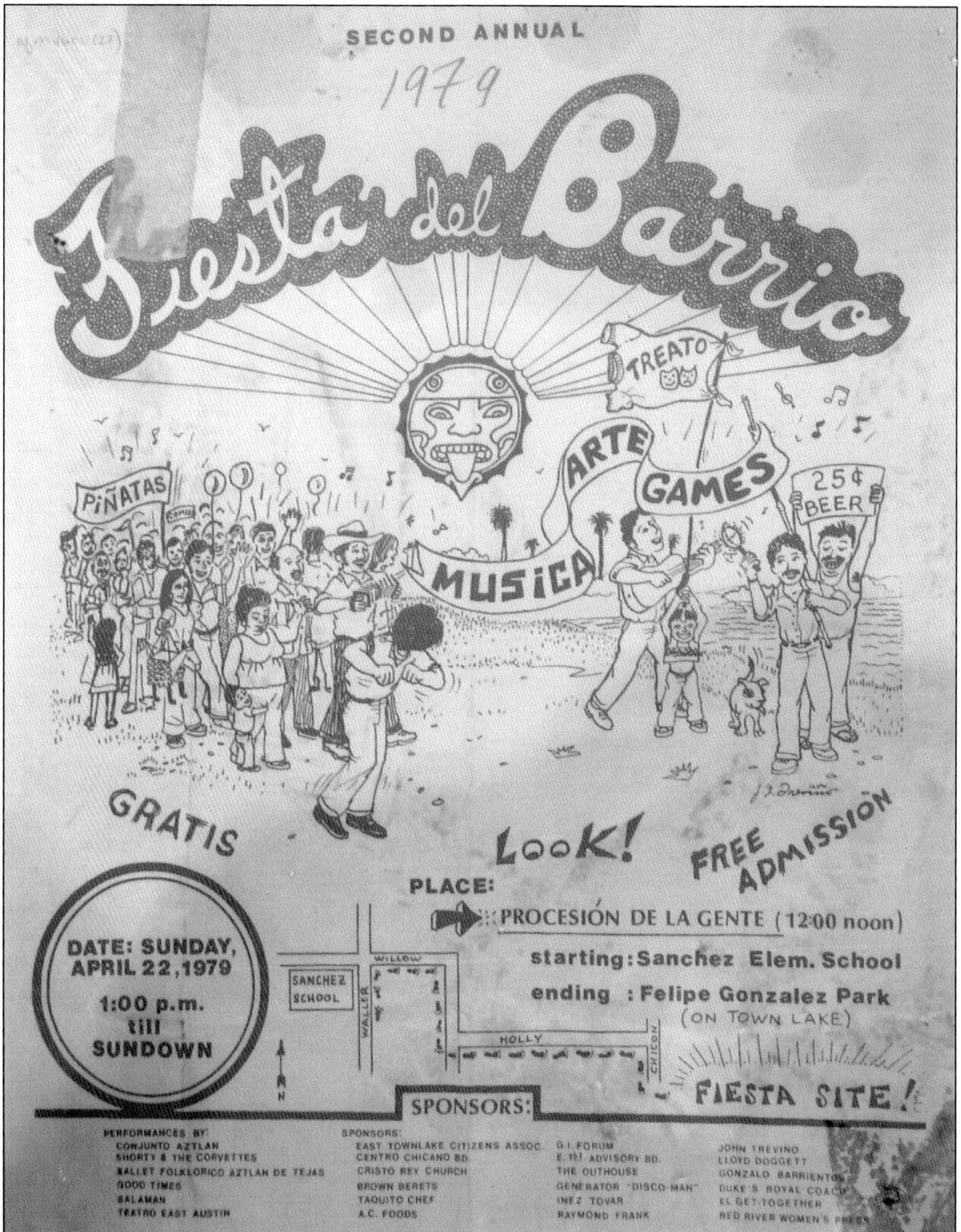


The 1979 Fiesta del Barrio featured free admission, music by Shorty and the Corvettes and Conjunto Aztlan, family games and art, and 25¢ beer.

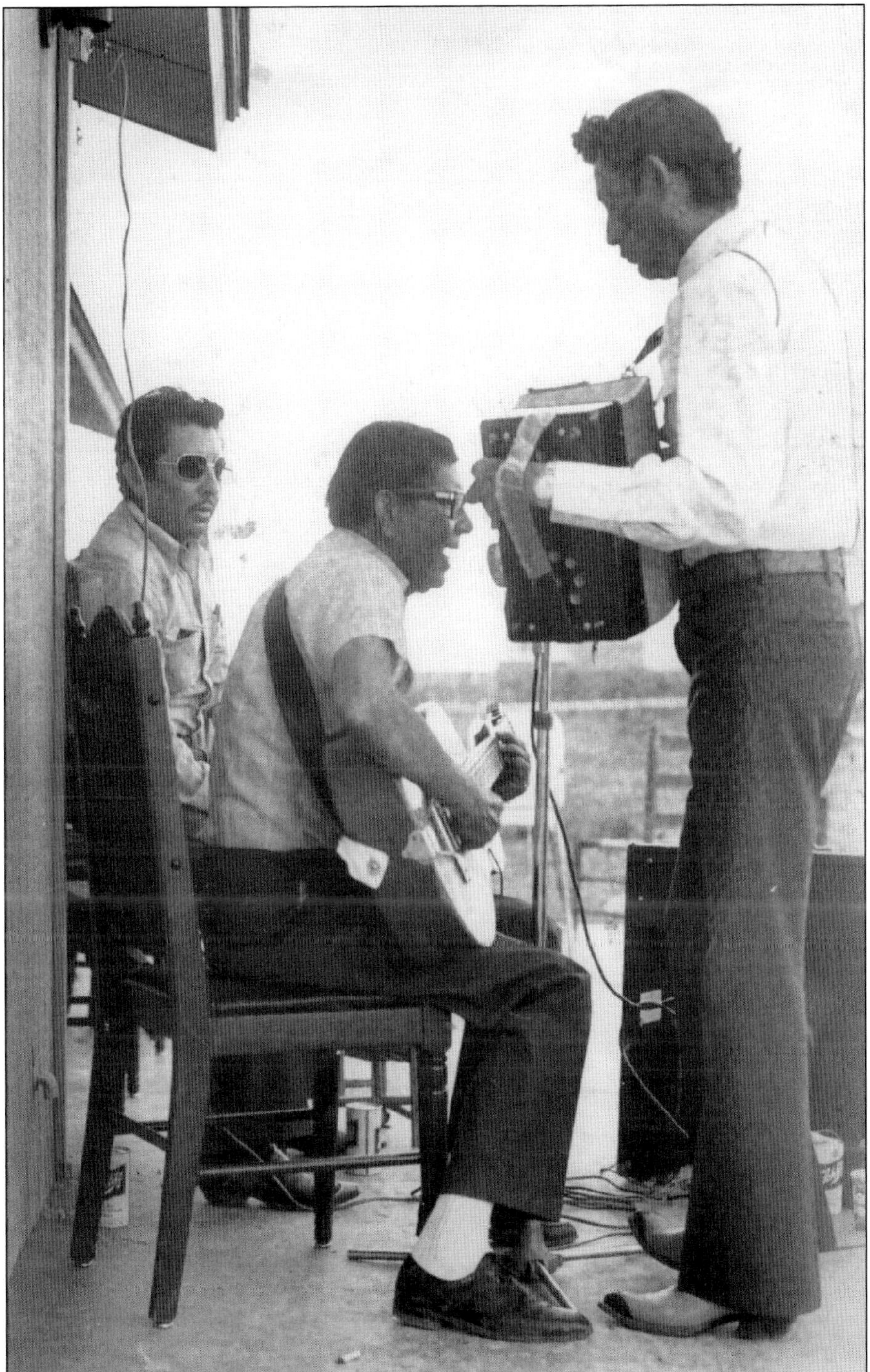

Montopolis conjuntos played, and continue to play, all manner of gatherings, including weddings, quinceañeras, political rallies, birthday parties, barbecues, fundraisers, museum openings, and cultural events. This 1970 photograph shows three musicians playing at a local event, with three cans of Schlitz beer at their feet.

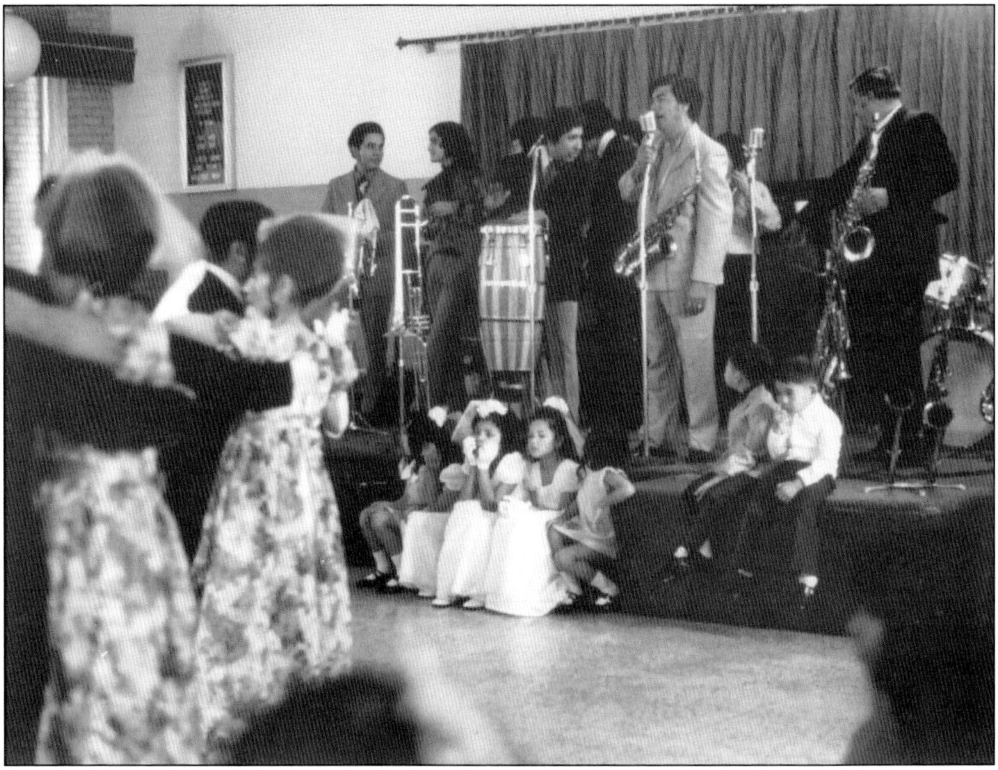

The Alfonso Ramos Band plays a wedding at the San Jose Community Center in Montopolis.

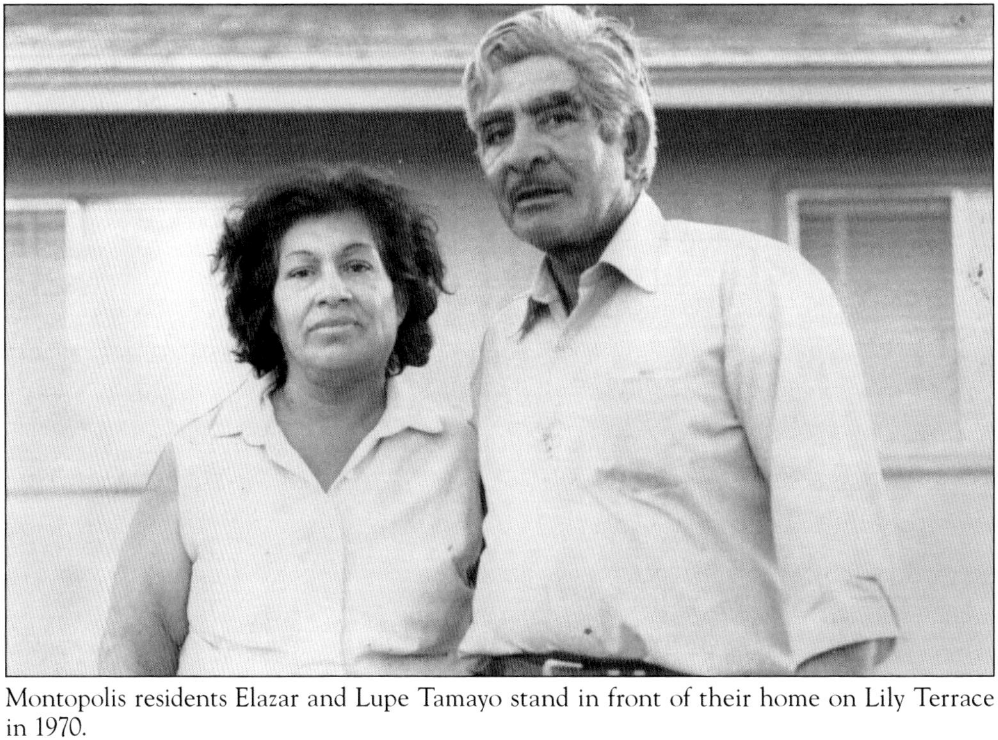

Montopolis residents Elazar and Lupe Tamayo stand in front of their home on Lily Terrace in 1970.

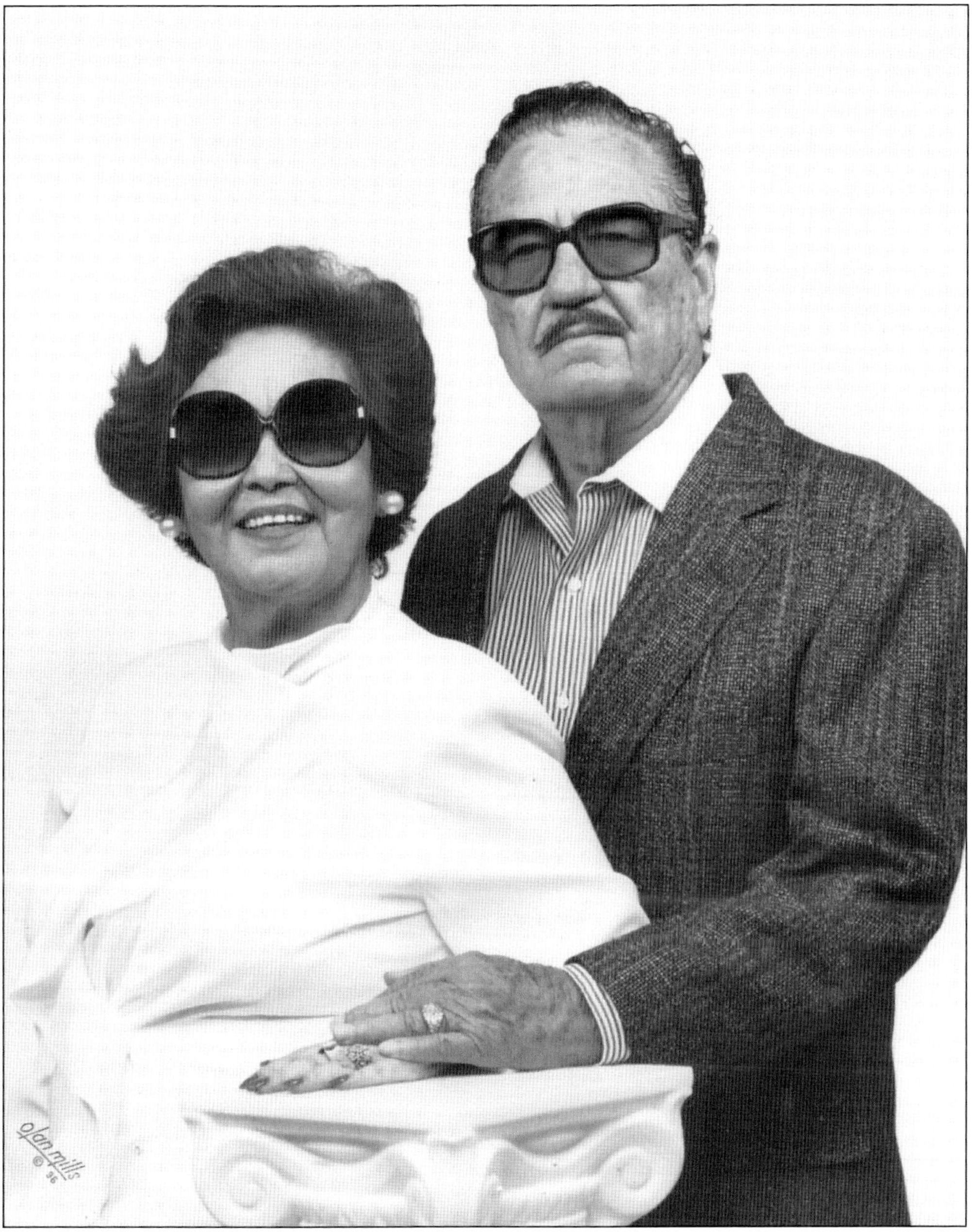


Felix and Amanda Benavides moved to Montopolis from the Rio Grande Valley in the early 1950s and have been a mainstay of the neighborhood for almost 60 years. Their multi-acre homestead was located in the rural southern portion of the neighborhood, along the Del Valle border, which allowed them to not only engage in subsistence farming, but also in deer, squirrel, and raccoon hunting. Their largely hidden portion of Montopolis was annexed by the City of Austin in the 1970s. (Courtesy of Felix and Amanda Benavides.)

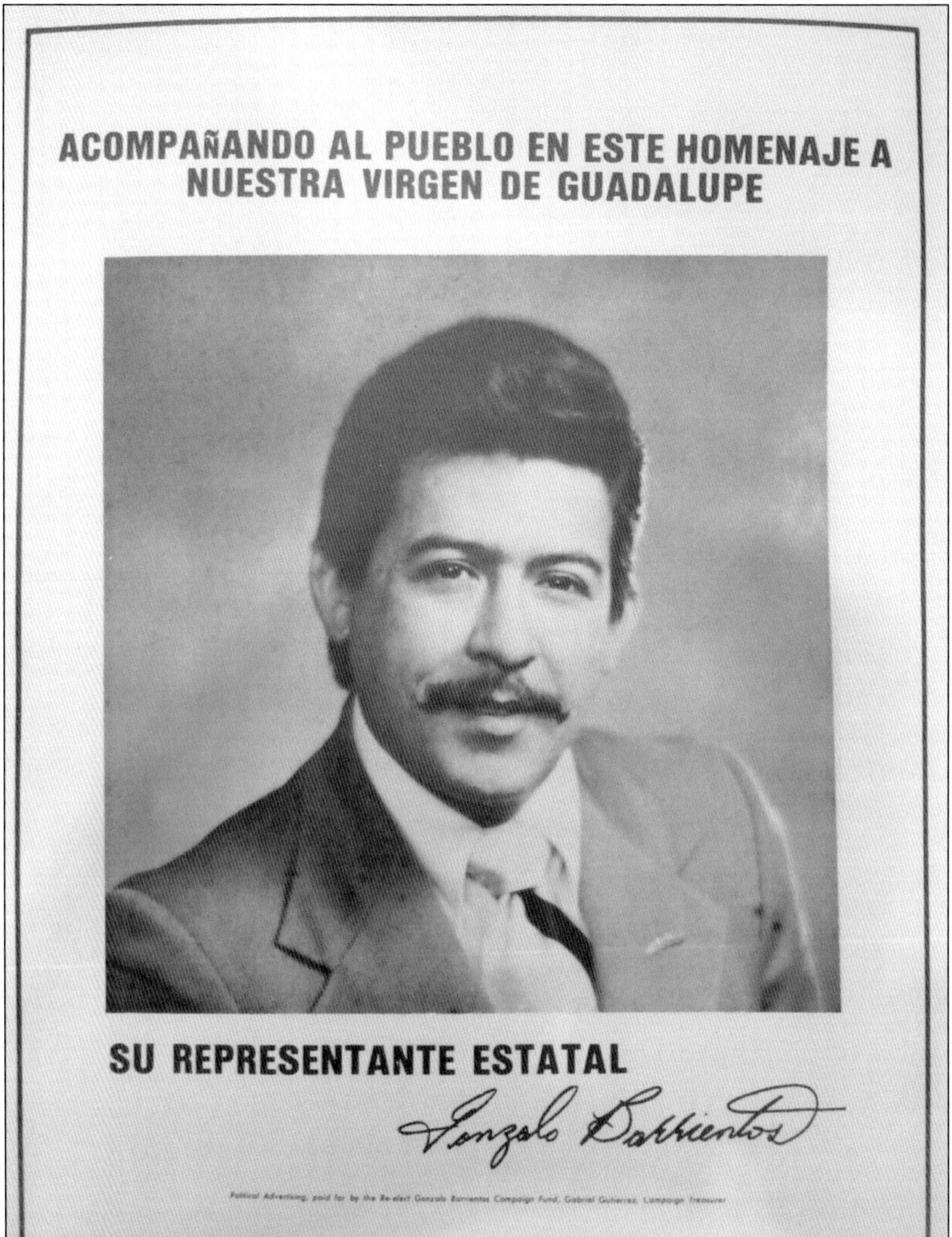


Gonzalo Barrientos, born in 1941, represented Montopolis and South Austin in the Texas House of Representatives (Districts 37 and 51) from 1975 to 1984 and in the Texas State Senate (District 14) from 1985 to 2006, and he continues to remain active in local and state politics. This campaign advertisement is from the 1977 Homanje del Pueblo a La Guadalupana, an important event sponsored by the religious society for women at San Jose Parish, the Sociedad de Nuestra Señora de Guadalupe.

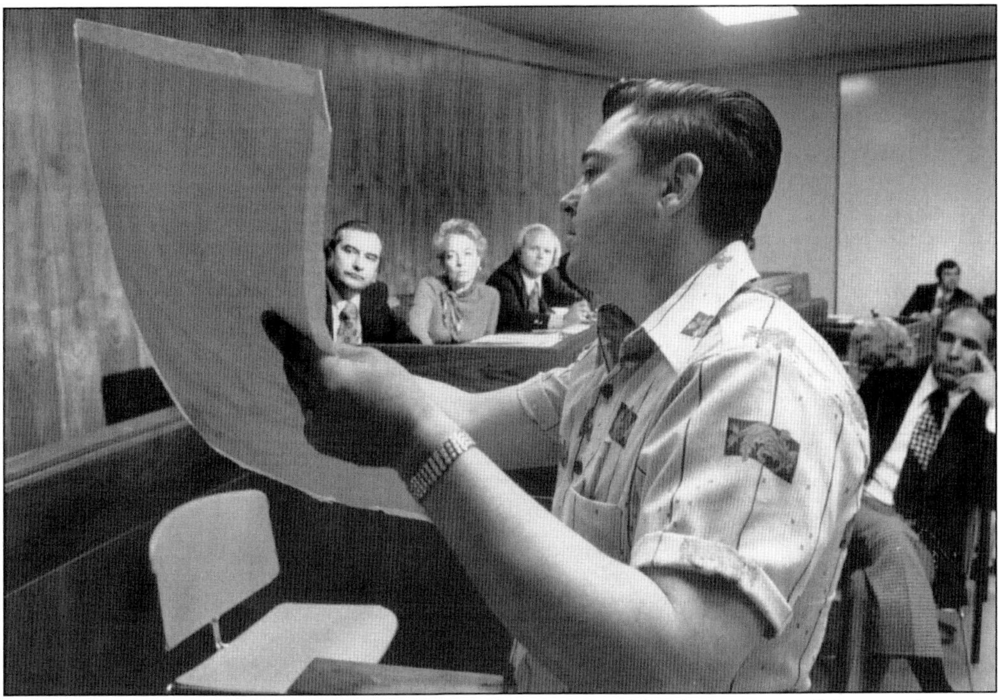

Travis County commissioner Richard Moya explains some of the finer points of county planning to commissioner Ann Richards, county judge Mike Renfro (to the right of Richards), and others at a 1975 meeting.

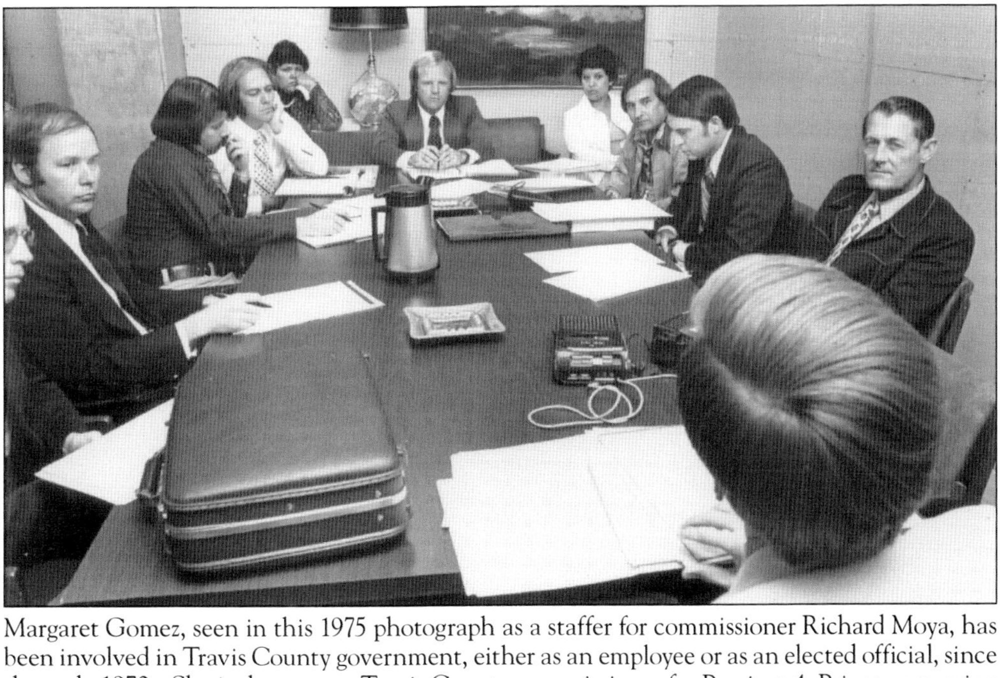

Margaret Gomez, seen in this 1975 photograph as a staffer for commissioner Richard Moya, has been involved in Travis County government, either as an employee or as an elected official, since the early 1970s. She is the current Travis County commissioner for Precinct 4. Prior to assuming her current position, Gomez served as county constable for southeast Travis County for over 12 years. That post is now held by Maria Canchola.

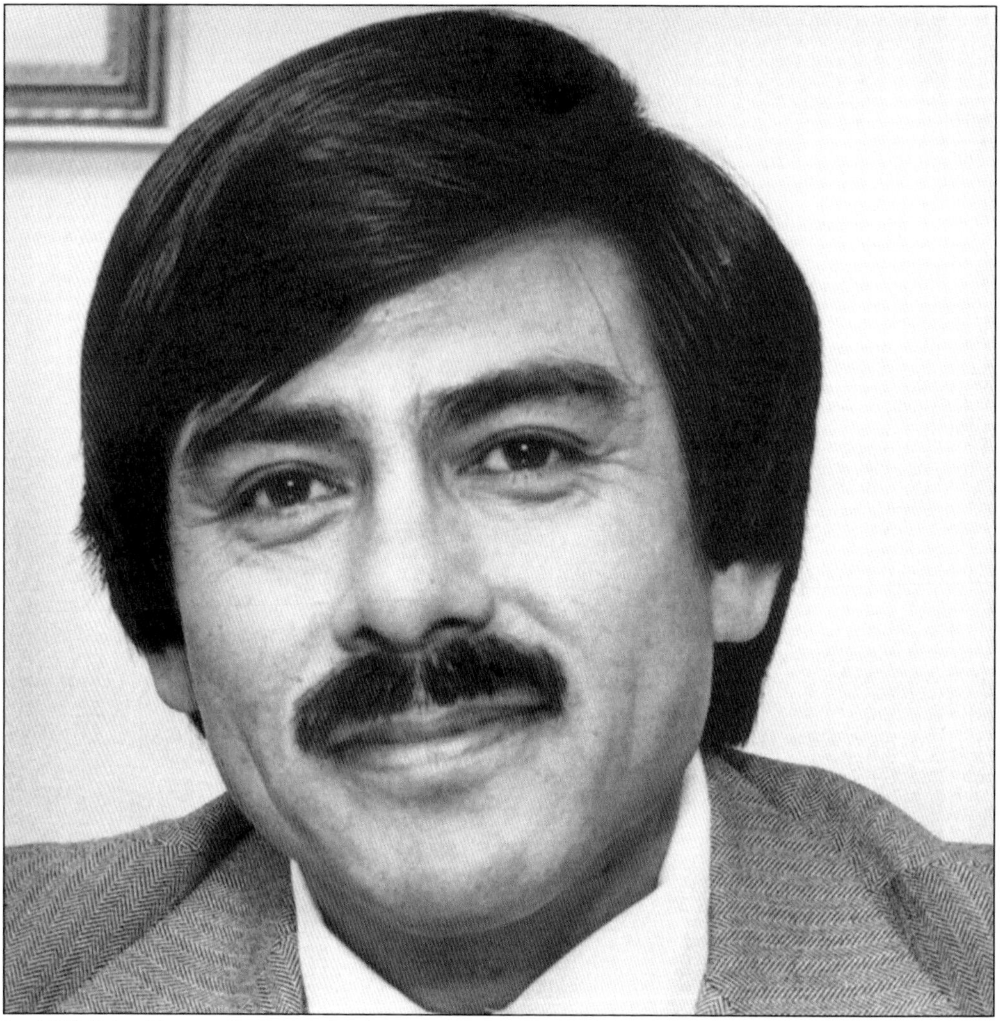

In 1975, John Treviño became the first Hispanic person elected to the Austin City Council. He served for more than 13 years, eventually becoming mayor pro tem. He has vivid recollections of first meeting Father Underwood, saying, "I had heard about a new priest, a young priest being assigned to the Dolores Parish. I had not met him before and had no idea what he looked like . . . and so sometime after the meeting that night I see this guy driving up in the parking lot in a motorcycle and a T-Shirt . . . and the first thing I recall is seeing that he was white . . . and I kept saying 'What's a white guy in a motorcycle doing over here?' It turns out that that was my introduction to Father Fred Underwood." Treviño partnered with Father Underwood in operating and supervising the newly created War on Poverty initiative known as VISTA (Volunteers in Service to America) in Montopolis, as well as many other initiatives.

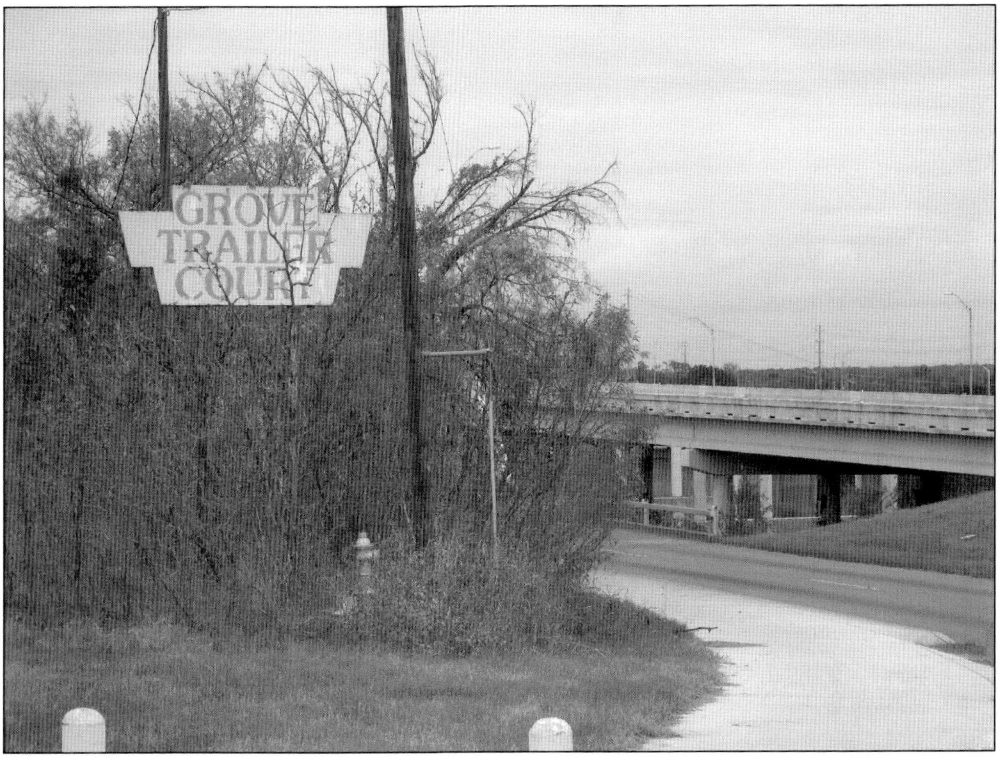


A faded sign is all that remains of the Grove Trailer Court, which was located along the southwest bank of the Montopolis Bridge. Vernon Grove operated a cattle operation down the street at what is now Roy G. Guerrero Park and also built the trailer park in the 1940s and 1950s. Southeast Austin continues to house a high concentration of manufactured home and trailer park communities due to its historically cheaper cost of land and living. (Courtesy of the author's collection.)

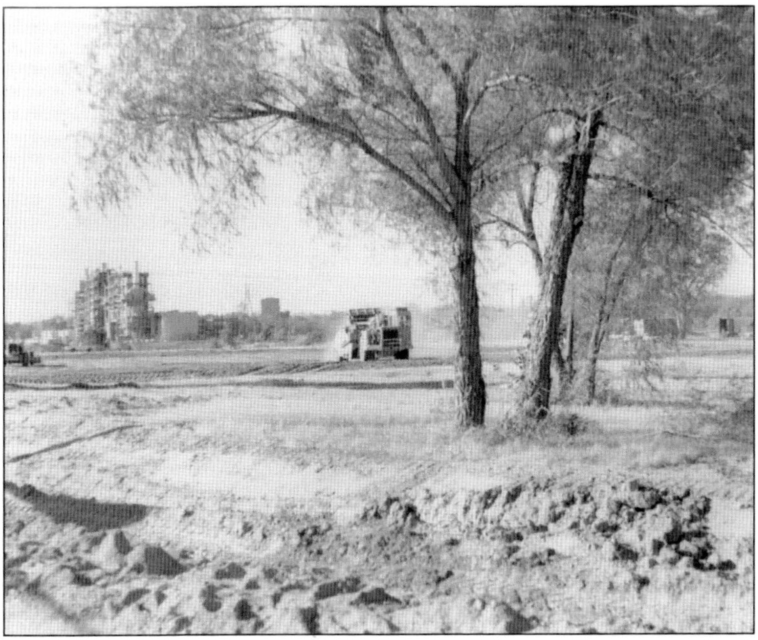

The 400-acre property comprising the Roy G. Guerrero Colorado River Metropolitan Park has been developed in stages. In this November 1979 photograph, land for Krieg Field is being smoothed out. The Holly power plant is in the background.

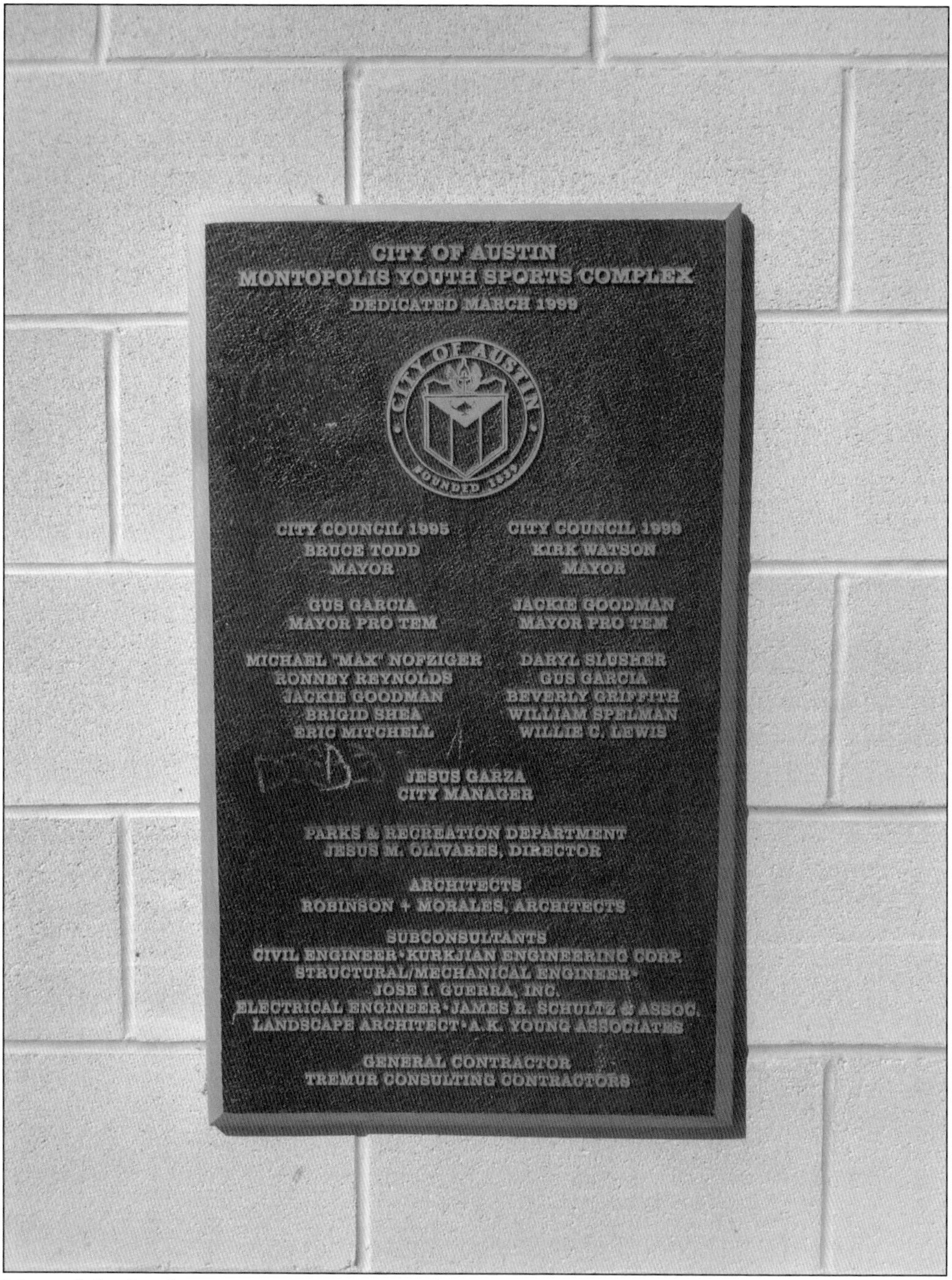


Most of the land comprising Guerrero Park was acquired in 1994, with funding for the park approved in 1998. The Montopolis Youth Sports Complex was dedicated in March 1999 and serves as the headquarters for Montopolis Little League and other team sports. (Courtesy of the author's collection.)

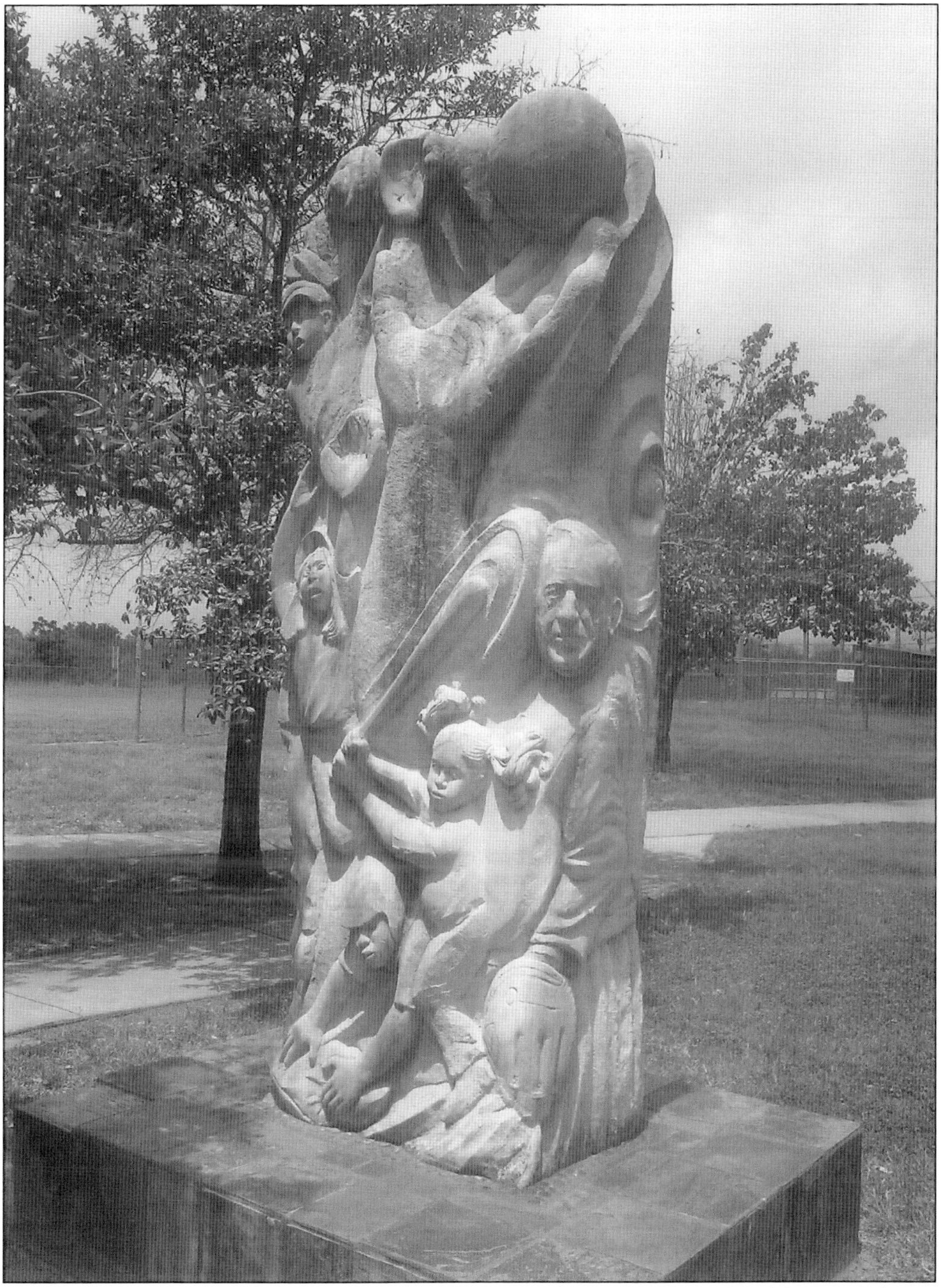

*Reach for Your Dreams* is a hand-carved limestone, slate tile, and river rock public art sculpture that was installed at the Montopolis Youth Sports Complex in 2002. The sculptor is Ambray Gonzales, a longtime Austin mixed-media artist. (Courtesy of the author's collection.)

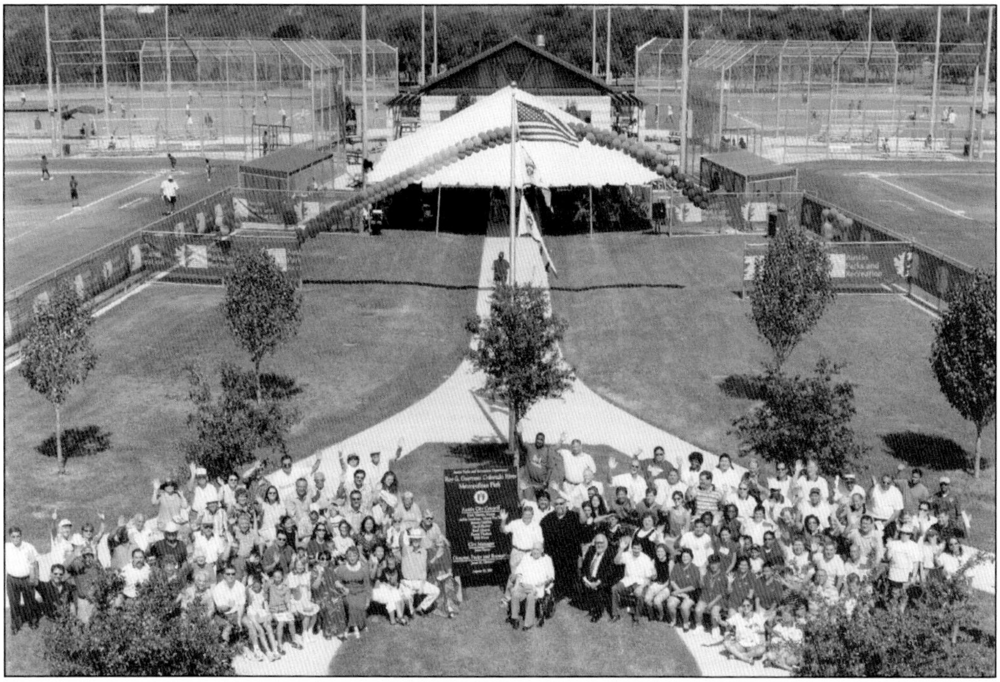

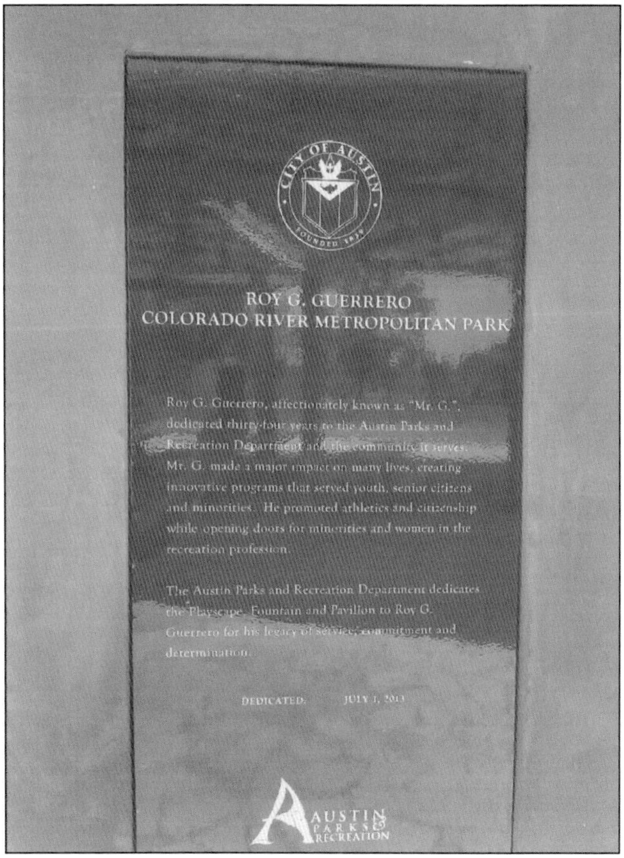


Roy G. Guerrero Colorado River Metropolitan Park was officially dedicated on August 25, 2001, in honor of Roy "Mr. G." Guerrero, a 34-year employee of the Austin Parks and Recreation Department.

After moving one of Austin's most highly regarded disc golf courses from Pease Park to Guerrero Park in 2012, the Austin Parks and Recreation Department finished work on the "metropolitan" portion of the park in 2013. The park now boasts a new walking trail, restrooms, a pavilion, and one of the best playscapes in Austin. The park is coming along nicely and is well positioned for further development in the future. (Courtesy of the author's collection.)

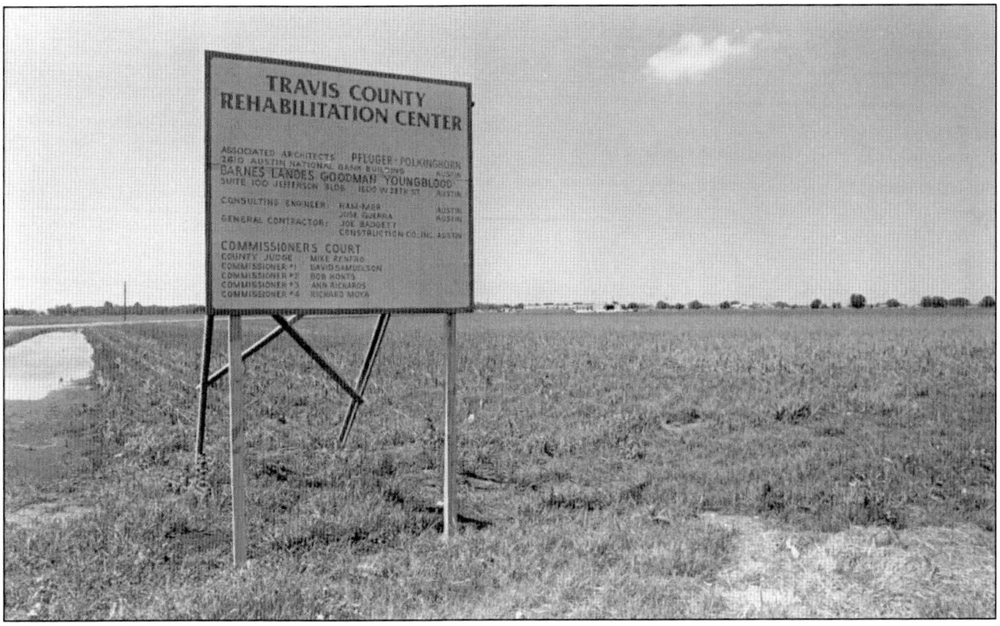


Outside of the construction of Bergstrom Air Base, one of the biggest public works projects in the history of the Montopolis-Del Valle region has been the construction of the Del Valle Rehabilitation Center, now known as the Travis County Correctional Complex.

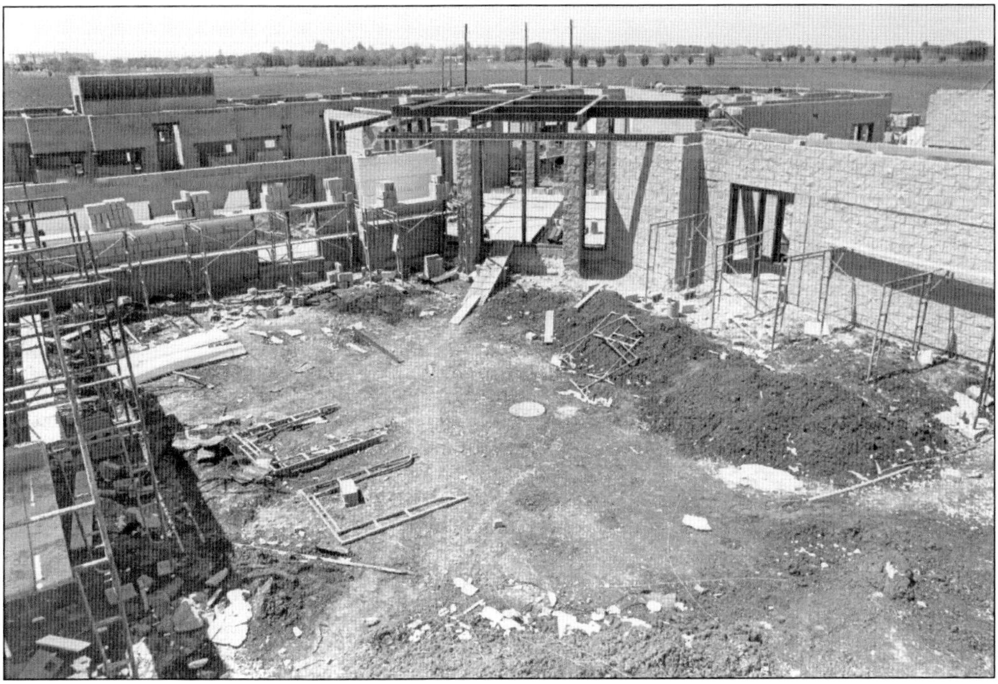

Construction for the Del Valle Rehabilitation Center began in the mid-1970s. It was opened in 1977 as a campus-style county correctional facility that focused on intensive inmate rehabilitation under direct staff supervision.

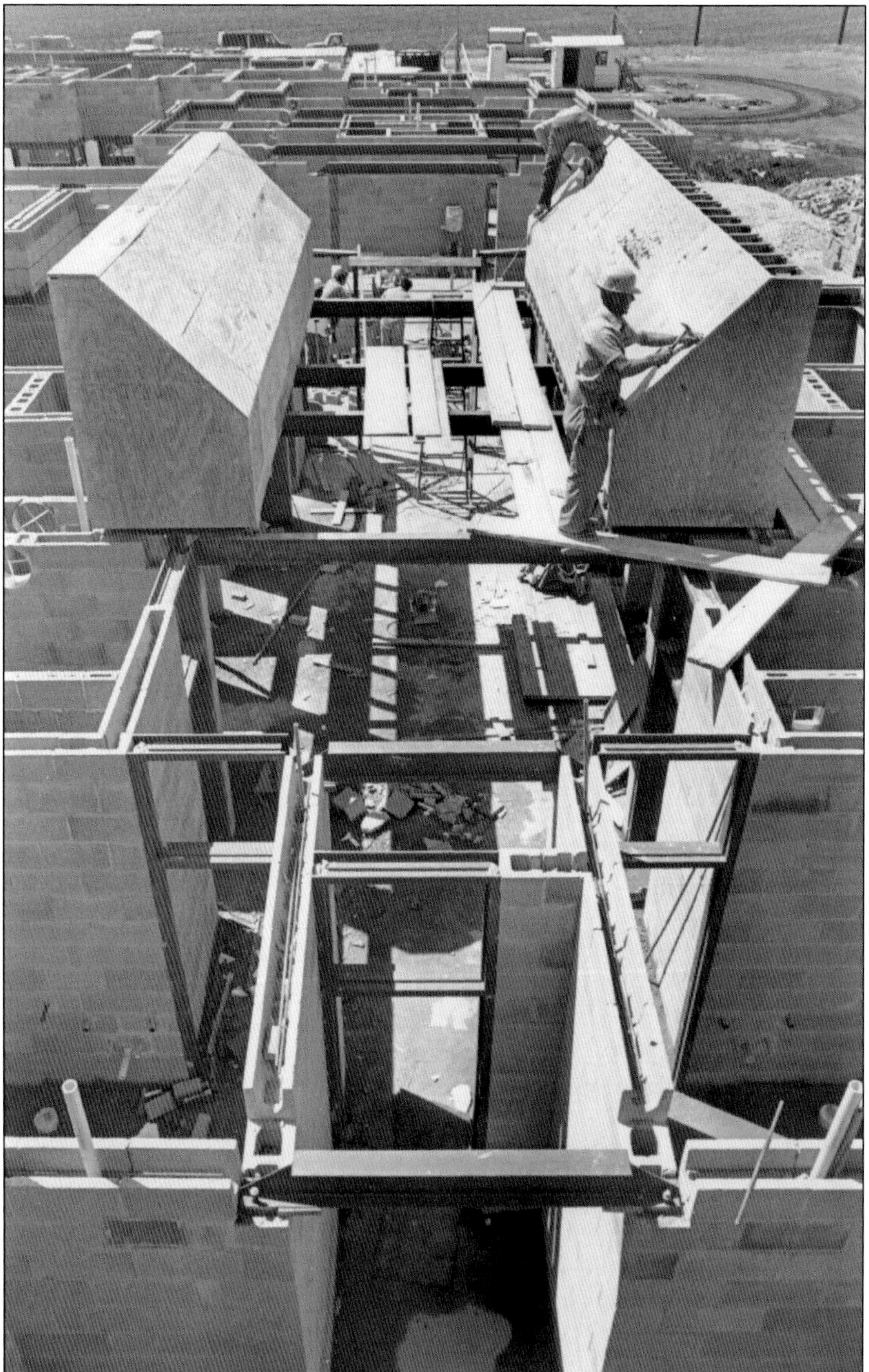

The Travis County Correctional Complex's origins as a rehabilitation center continue into the present. The facility in Del Valle continues to employ innovative rehabilitation strategies for inmates, including yoga classes, green-built facilities, community gardening, theater arts programs, anger management classes, and others.

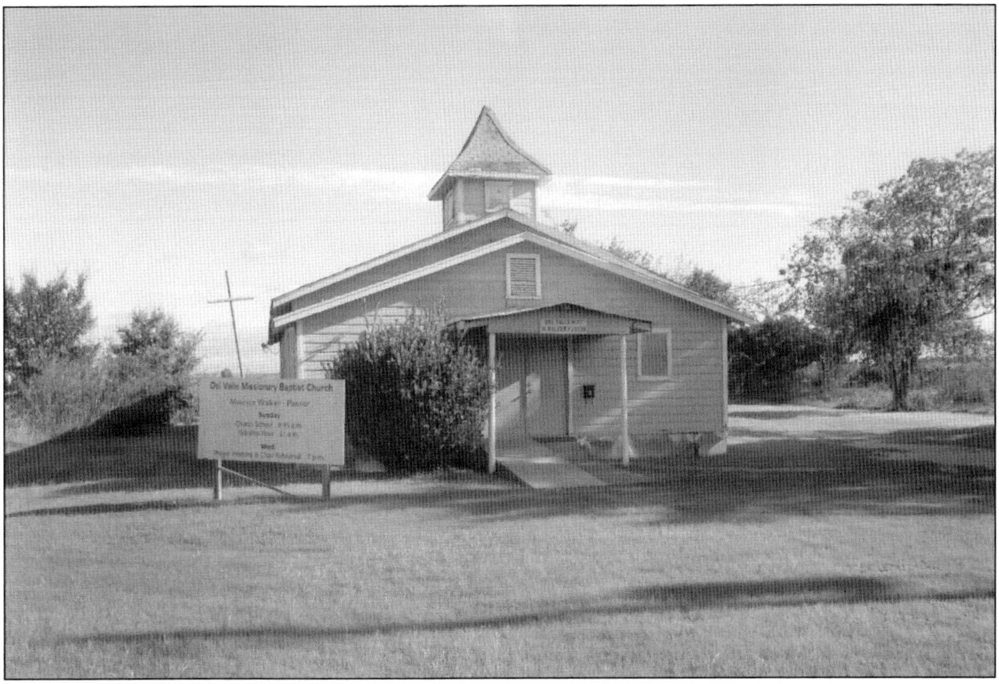


St. Edward's Baptist Church in Montopolis is the oldest black Baptist church in Travis County, and Del Valle Missionary Baptist Church, located on East Highway 71, is the second oldest. The two churches have similar origins and serviced the post-emancipation African American population of southeastern Travis County. (Courtesy of the author's collection.)

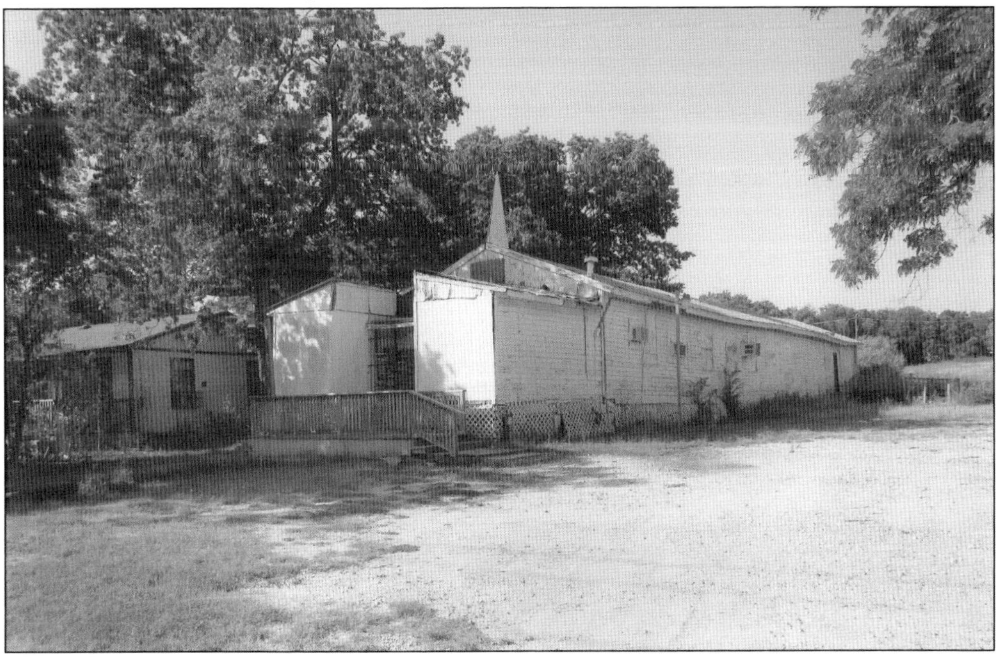

The New Jerusalem Baptist Church, located on Riverside Drive, continues to have an active congregation. Located along the East Riverside Corridor, which city officials have slated for intensive development, the church's days may be numbered. (Courtesy of the author's collection.)

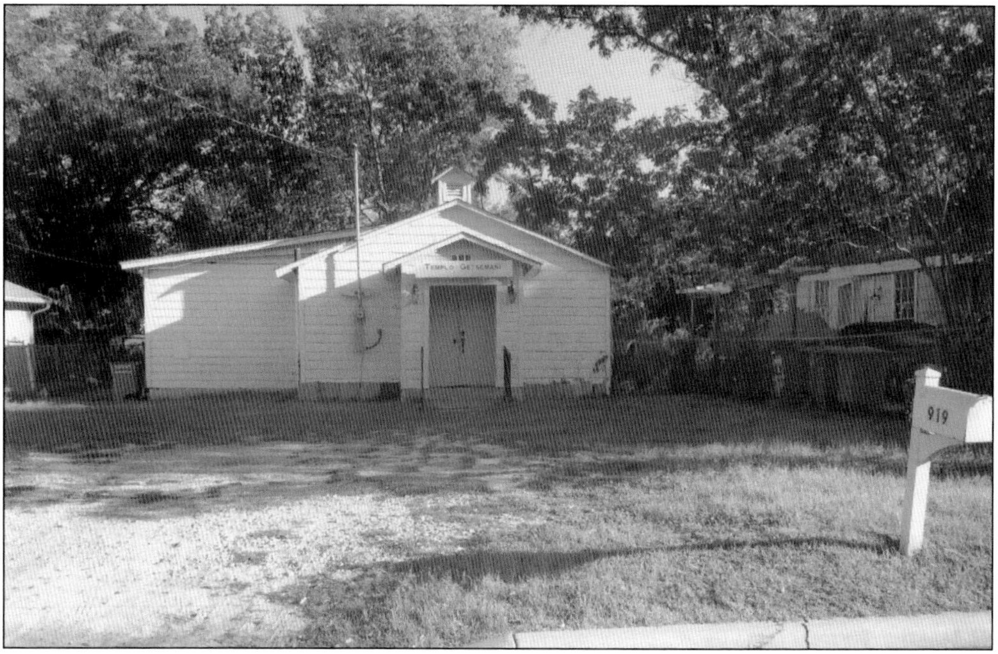


The Gethsemane Assembly of God Church, which stands on Valdez Street, has been in operation since the 1950s and maintains an active congregation that adds to the religious diversity of the Montopolis neighborhood. (Courtesy of the author's collection.)

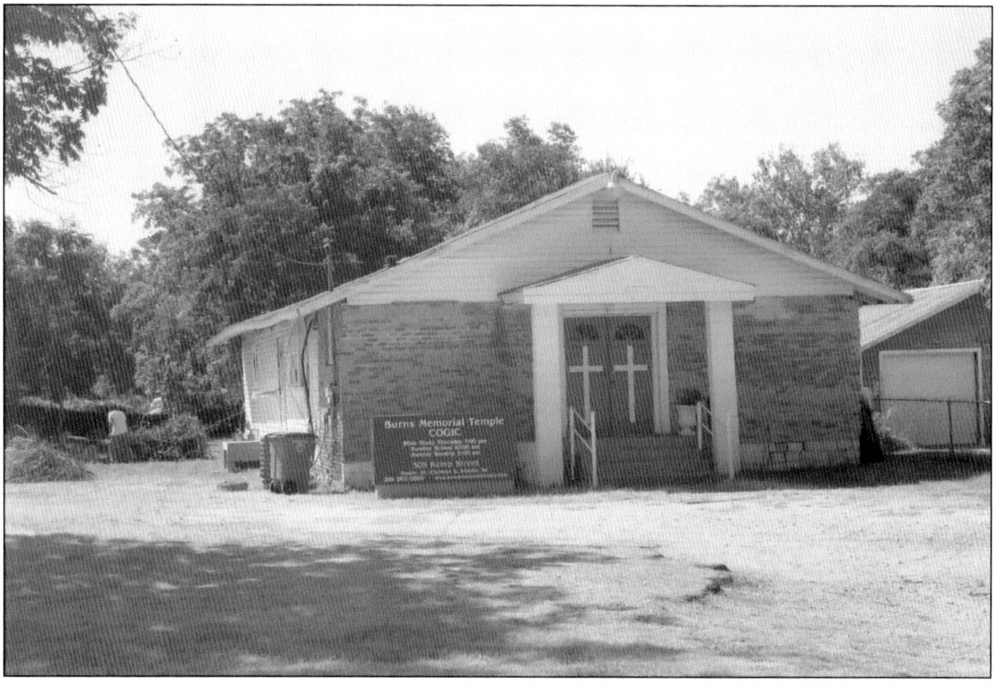


The Burns Memorial Temple Church, located on Kemp Street, has also operated as Holy Temple Church of God in Christ over the years, and it continues to maintain a predominantly African American congregation under the leadership of pastor Dr. Clarence B. Alberts Sr. and his wife, Dr. Terry J. Alberts. (Courtesy of the author's collection.)

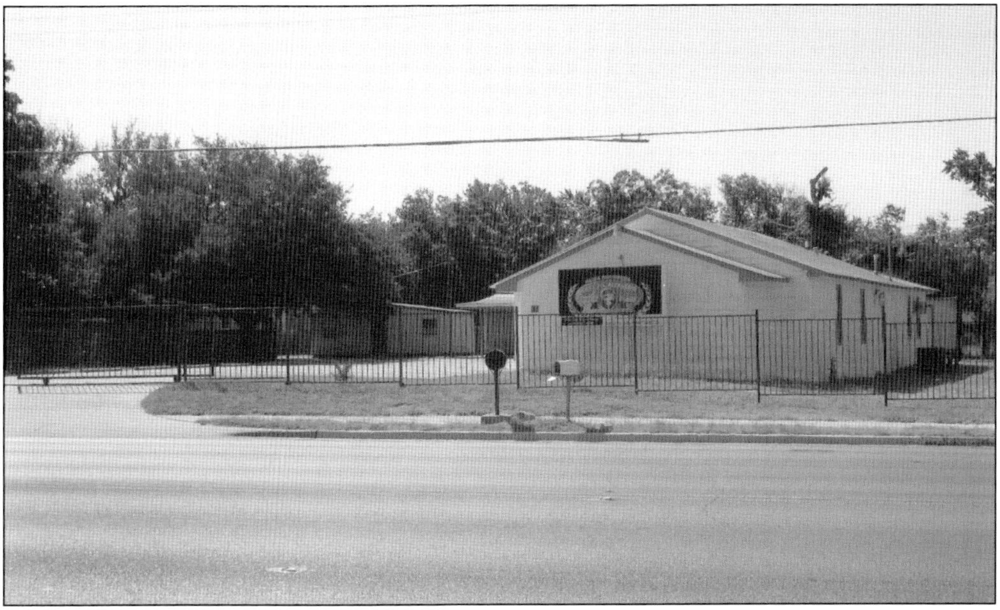

The Casa Del Aflarero Pentecostal Church, situated at 415 Montopolis Drive, has also operated as Peña de Horeb Ebenezer Church since coming under the ownership of Buenas Nuevas Assembly, Inc., in 1996. (Courtesy of the author's collection.)

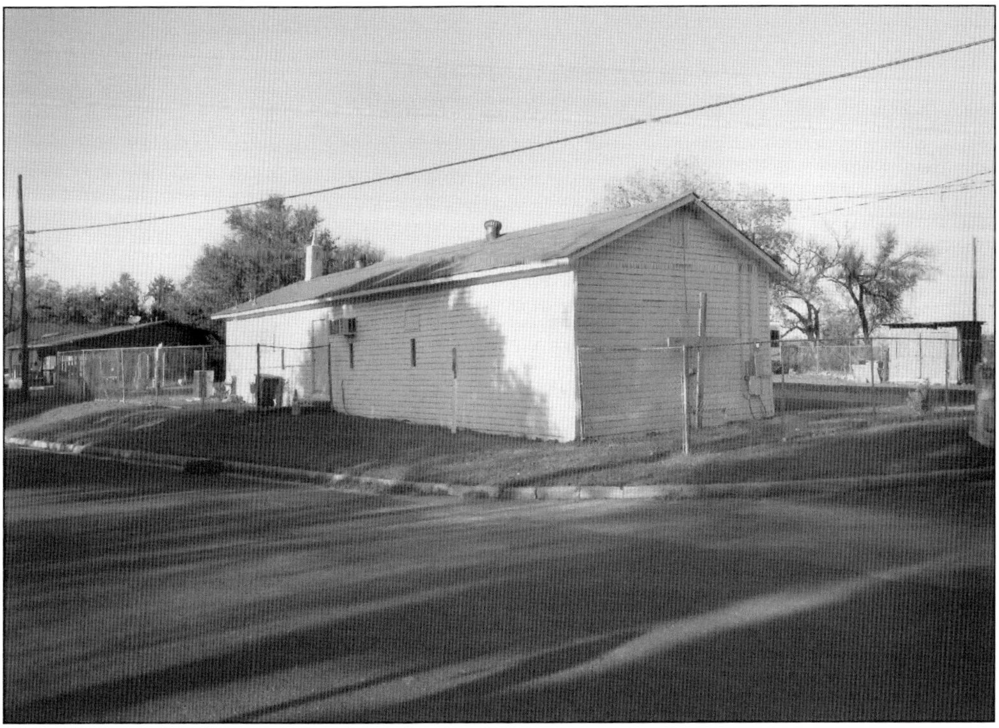

The Morning Glory Church of God in Christ, located at 208 Bonnett Street in the northern portion of the Montopolis neighborhood, is one of the community's distinguished African American congregations. Since 2003, it has been under the leadership of pastor Frederick O'Neal Patterson and his wife, Lisa. (Courtesy of the author's collection.)

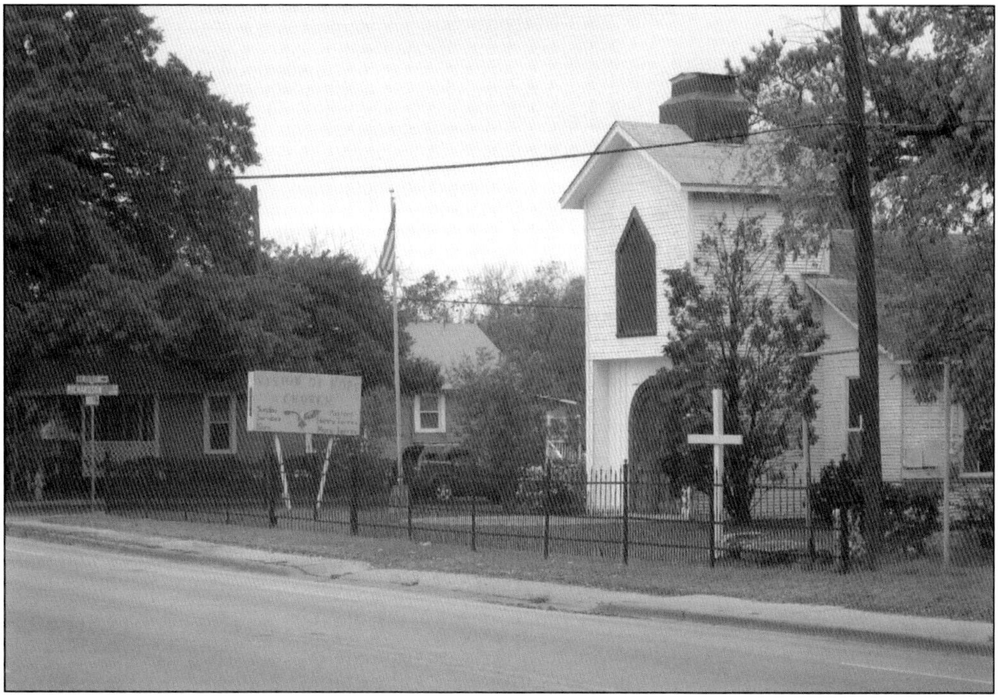

The Vision of Hope Church, which stands on the corner of Montopolis Drive and Richardson Lane next to the San Jose Cemetery, is owned and operated by the Texas Conference of Seventh-day Adventists. (Courtesy of the author's collection.)

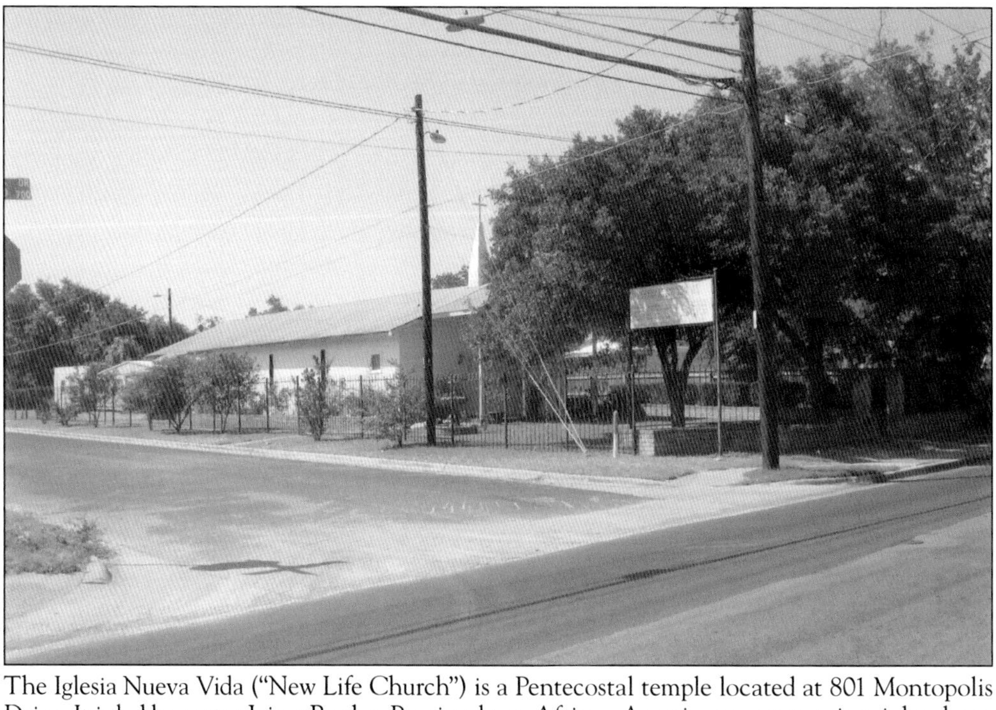

The Iglesia Nueva Vida ("New Life Church") is a Pentecostal temple located at 801 Montopolis Drive. It is led by pastor Jaime Rocha. Previously an African American congregation, it has been in operation in its present incarnation since 1994. (Courtesy of the author's collection.)

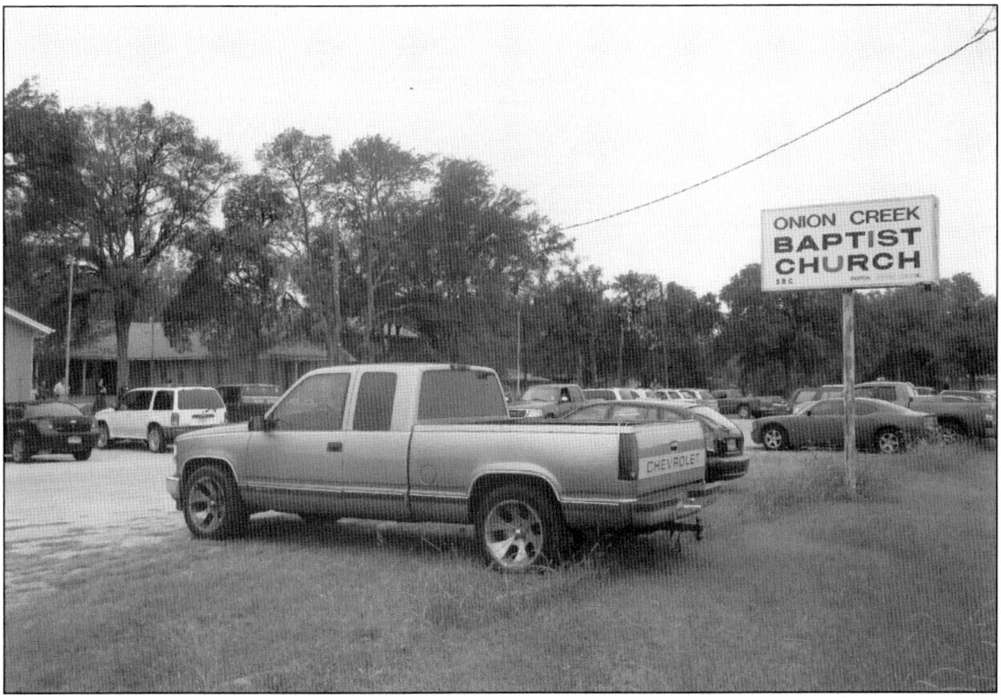


Located at 8214 Riverside Drive, Onion Creek Baptist Church was founded as a Euro-American Baptist congregation in the years prior to the Civil War, but it is now a proud and active multiethnic church with many Montopolis and Del Valle residents as parishioners. (Courtesy of the author's collection.)

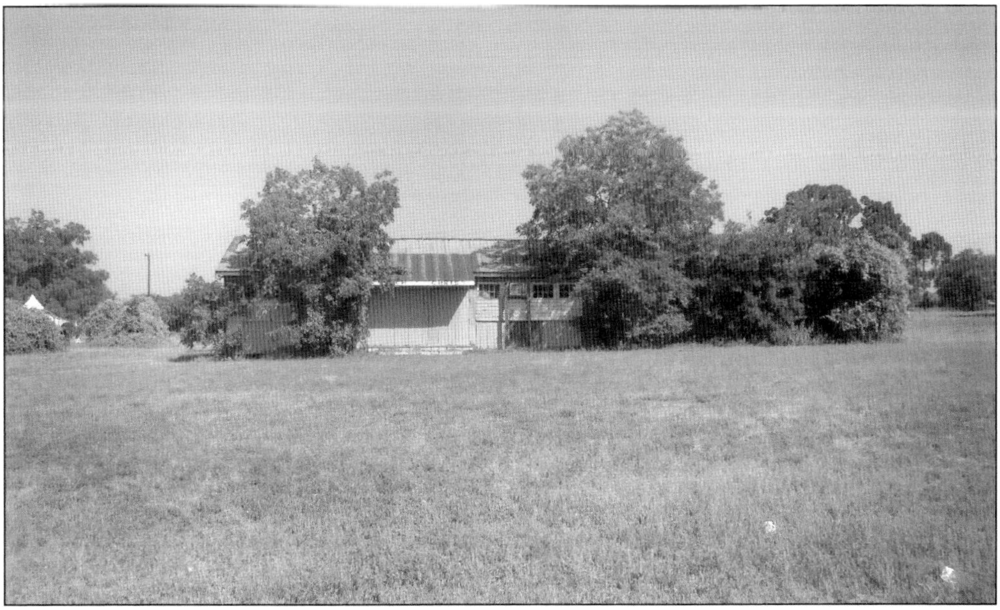

The Montopolis Church of Christ, located at 500 Montopolis Drive, continues to occupy its old but dignified position on a large and formerly rural lot that is highly visible to motorists. The church shuttered its doors in 1968, and the present owners have kept the land and building in trust since. (Courtesy of the author's collection.)

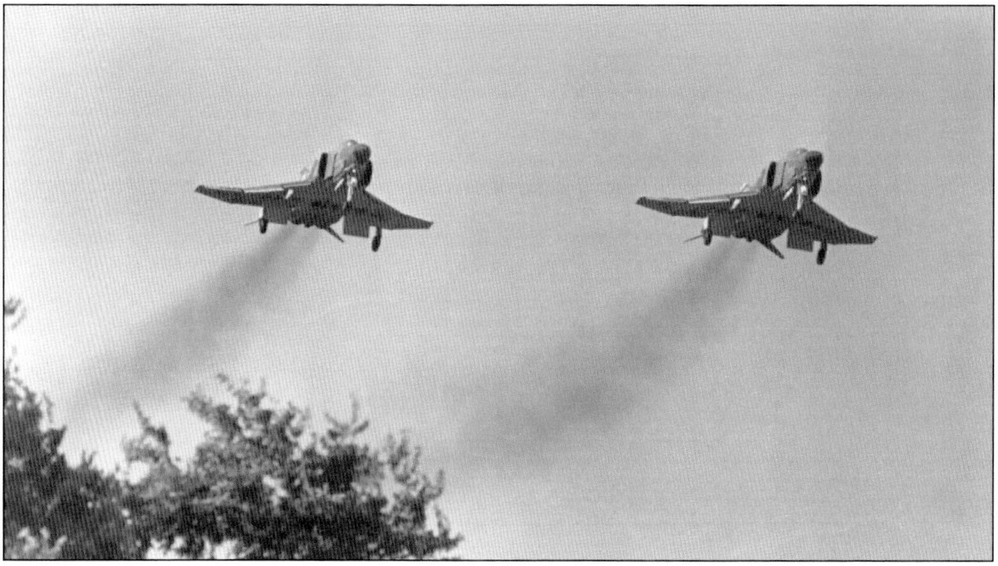

Aircraft operations at Bergstrom Air Force Base were the source of perennial frustration for Montopolis and Del Valle residents. Not only were the jets noisy, disrupting schools, churches, and homes, but periodic neighborhood plane crashes also kept the community on edge. By the early 1980s, the Montopolis Neighborhood Association grew frustrated at having to negotiate a new agreement every time the base leadership changed hands and began to appeal to the larger Austin community for help. The base was eventually closed in the early 1990s and converted into Austin's new international airport. Unfortunately, the noise and flight path concerns remain.

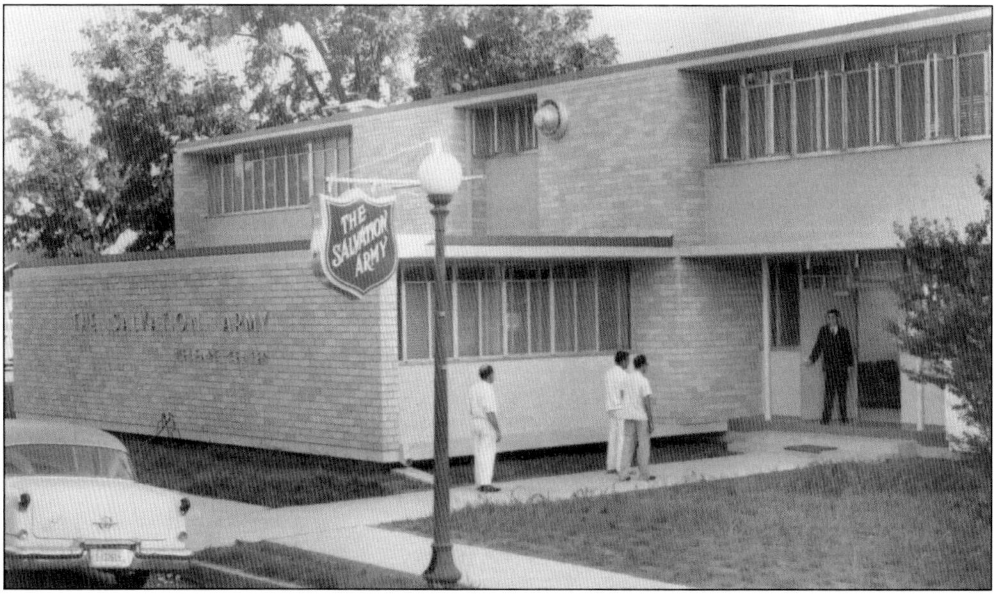


In 1984, the Salvation Army proposed to move its social services center from downtown Austin into the Montopolis neighborhood. It requested light industrial zoning for its new facility. The Montopolis Neighborhood Association, under the leadership of Enrique Lopez, opposed the move and, in vigorous testimony before the Austin City Council, conveyed the message that Montopolis was a historic neighborhood older than Austin itself and with a unique community integrity. This 1962 photograph shows the Salvation Army headquarters in Austin.

# *Four*

# The Present and Future

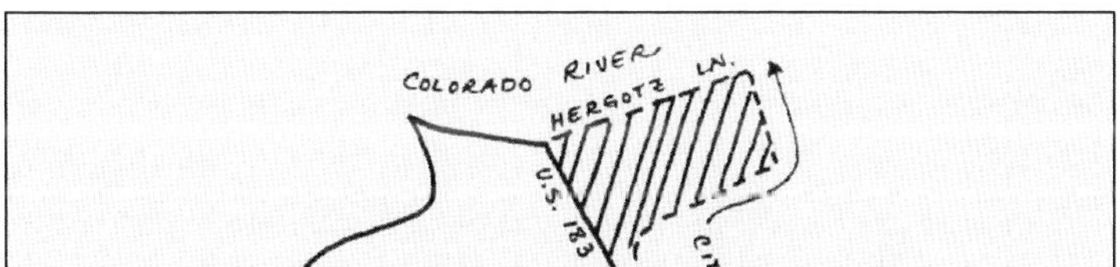


The planning boundaries of the Montopolis neighborhood have shifted over the years. This map from the 1979 Montopolis neighborhood plan shows that the neighborhood's western boundary at the time was Country Club Road and that the neighborhood's eastern and southern boundaries were envisioned to expand to Ben White Boulevard and what was then the city-county line. (Courtesy of the City of Austin.)

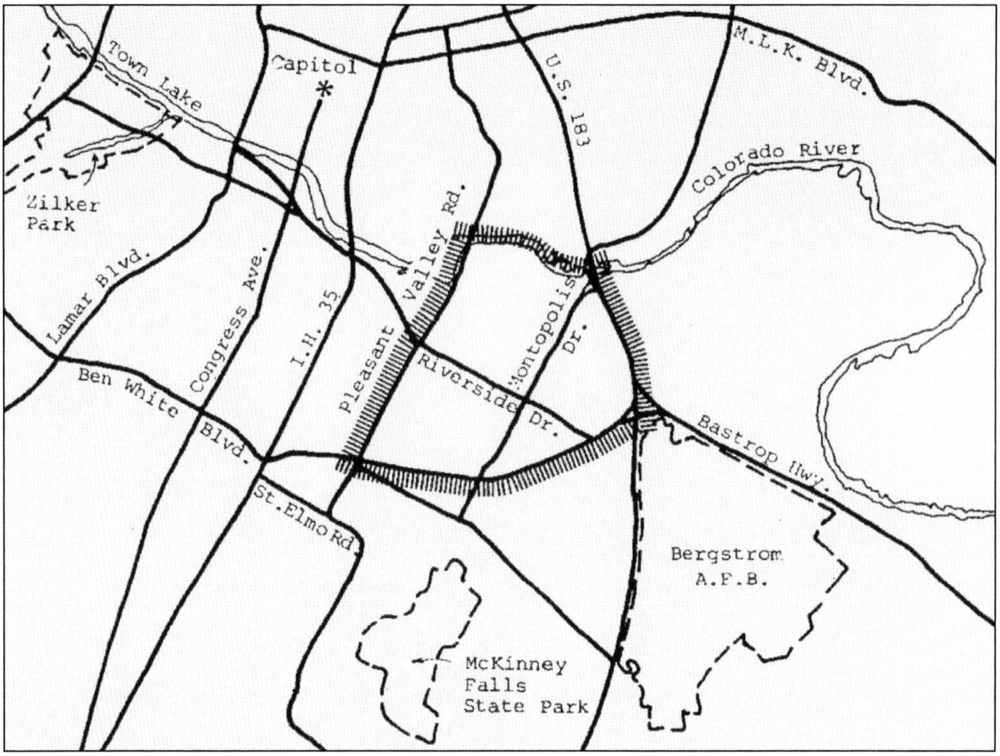


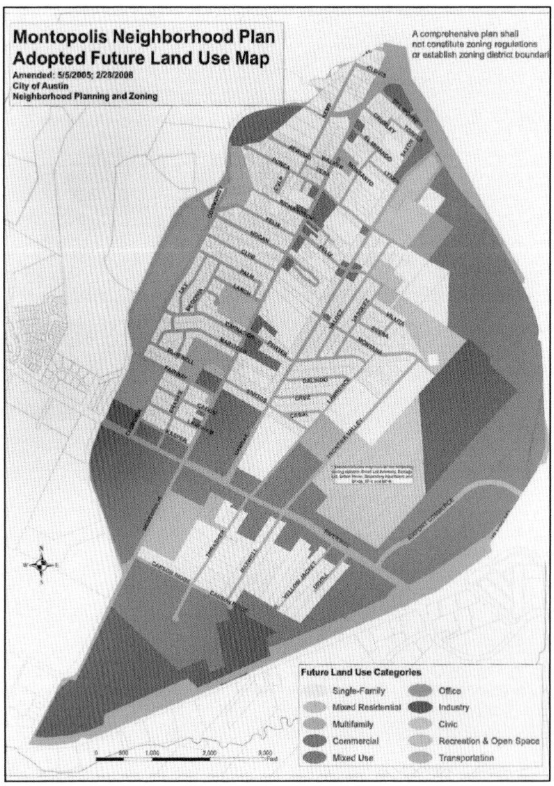


In 1985, the City of Austin's Office of Land Development Services conducted a study of the Montopolis neighborhood in response to neighborhood concerns that the area was being developed too rapidly. The western boundary of the neighborhood at the time was fixed at Pleasant Valley Road, although this changed once planners began to identify portions of the East Riverside Corridor area as ripe for multifamily development for University of Texas students. (Courtesy of the City of Austin.)

The present Montopolis planning area was adopted by the Austin City Council in September 2001. The neighborhood continues to vigorously defend its single-family zoning. Montopolis has a high degree of commercial and light industrial zoning—about twice the city average—and is also confronted by the challenges associated with development of the East Riverside Corridor. (Courtesy of the City of Austin.)

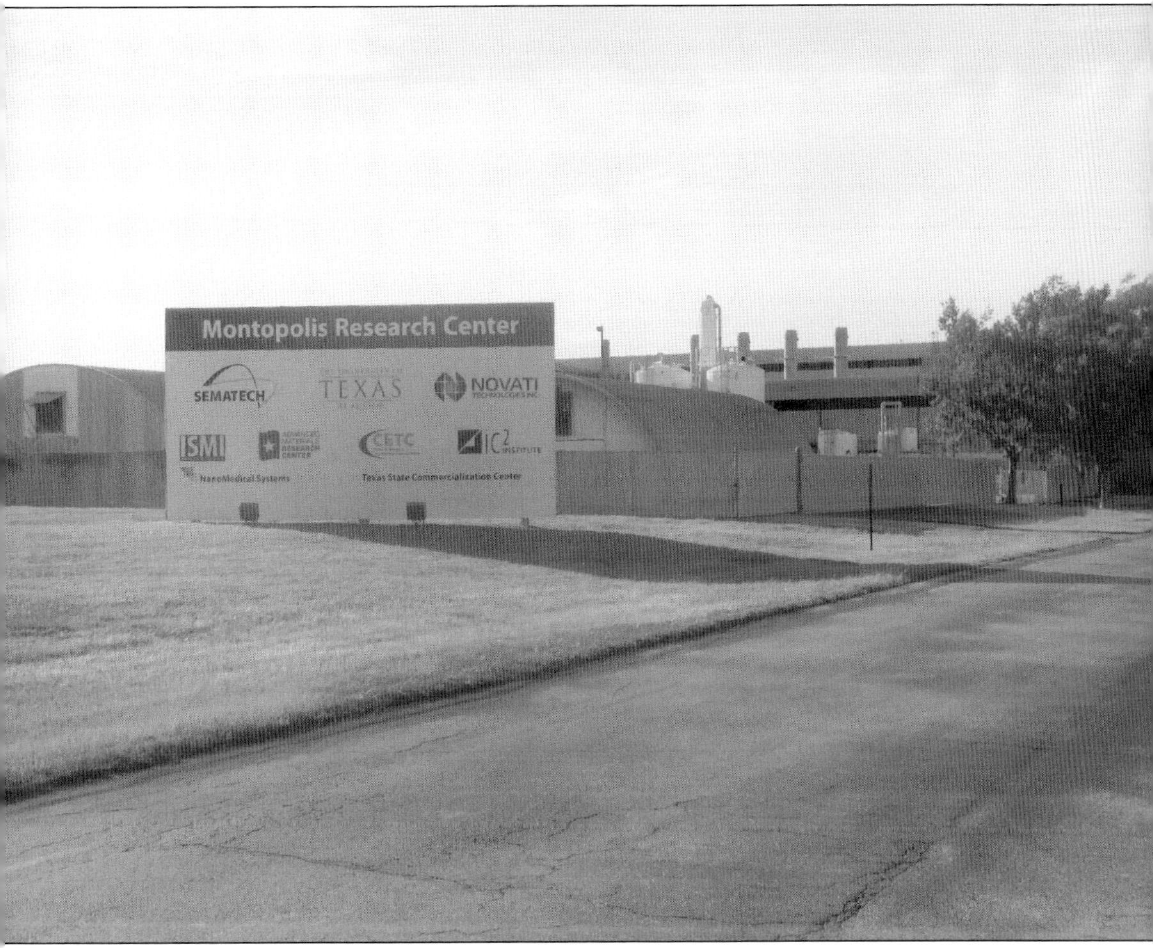


SEMATECH (Semiconductor Manufacturing Technology) was created in 1987 as a Department of Defense–funded partnership between the federal government and the US semiconductor industry, which had fallen behind Japanese industry by the mid-1980s. Austin won a national competition for its headquarters, edging out Phoenix and Boston, with $68 million in local and University of Texas incentives and a promise of more. Montopolis has been the consortium's home base for most of its existence, but in 2011, SEMATECH moved its headquarters to Albany, New York. The Austin facility continues in operation. (Courtesy of the author's collection.)

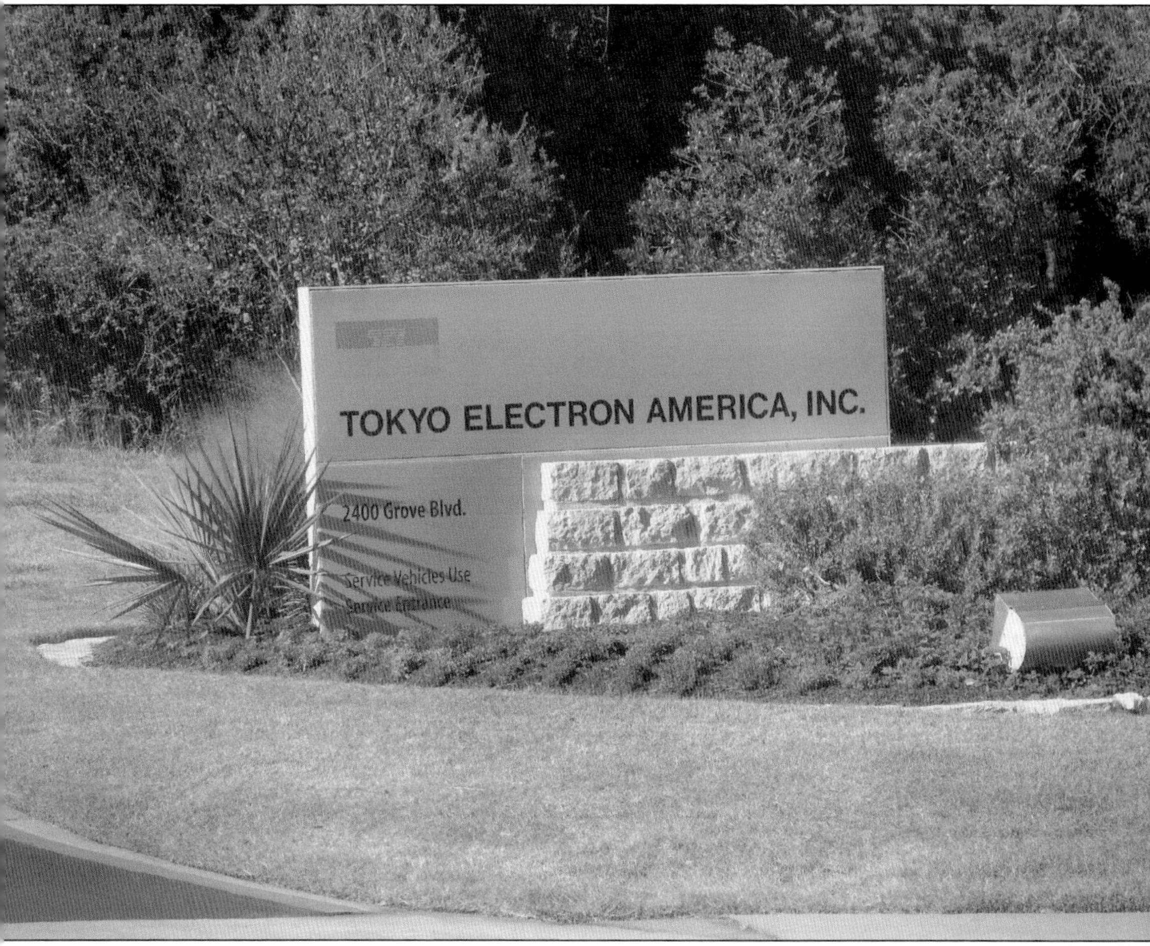


SEMATECH may have been created to compete with the Japanese semiconductor industry, but this did not stop Japanese firms such as Tokyo Electron from setting up shop down the street. Tokyo Electron has been a good Montopolis neighbor, funding a variety of neighborhood initiatives and allowing usage of its facilities for community board meetings. (Courtesy of the author's collection.)

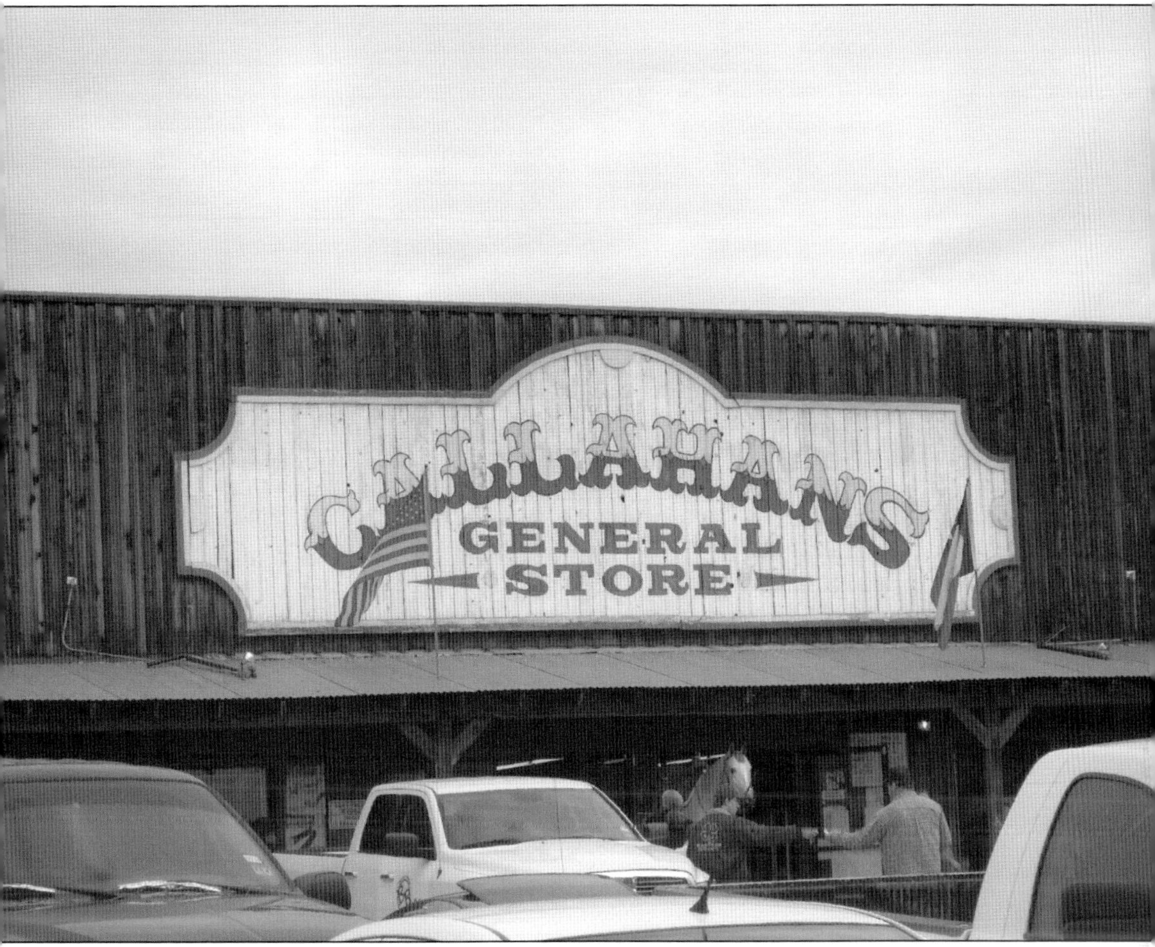


Callahan's General Store opened in June 1978 and is squarely in the tradition of area general stores that preceded it in the previous century, such as the iconic Givens General Store. It is located at the site of an old livestock sales barn. In addition to hardware, housewares, and western wear, the store also sells feed and live animals and is a True Value hardware store. (Courtesy of the author's collection.)

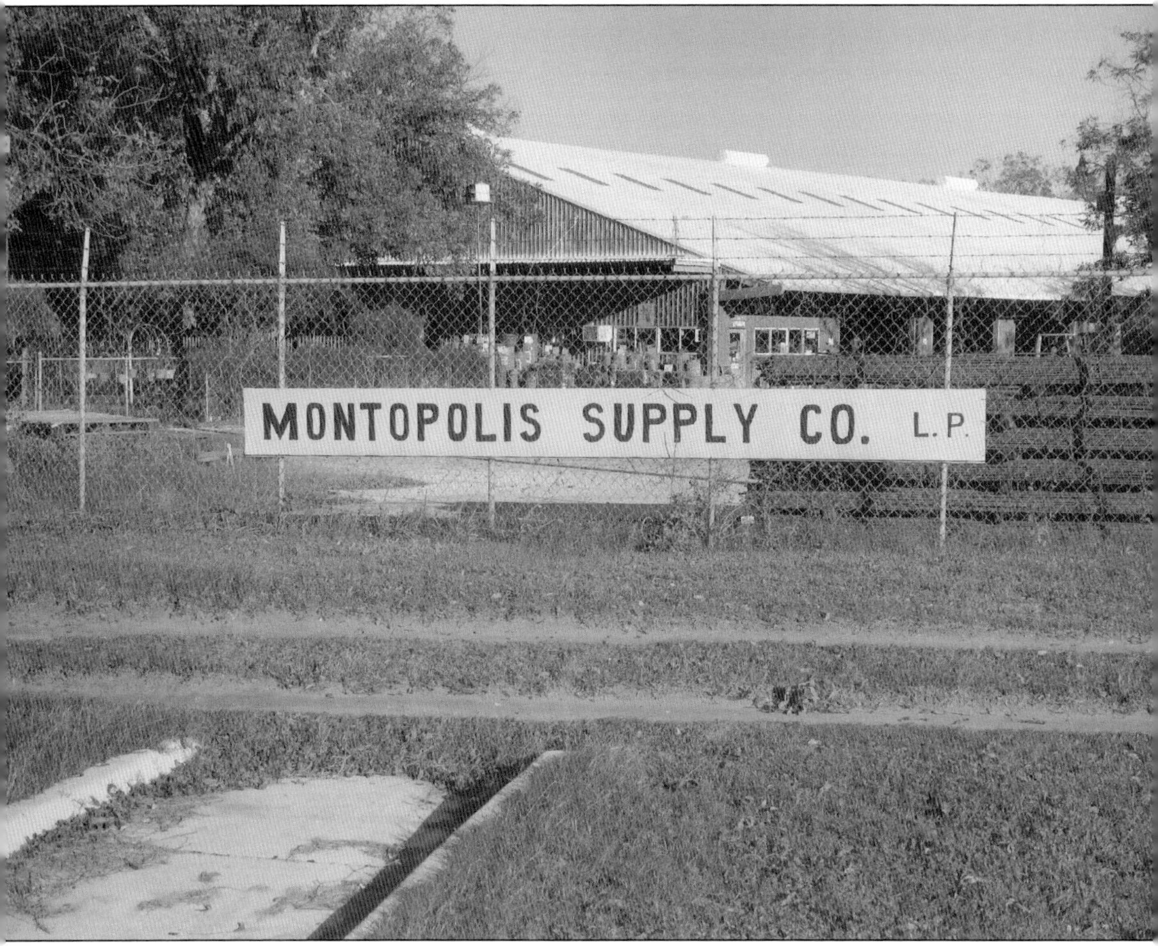


Located at 255 South Highway 183, Montopolis Supply Co. is situated at the site of the Colorado School for Negroes (No. 1), shown in historical maps. It was opened in the early 1950s by Ross R. Willhoite (1931–2013) and continues in business as a family operation. (Courtesy of the author's collection.)

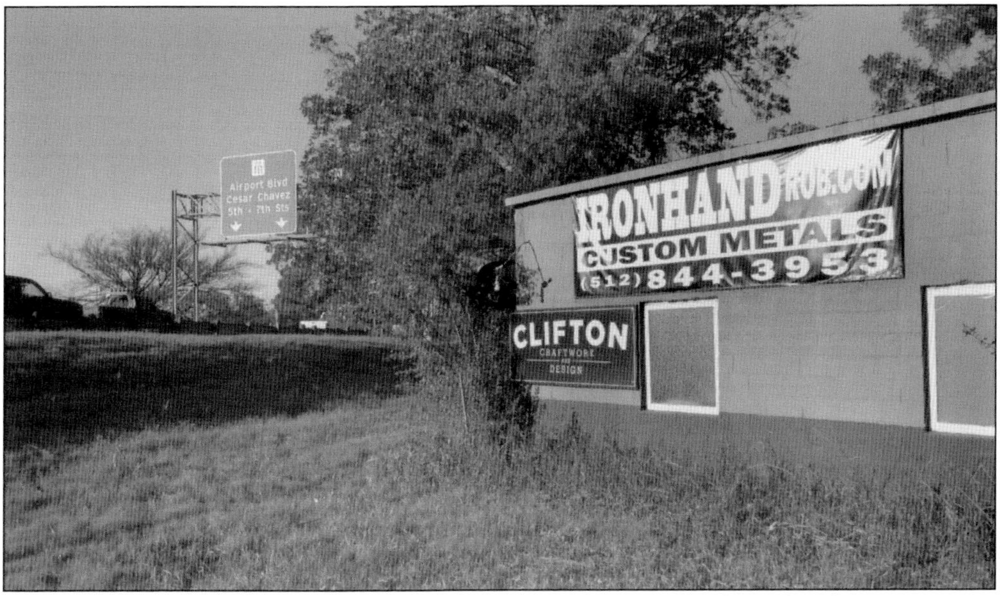


Since the 1990s, motorists traveling north on Highway 183 just before the Colorado River crossing have been able to appreciate a unique piece of public art also serving as memorable advertising: the rear end of a Mazda 626 crashing into a building. The building in question is the current business home of Ironhand Rob Custom Metals and Clifton Craftwork and Design. (Courtesy of the author's collection.)

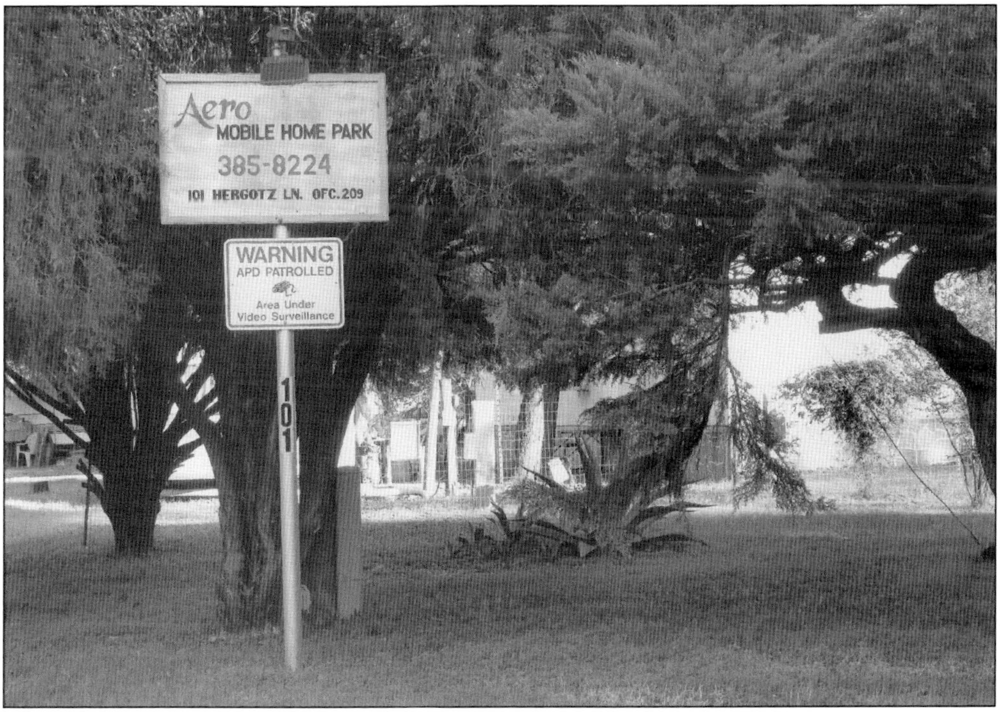


Montopolis is home to numerous historic trailer parks, with the Aero Mobile Home Park on Hergotz Lane chief among them. The park is over 60 years old and has been under the ownership of the Aero Mobile Home Corporation since 1988. (Courtesy of the author's collection.)

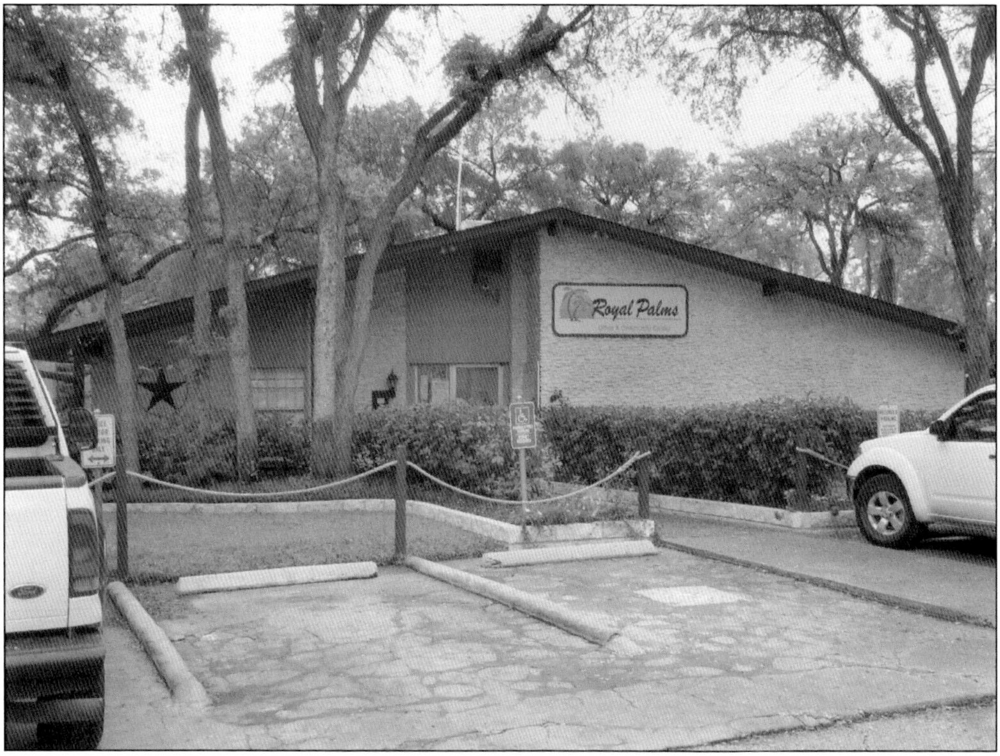


Another important trailer park is the Royal Palms Manufactured Home & RV Community, a business started by owner Sidney E. Lanier in the early 1980s. The park was in the local news in the summer of 2007 when local soul food icon Lozina E. Stephens, better known as "Nubian Queen Lola," was evicted from the trailer court for numerous minor violations. (Courtesy of the author's collection.)

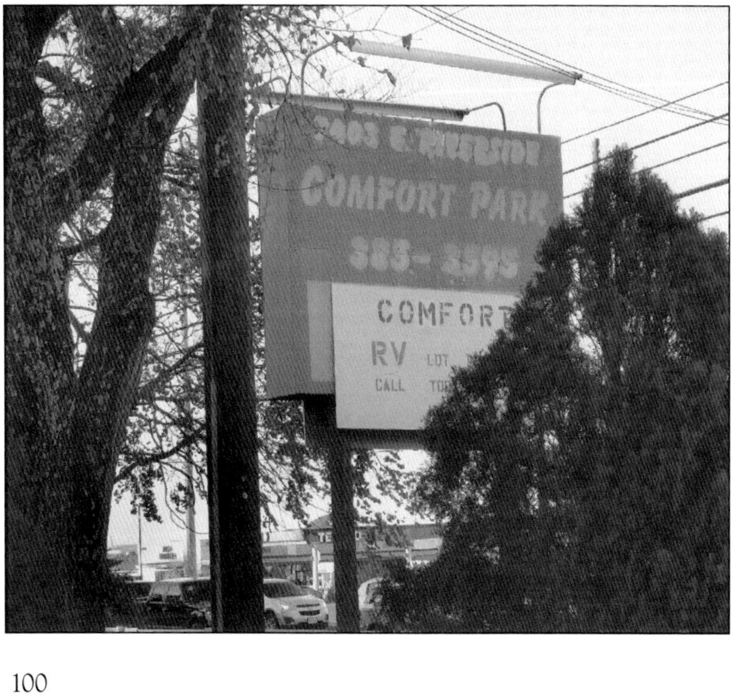


For years, the Comfort Trailer and RV Park on Riverside Drive has housed some of the poorest families in Montopolis. It is located along the East Riverside Corridor and is close to the Bergstrom Expressway project, so its days may be numbered. (Courtesy of the author's collection.)

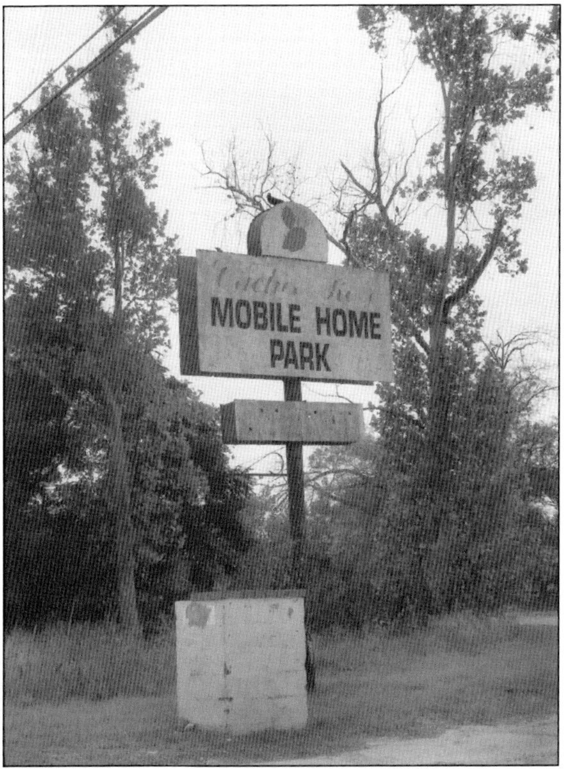


The Cactus Rose mobile home park, located at 500 Bastrop Highway, stopped accepting new visitors quite some time ago, but it continues in operation for longtime residents. (Courtesy of the author's collection.)

The working-class community living along Hoeke Lane in Montopolis–Del Valle is now neatly tucked away amidst burgeoning industrial development, but its rural origins are amply evident. This photograph shows the Village Park Trailer Park, located on Hoeke Lane. (Courtesy of the author's collection.)

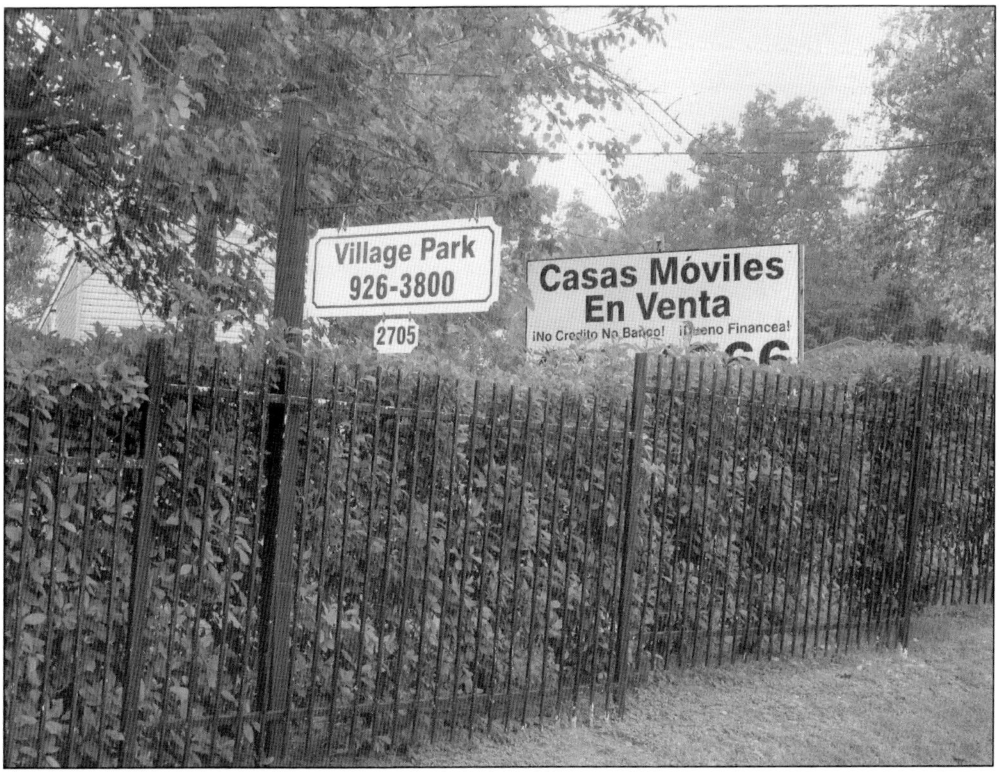

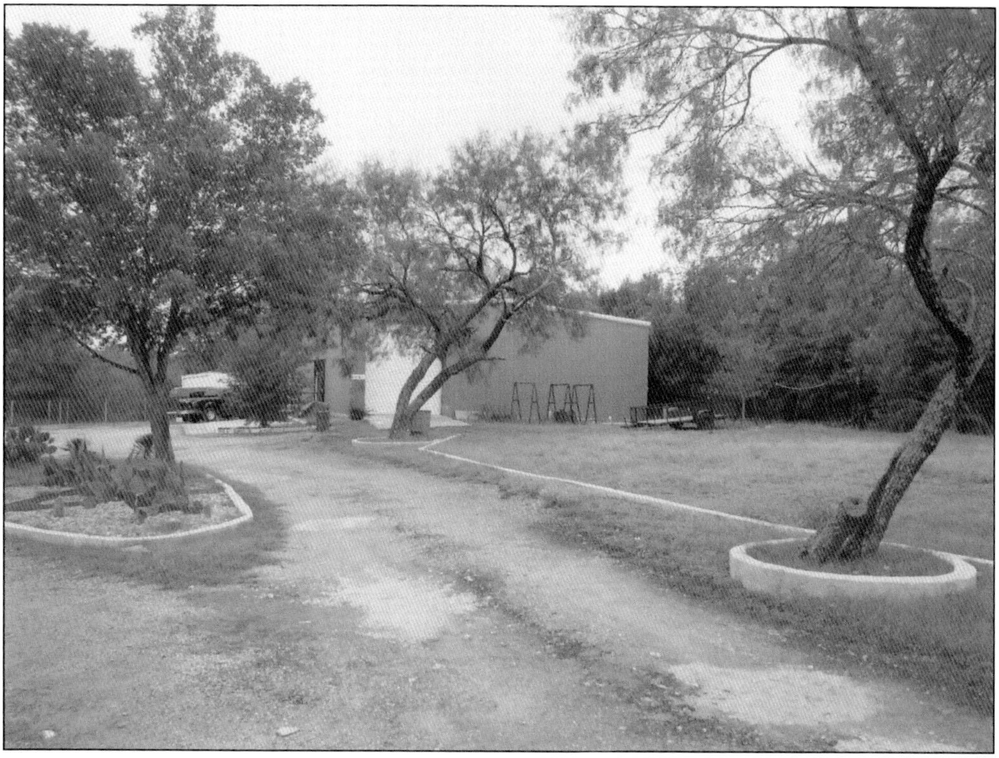

Behind this unassuming blue warehouse building between Posten Lane and Ella Lane lies the San Jose Cemetery No. 2, also known as the Montopolis Cemetery. The four-acre property is almost completely overgrown and has never been properly surveyed by an archaeologist. (Courtesy of the author's collection.)

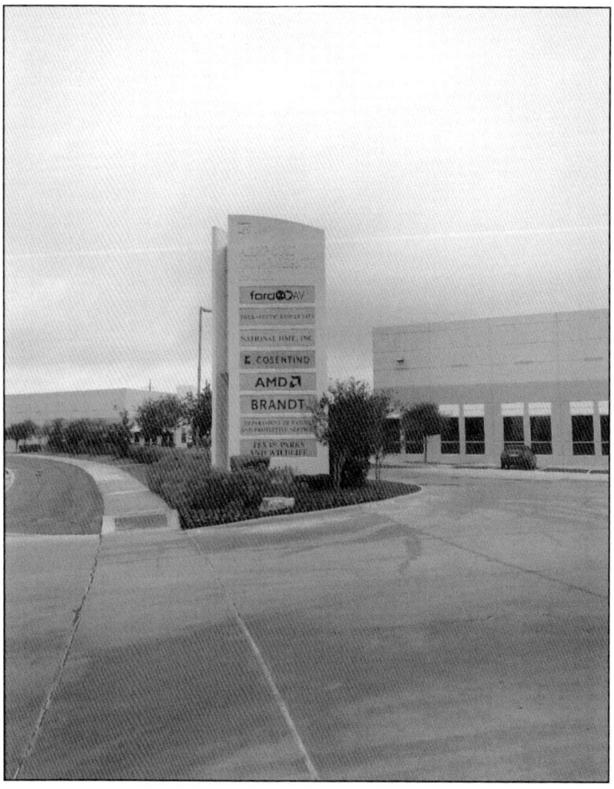


The Airport Commerce Park, located along Route 71 and Highway 183, houses the offices of numerous important organizations, including the Texas Parks and Wildlife Department and Advanced Micro Devices. (Courtesy of the author's collection.)

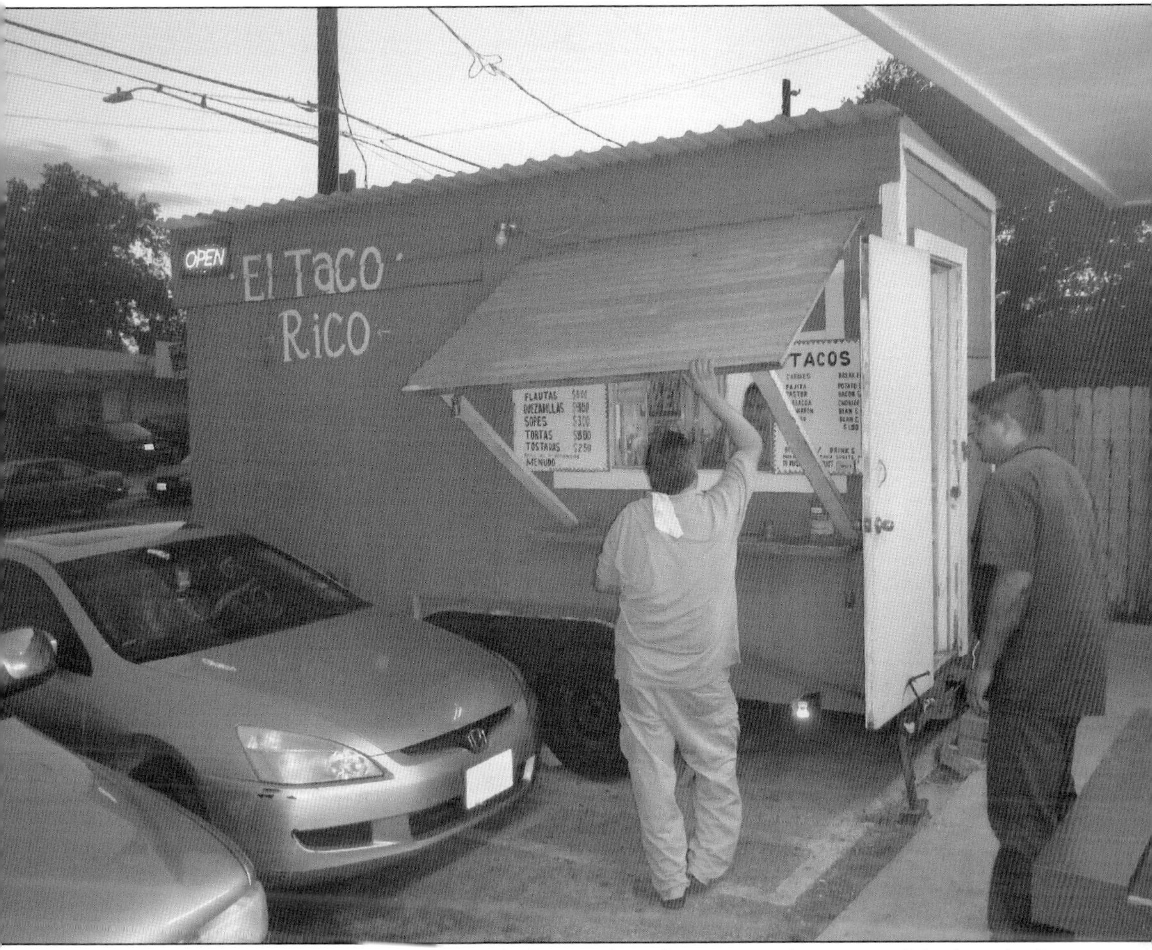


Food trailers are currently very popular, and Montopolis is fortunate to have one of the best food trailers in Austin. This photograph shows El Taco Rico's Yolanda Sanchez Cornejo at work. Whenever Anthony Bourdain is in town, this is where he goes. (Courtesy of the author's collection.)

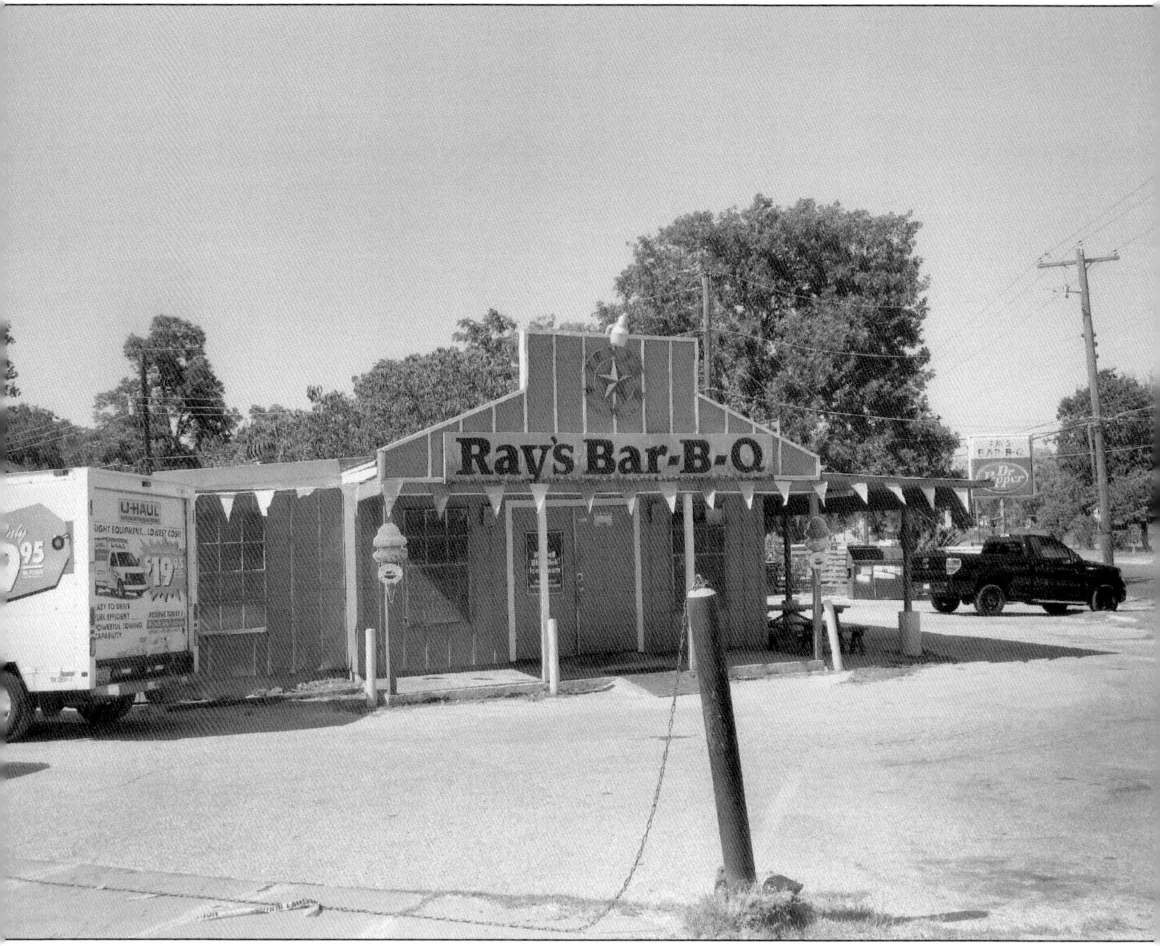


Ray's Bar-B-Q, located on Montopolis Drive, serves authentic Texas barbecue, Blue Bell ice cream, and down-home drinks. It was featured in the television show *Friday Night Lights*—and yes, the owners are football fans. (Courtesy of the author's collection.)

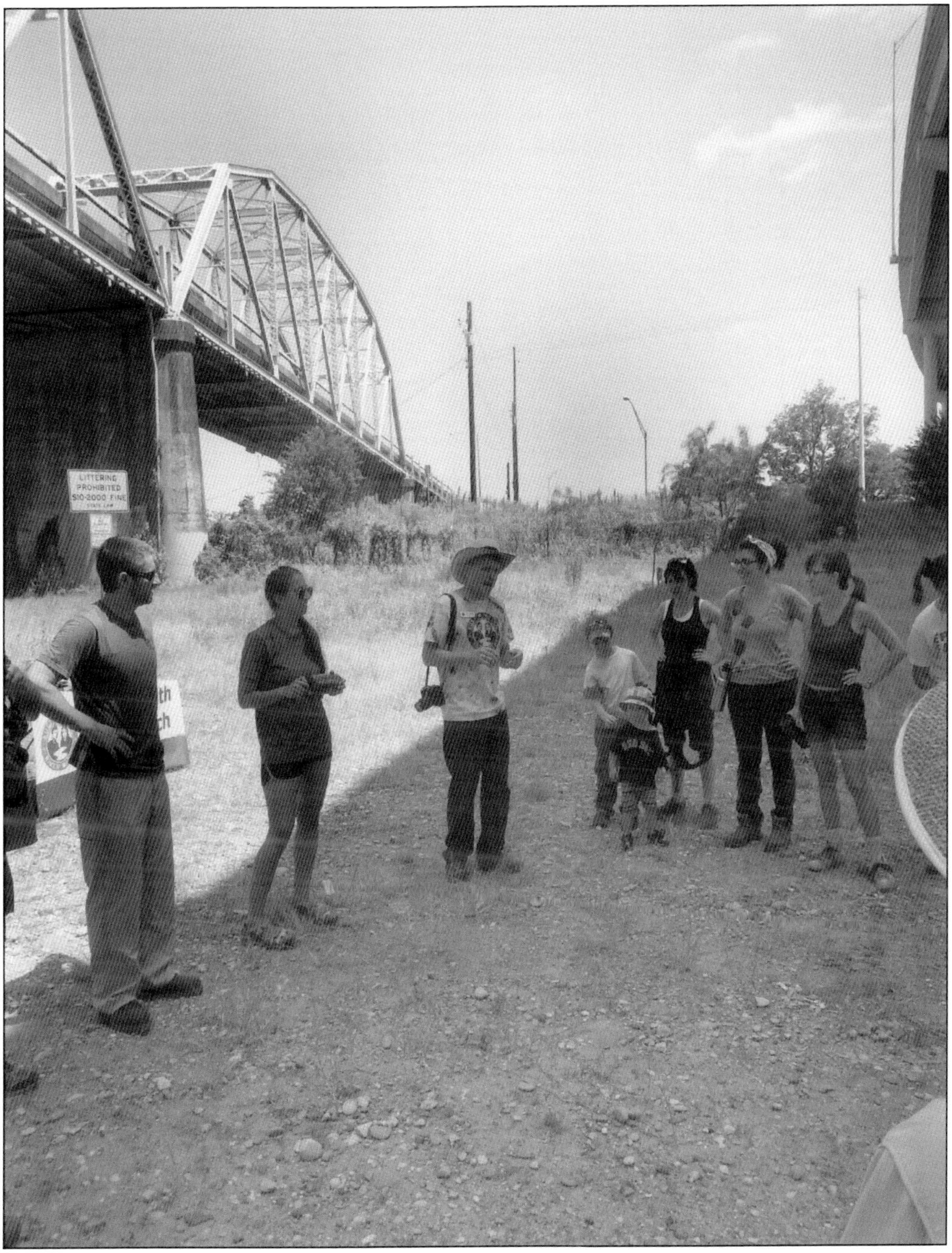


Since 1992, Austin Youth River Watch has been advancing personal and academic achievement through environmental monitoring, education, and adventure. With initial funding and long-term support from the City of Austin and the Lower Colorado River Authority, the organization has taught hundreds of high schools students to collect and track water-quality data. Environmental stewardship training is combined with dropout prevention; the organization has close to a 100-percent dropout prevention rate. In this photograph, Austin Youth River Watch executive director Brent Lyles shows participants about water-quality monitoring initiatives beneath the Montopolis Bridge. (Courtesy of the author's collection.)

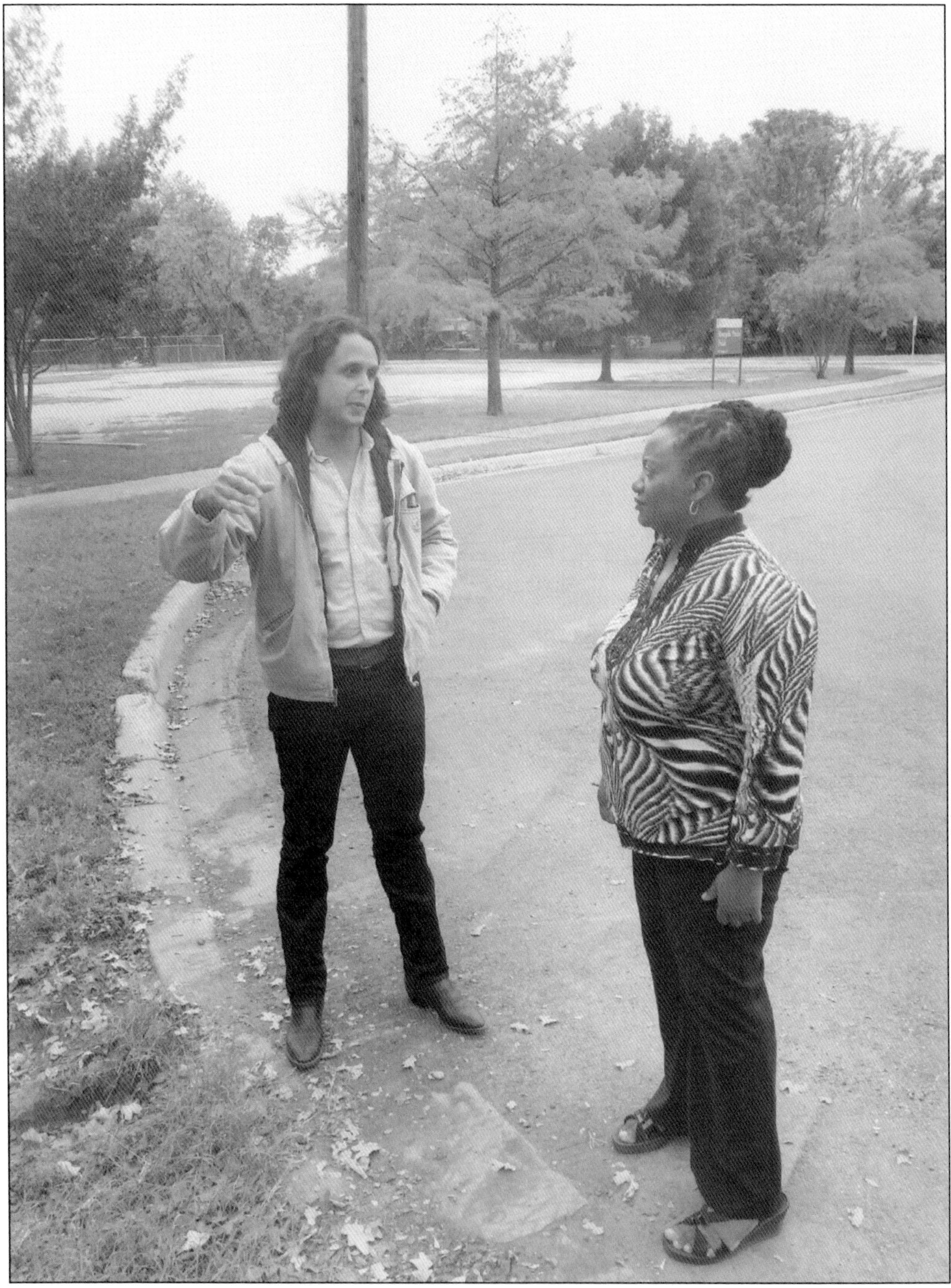

Joaquin Mariel of Ecology Action and Adama Brown of the Burdett Prairie Cemetery Association discuss a potential collaboration to train Americorps and VISTA volunteers in the finer points of Montopolis history, as well as cemetery maintenance and restoration. (Courtesy of the author's collection.)

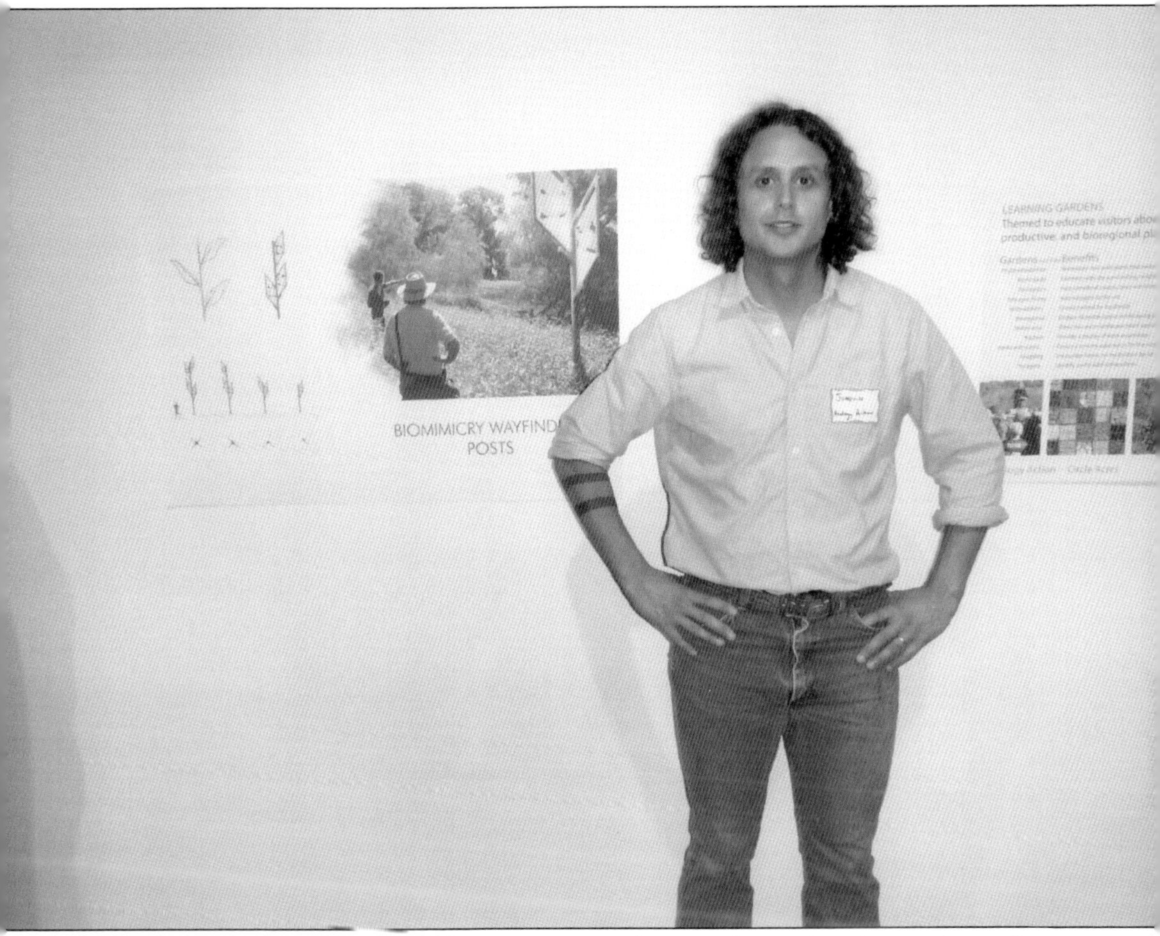


Ecology Action is one of Austin's oldest environmental nonprofits, and it pioneered recycling advocacy in the 1970s and 1980s. In 2012, the group acquired a former EPA brownfield in Montopolis, adjacent to Roy G. Guerrero Park, and it has produced an innovative management plan for the property designed by the Center for Maximum Potential Building Systems. Urban environmental education is a major component of the plan. Here, Ecology Action executive director Joaquin Mariel stands next to a poster showing future "Biomimicry Wayfinding Posts." (Courtesy of the author's collection.)

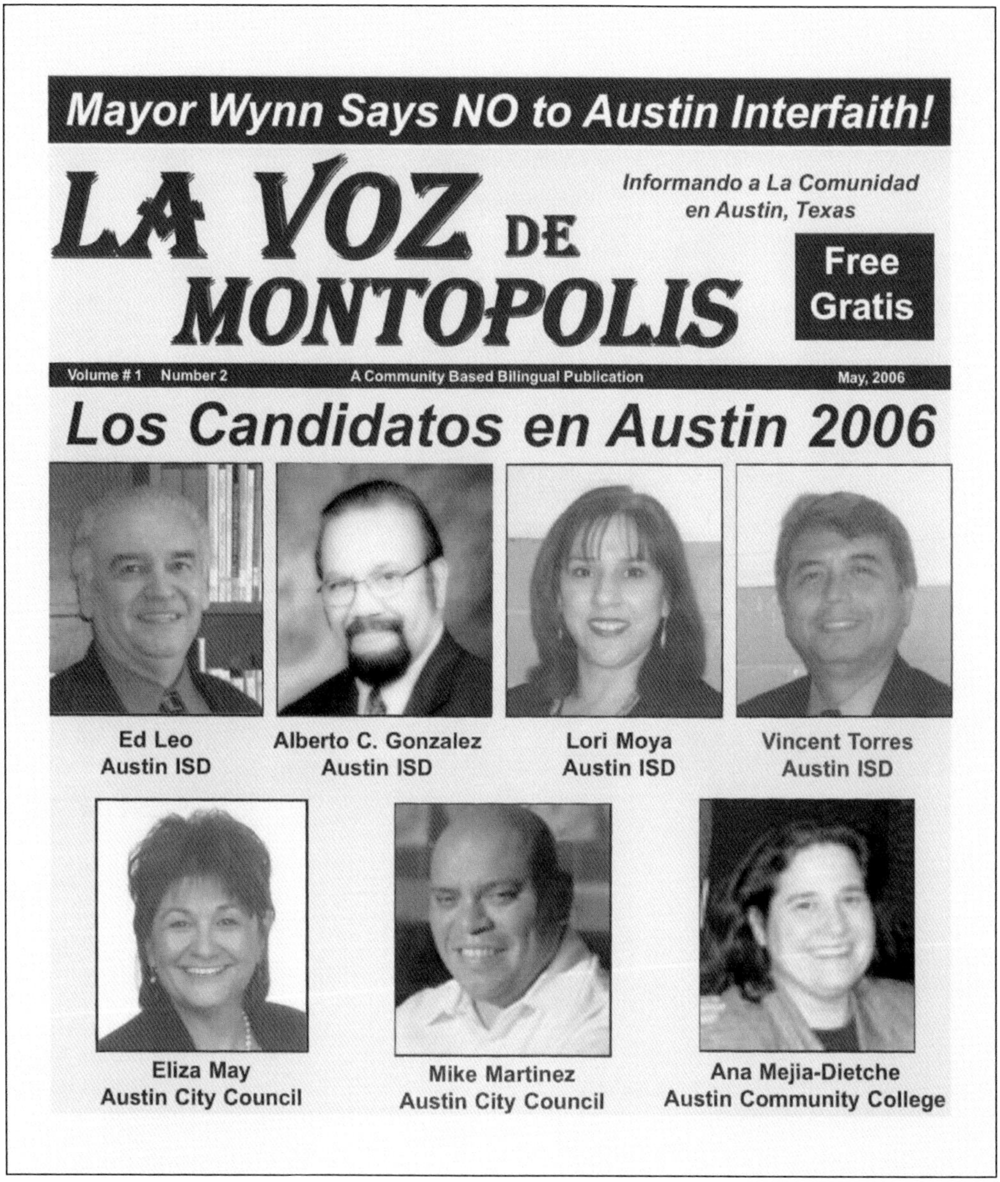

Mayor Wynn Says NO to Austin Interfaith!

LA VOZ DE MONTOPOLIS

Informando a La Comunidad en Austin, Texas

Free Gratis

Volume # 1 Number 2 | A Community Based Bilingual Publication | May, 2006

Los Candidatos en Austin 2006

Ed Leo
Austin ISD

Alberto C. Gonzalez
Austin ISD

Lori Moya
Austin ISD

Vincent Torres
Austin ISD

Eliza May
Austin City Council

Mike Martinez
Austin City Council

Ana Mejia-Dietche
Austin Community College

*La Voz* has evolved into a multicounty, bilingual community publication covering much of central Texas, but it began its life in neighborhoods such as Montopolis, Dove Springs, and East Austin. The indefatigable Alfredo R. Santos is the editor and publisher of the newspaper. (Courtesy of *La Voz*.)

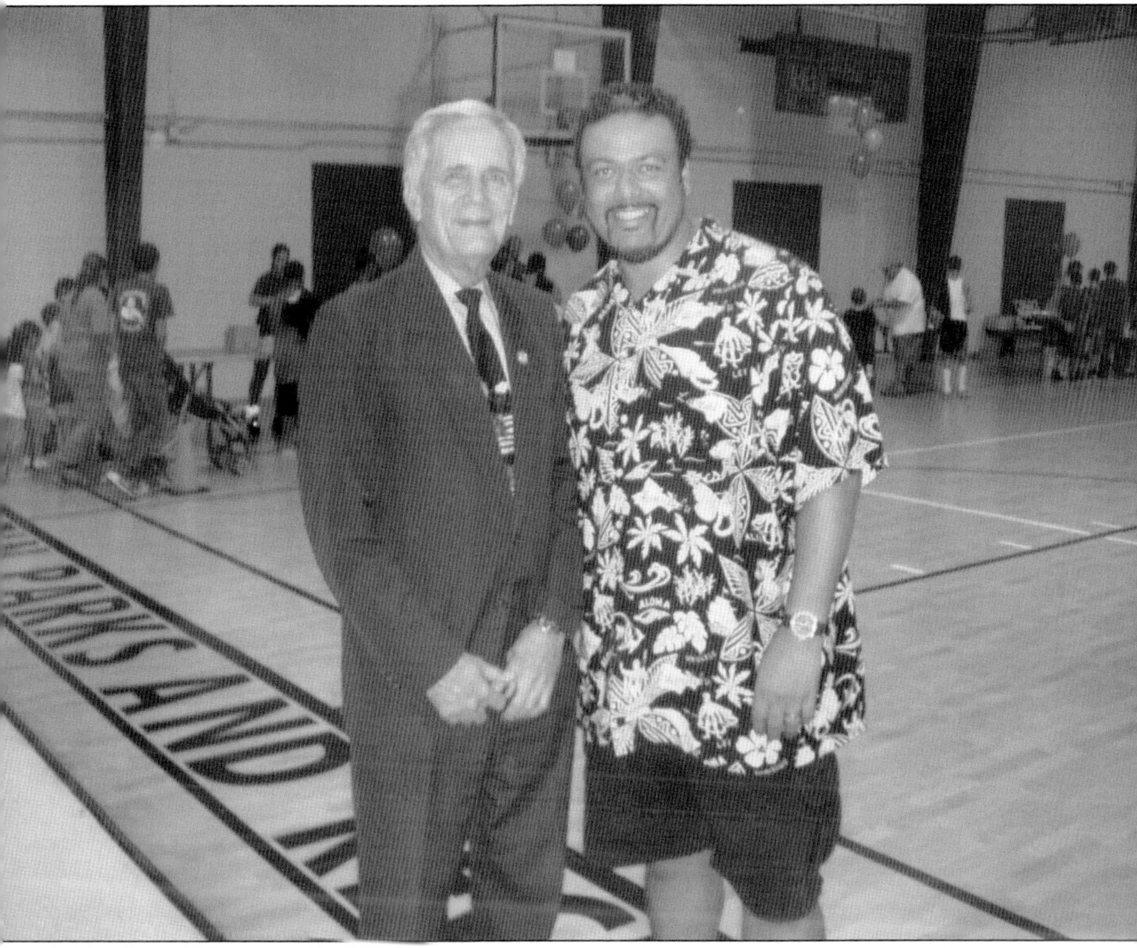


Congressman Lloyd Doggett has been a steadfast friend of the Montopolis neighborhood for decades. The neighborhood continues to show its appreciation for its congressman by repeatedly reelecting him by overwhelming margins, despite repeated efforts to gerrymander him out of office on the part of the Texas Legislature. This photograph of the author (right) with Congressman Doggett was taken at the Montopolis Recreation Center. (Courtesy of the author's collection.)

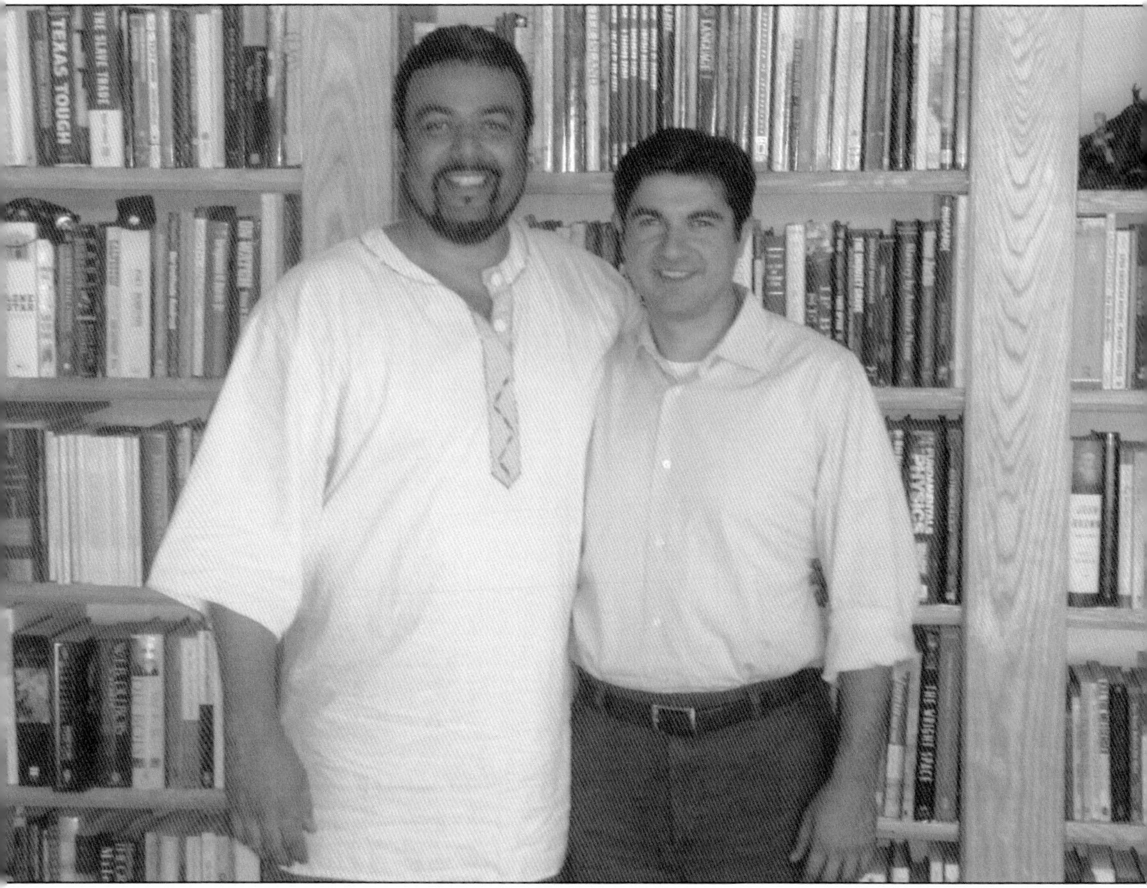

Serving in the tradition of former officeholders Gonzalo Barrientos and Glen Maxey, State Rep. Eddie Rodriguez has ably represented Montopolis and the rest of House District 51 in the Texas Legislature since 2002. He is seen here with the author. (Courtesy of the author's collection.)

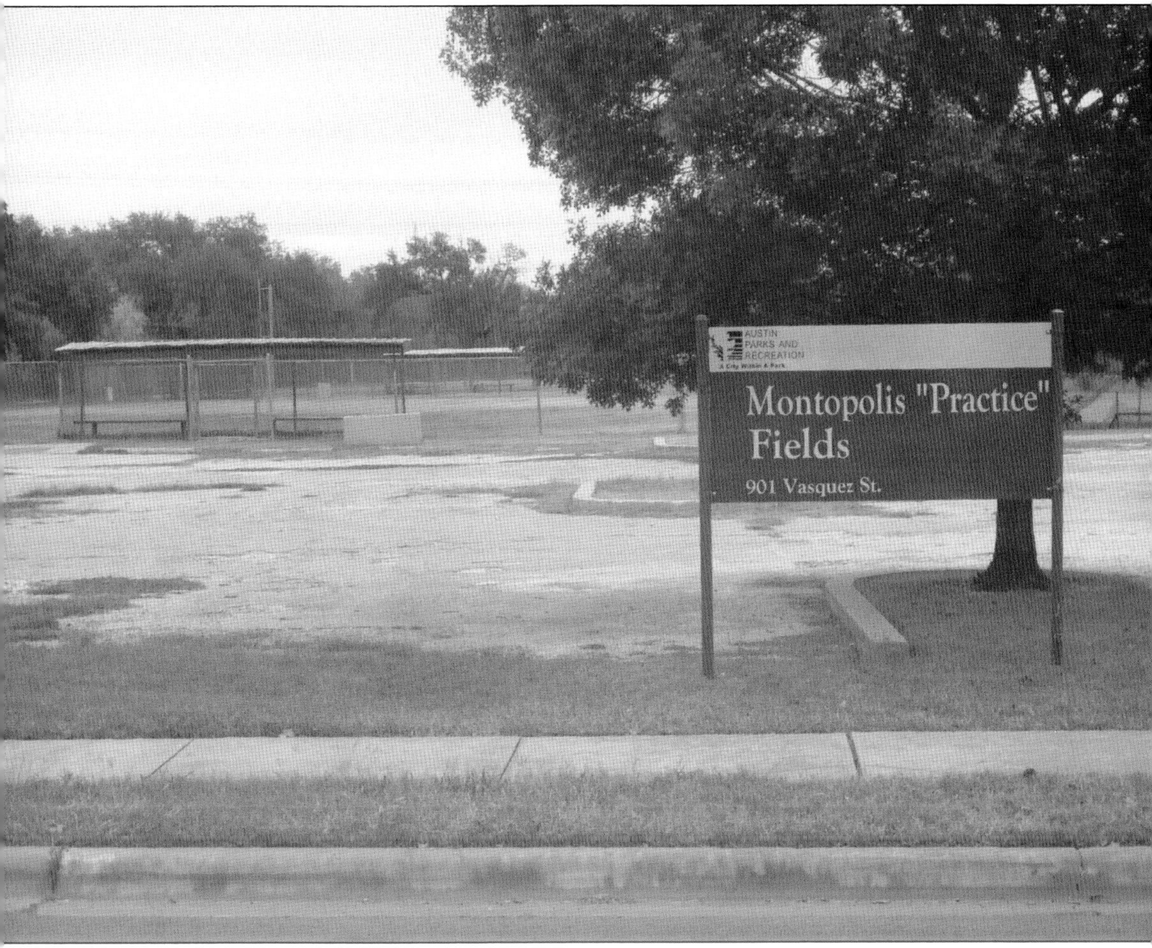


The funding and construction of the Montopolis "Practice" Fields in the early 1990s proved somewhat controversial because the eastern section of the Burdett Prairie Cemetery and the western edge of the ball field site share a common boundary of about 200 feet. Archival and oral history investigations revealed a great deal of information about the cemetery, but the site still awaits proper archaeological examination. Meanwhile, the practice fields were built and are still in active use. (Courtesy of the author's collection.)

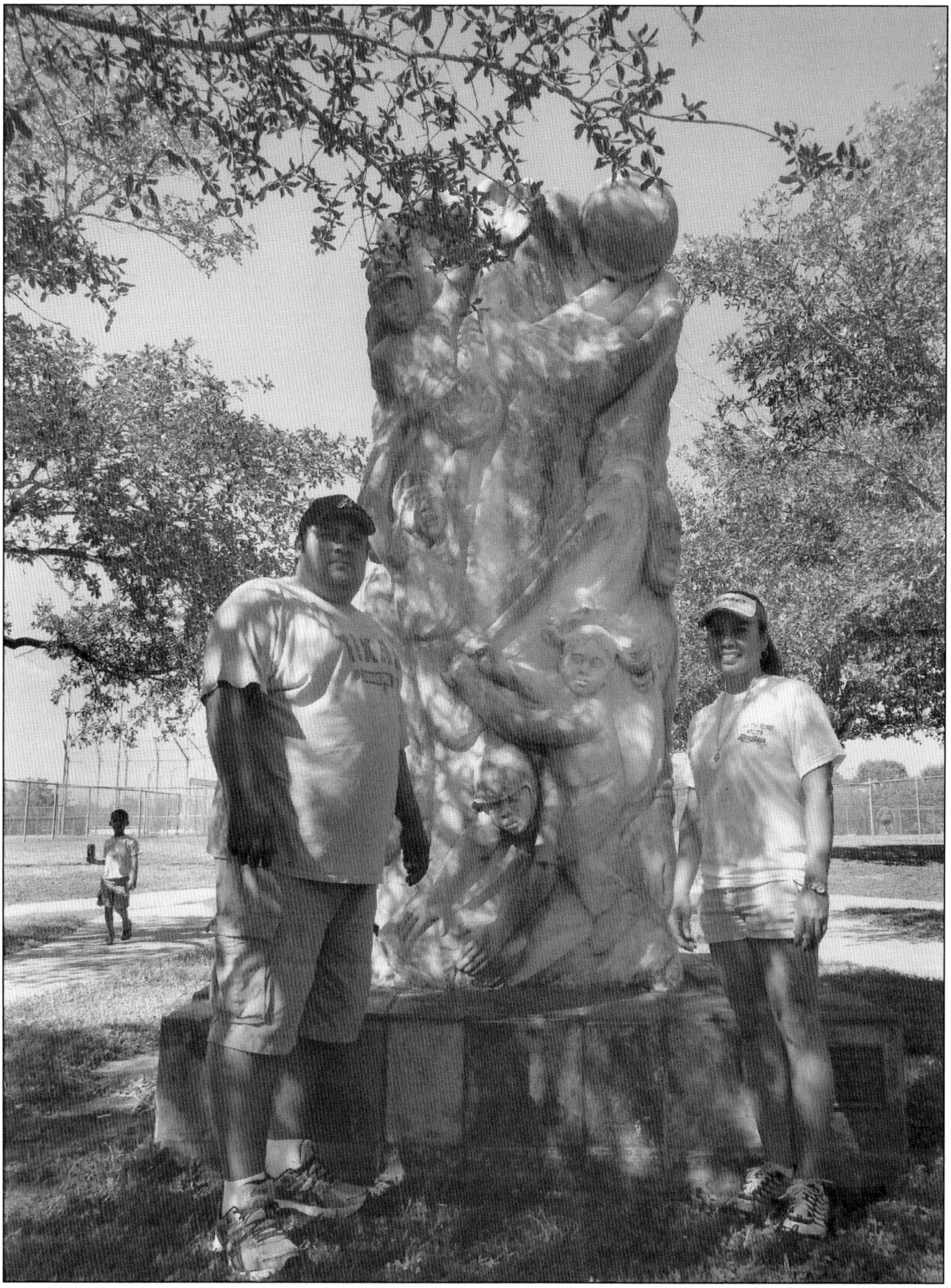

Israel Lopez, a Montopolis native, is the president of Montopolis Little League. His tireless advocacy on behalf of the neighborhood's youth has won him awards and considerable community regard and respect. In this November 2013 photograph, he stands next to Gracie Rodriguez in front of the *Reach for Your Dreams* sculpture at the Montopolis Youth Sports Complex in support of victims of the most recent Onion Creek flood in 2013. (Courtesy of the author's collection.)

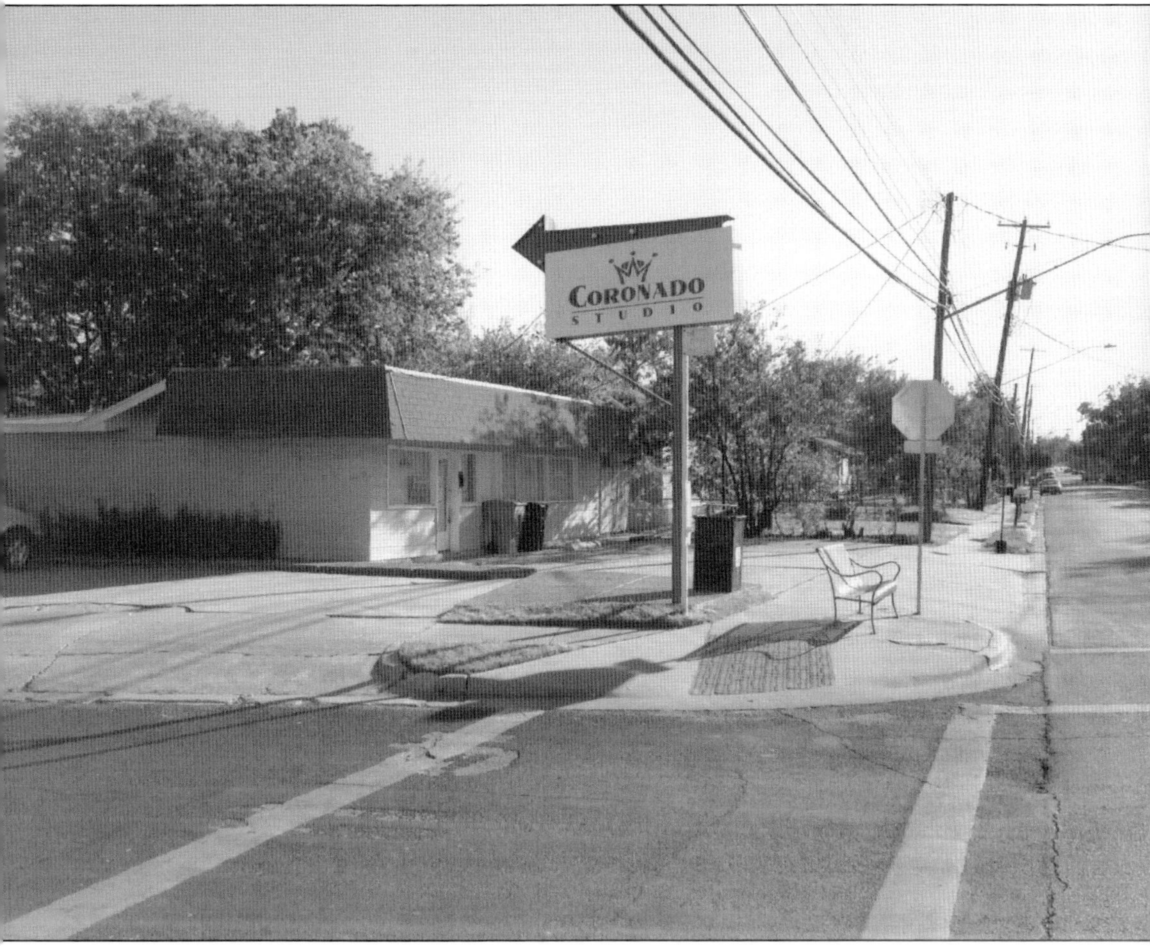


The sudden death of Latino arts icon Sam Coronado in November 2013 from complications after a stroke came as a shock. Coronado was a highly regarded community leader and visual artist whose studio, seen here, had been located in the heart of the Montopolis community since 1998. In addition to teaching at Austin Community College since 1986, he cofounded the Mexic-Arte Museum in 1984 and the Serie Project in 1993. (Courtesy of the author's collection.)

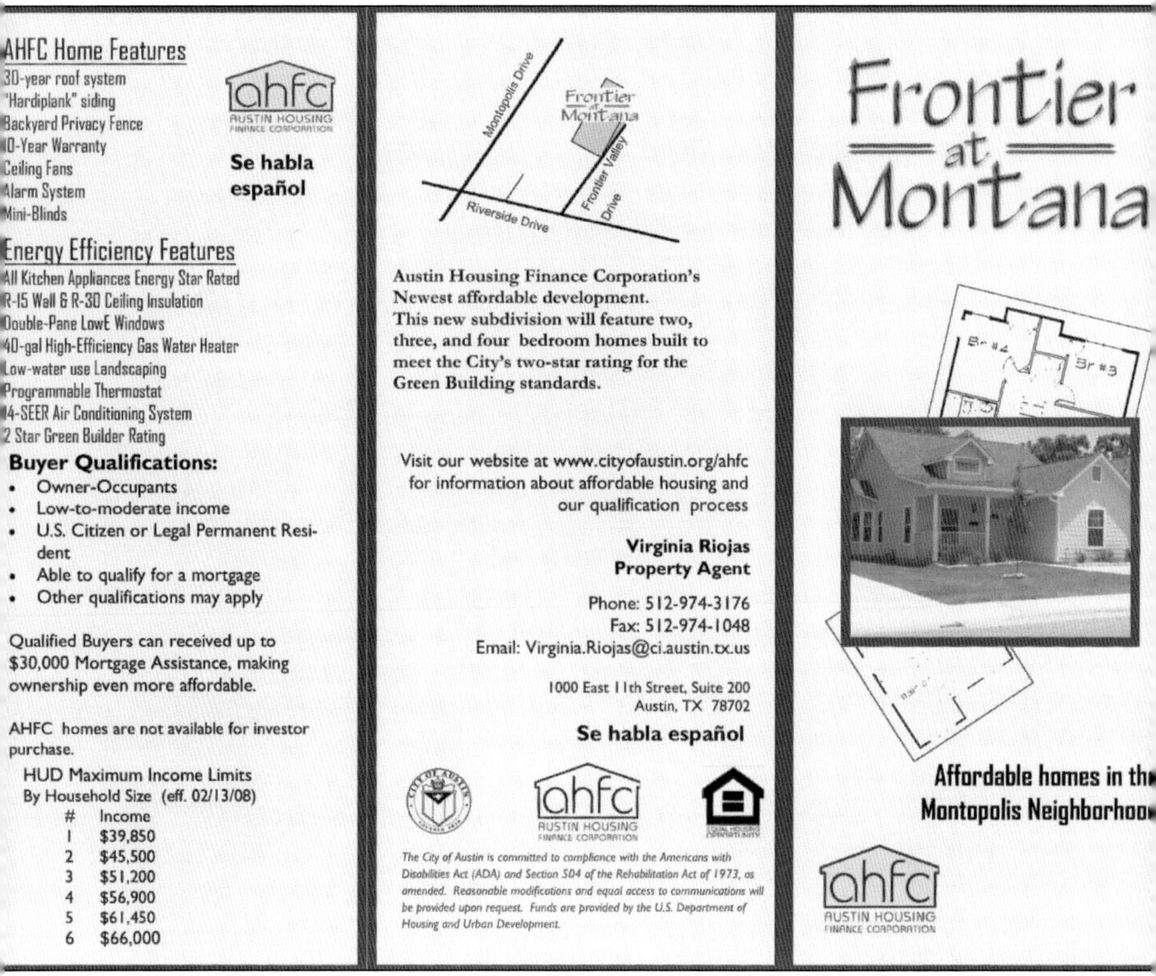


Frontier at Montana began as an affordable housing "laboratory" for three City of Austin departments—the Neighborhood Housing and Community Development Department, the Austin Housing Finance Corporation, and Austin Energy's Greenbuilding Program—to develop one of the country's first zero-energy affordable housing developments. The plan was to develop about 100 units within two years. As this brochure shows, the effort fell short. While the development, after many rookie mistakes by the general contractor, was eventually built, none of the buildings are zero-energy. They did, however, qualify for a two-star rating, with some rated higher, and they were reserved for low-to-moderate-income homebuyers. (Courtesy of the City of Austin.)

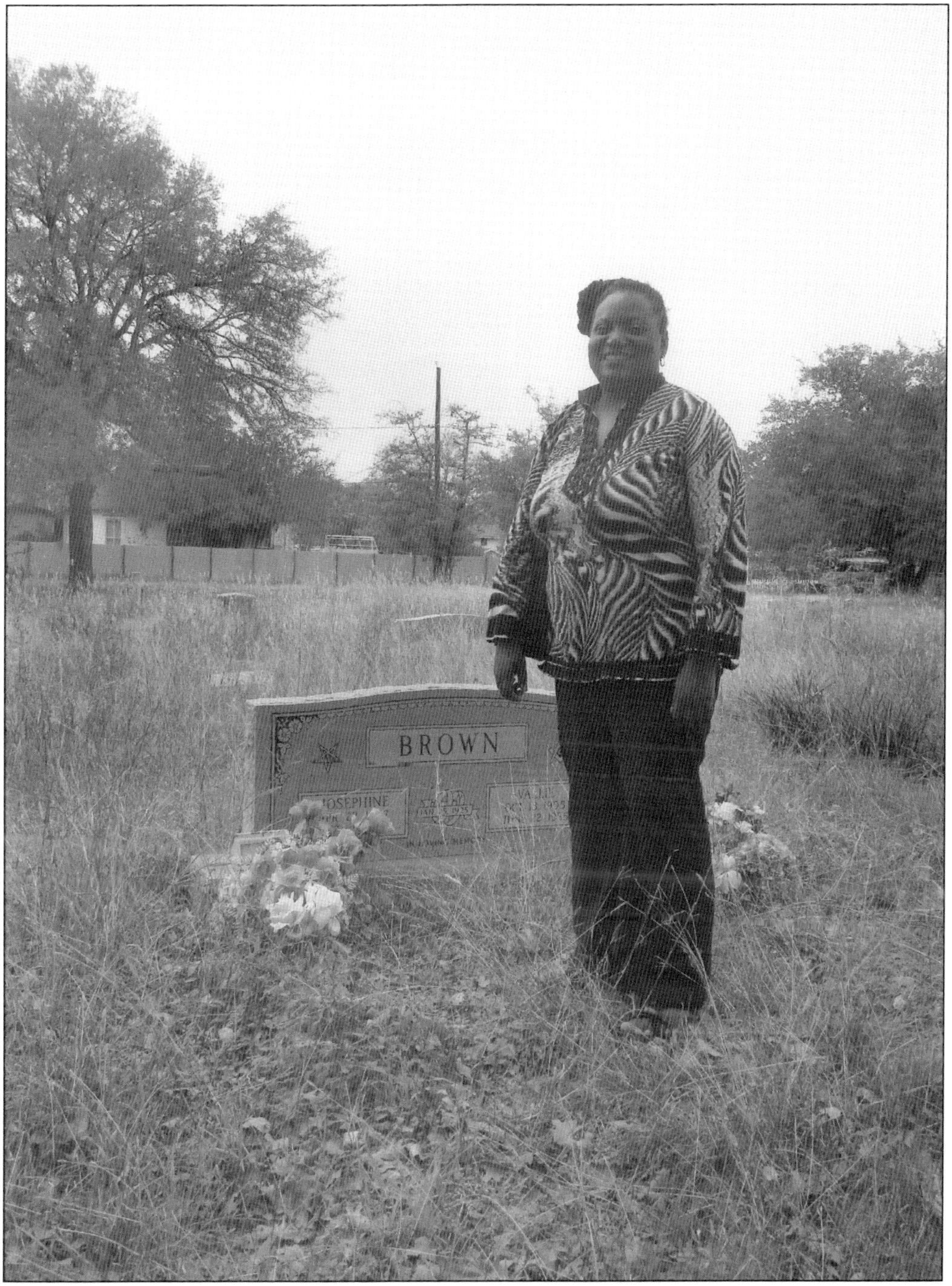


Adama Brown of the Burdett Prairie Cemetery Association has collaborated with the author and other individuals and groups to help preserve the final resting ground of her ancestors. A preservation plan for the historic cemetery is currently in development. (Courtesy of the author's collection.)

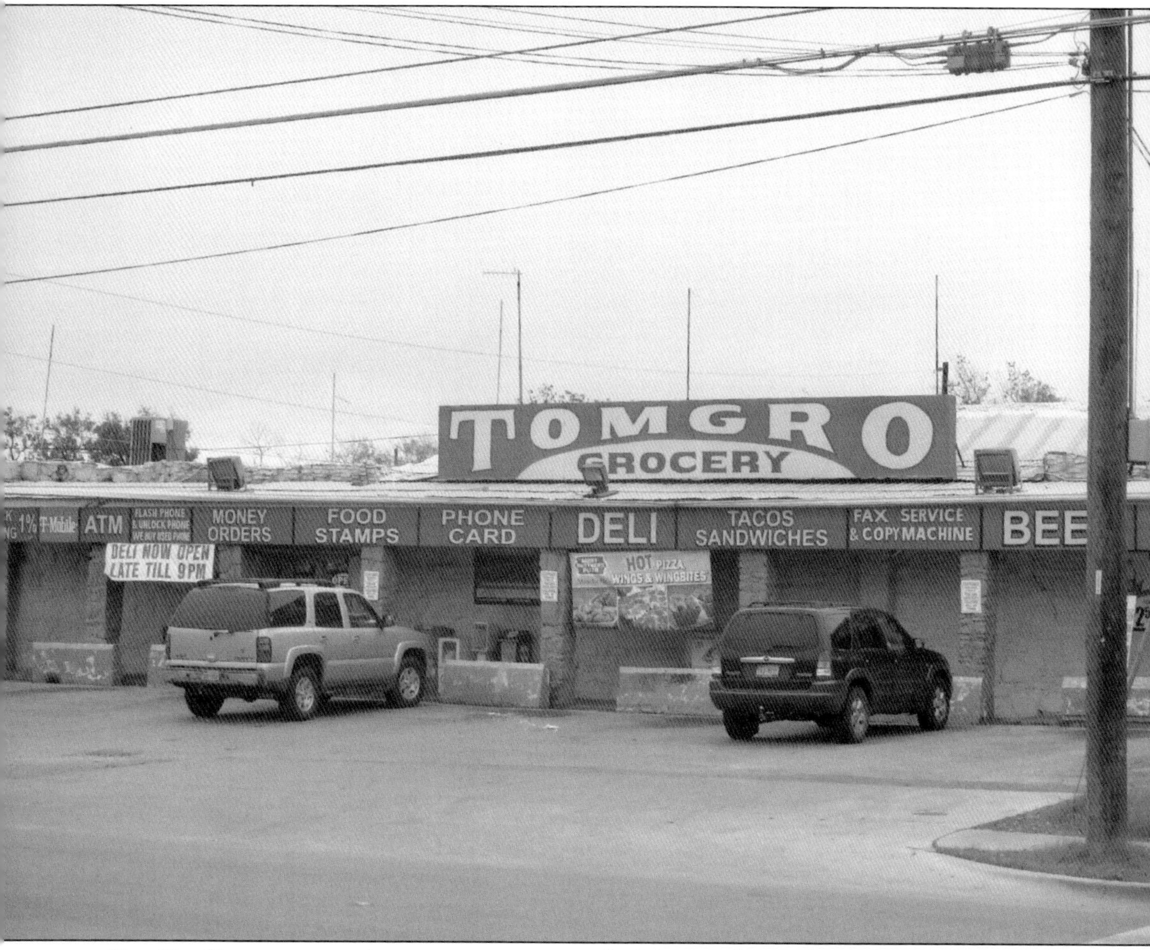


TomGro Grocery not only serves as a grocery for Montopolis residents, but also as a de facto general store and mobile office location. The property has also hosted weekend flea markets over the years. (Courtesy of the author's collection.)

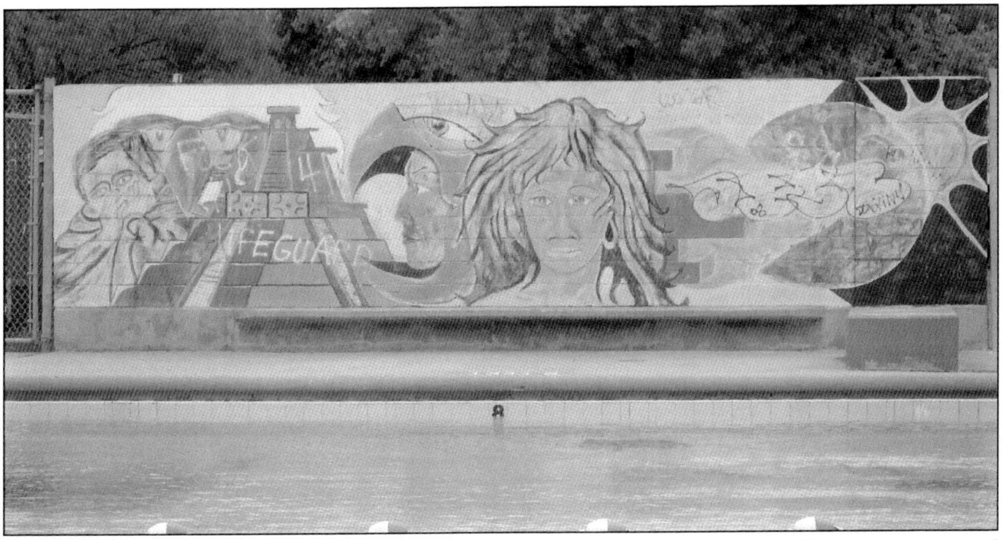

Montopolis is the location of some of the most interesting mural art in Austin. This mural is located at the Montopolis Pool, next to the recreation center. (Courtesy of the author's collection.)

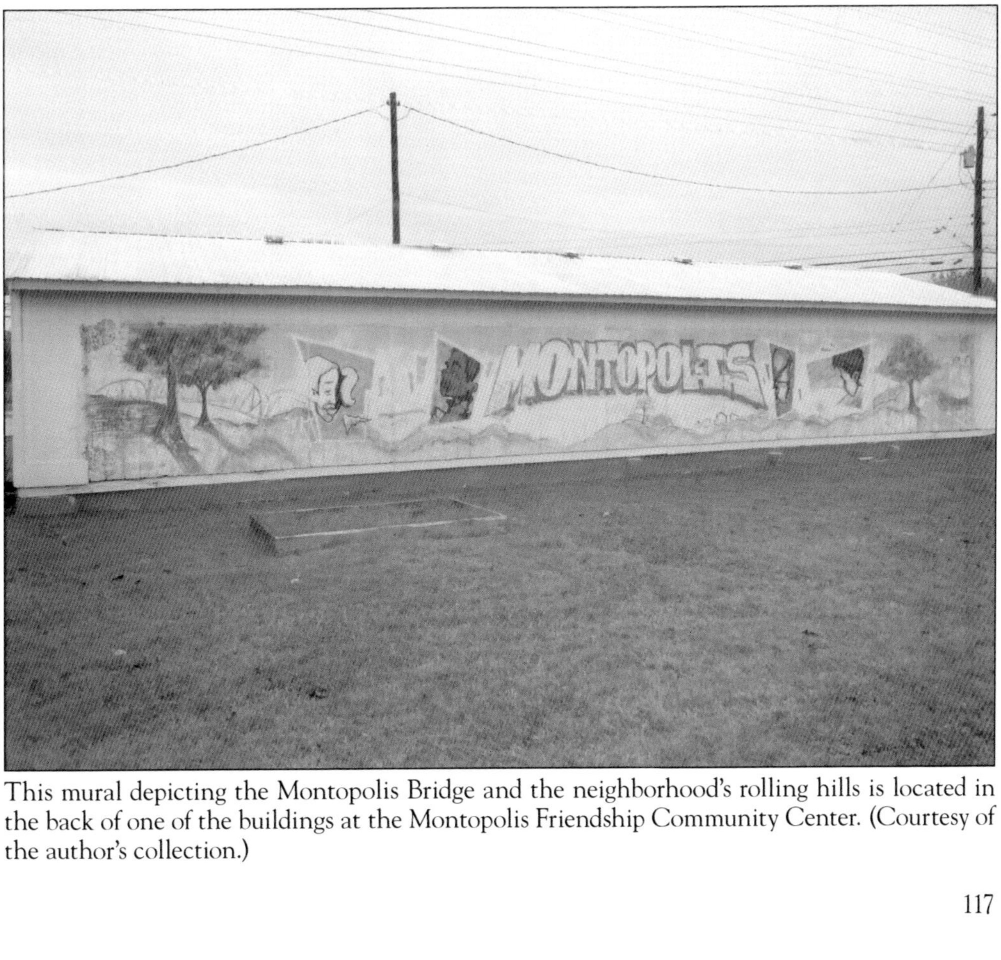


This mural depicting the Montopolis Bridge and the neighborhood's rolling hills is located in the back of one of the buildings at the Montopolis Friendship Community Center. (Courtesy of the author's collection.)

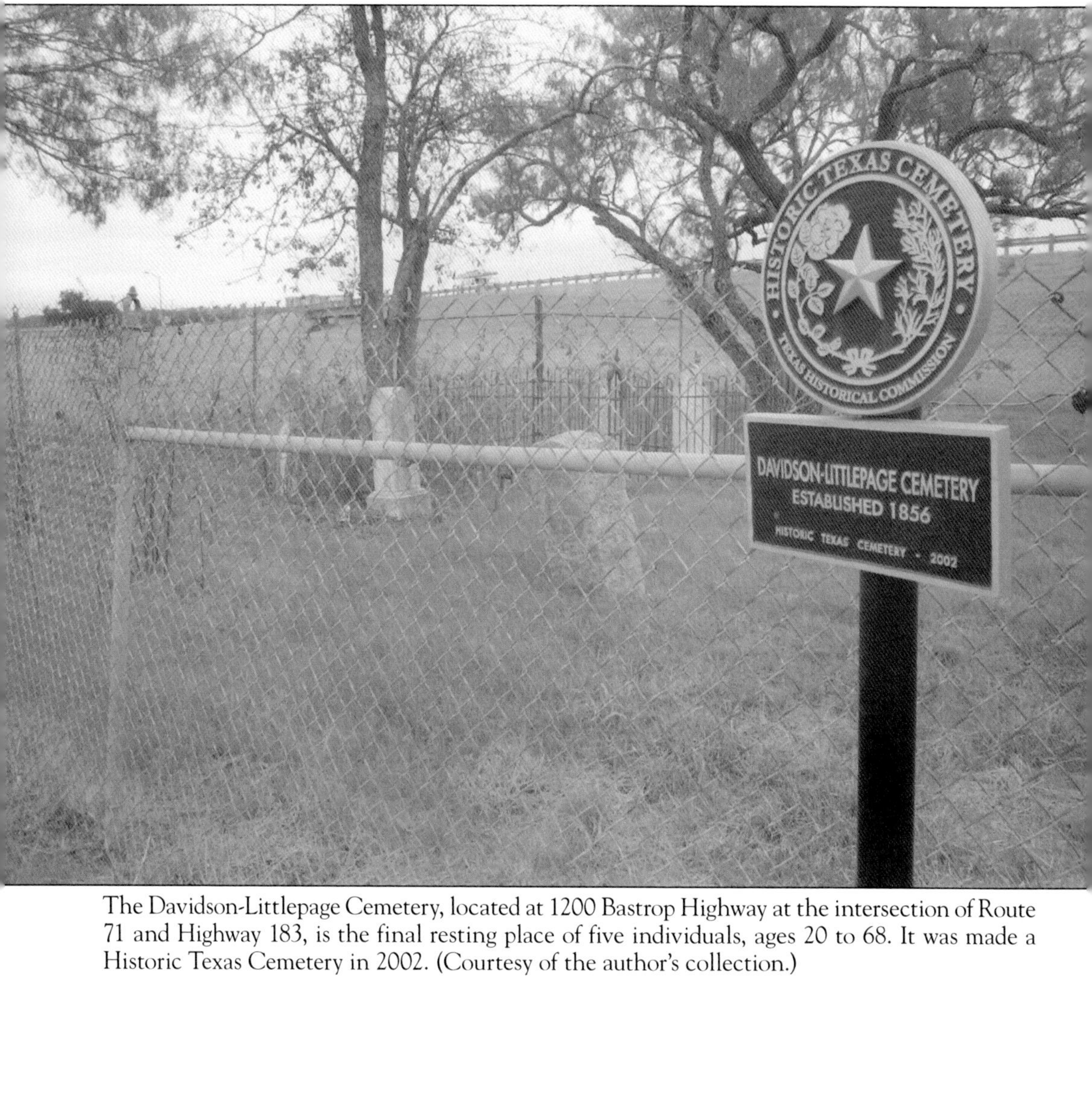


The Davidson-Littlepage Cemetery, located at 1200 Bastrop Highway at the intersection of Route 71 and Highway 183, is the final resting place of five individuals, ages 20 to 68. It was made a Historic Texas Cemetery in 2002. (Courtesy of the author's collection.)

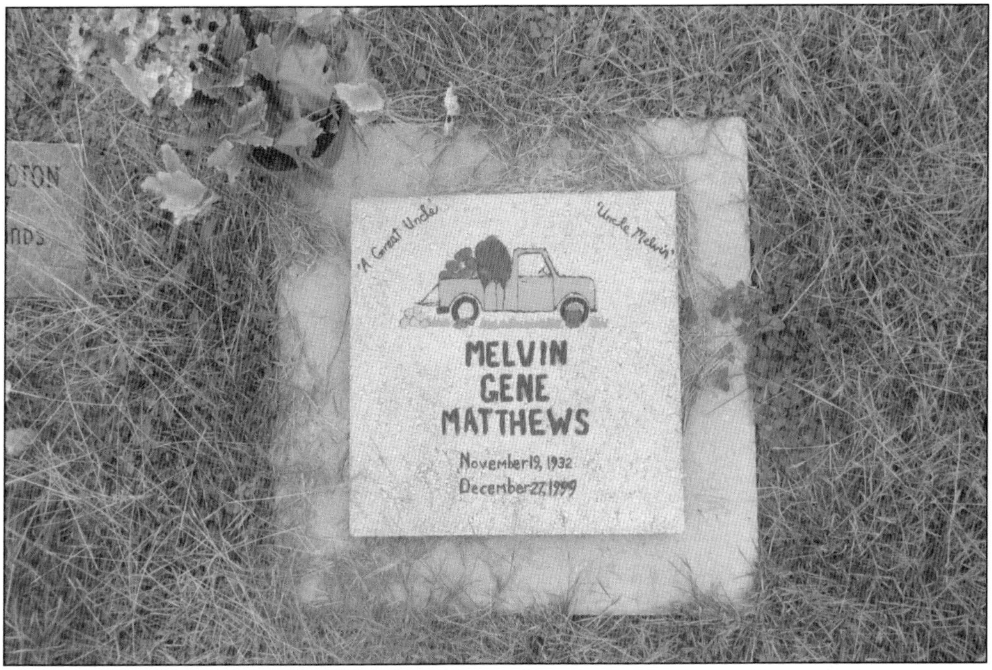


The Greenwood Cemetery is located at 8600 Riverside Drive, next to Austin-Bergstrom International Airport. Despite its unique flight path location, the cemetery is a place of considerable repose, and furnishes a window into the rural origins of southeast Austin prior to the construction of Bergstrom Air Base. The cemetery continues in active use, as this touching headstone shows. (Courtesy of the author's collection.)

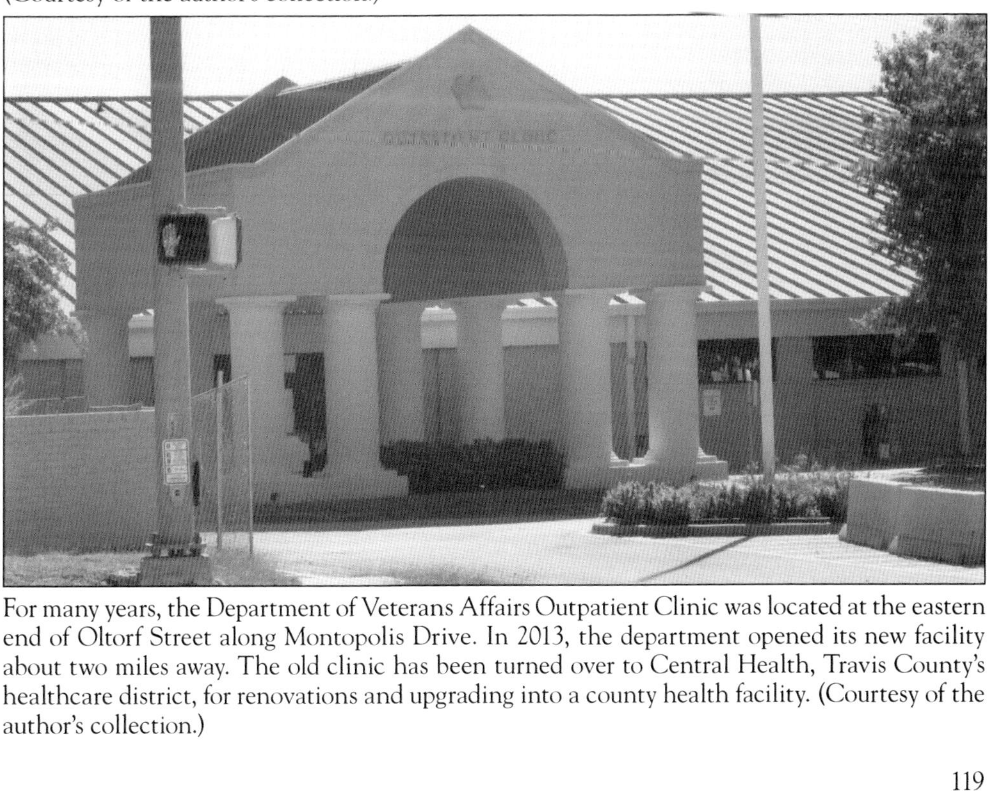

For many years, the Department of Veterans Affairs Outpatient Clinic was located at the eastern end of Oltorf Street along Montopolis Drive. In 2013, the department opened its new facility about two miles away. The old clinic has been turned over to Central Health, Travis County's healthcare district, for renovations and upgrading into a county health facility. (Courtesy of the author's collection.)

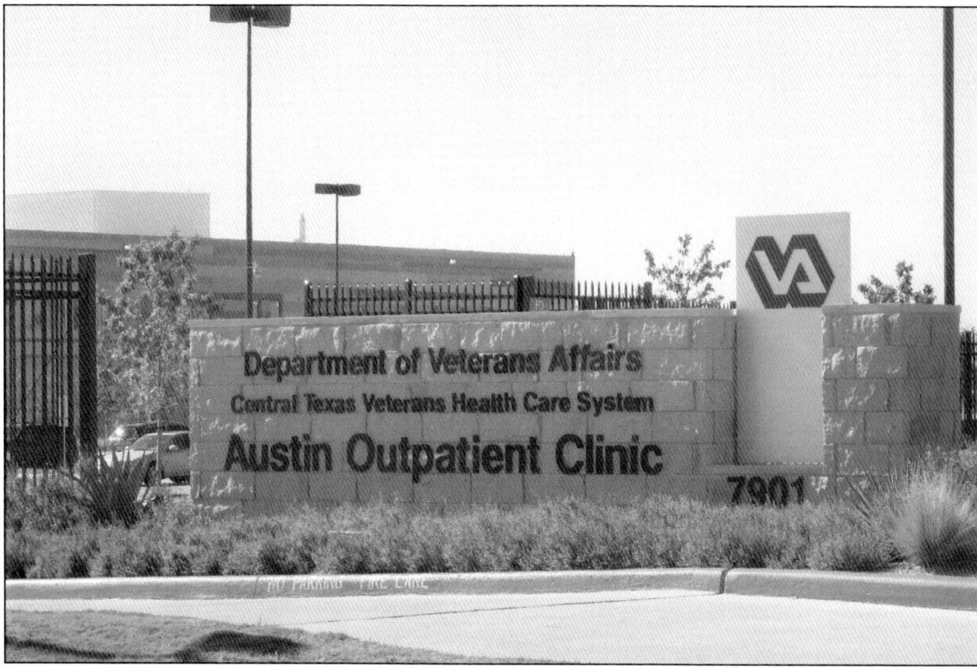

The small size of the previous outpatient clinic necessitated long and inconvenient shuttle trips by veterans to the Olin Teague Veterans' Medical Center in Temple for MRIs and CT scans, as well as other medical services. The new clinic is located along Metropolis Drive, and as the largest VA outpatient clinic in the United States, it also features mental health and women's health services the previous clinic did not offer. (Courtesy of the author's collection.)

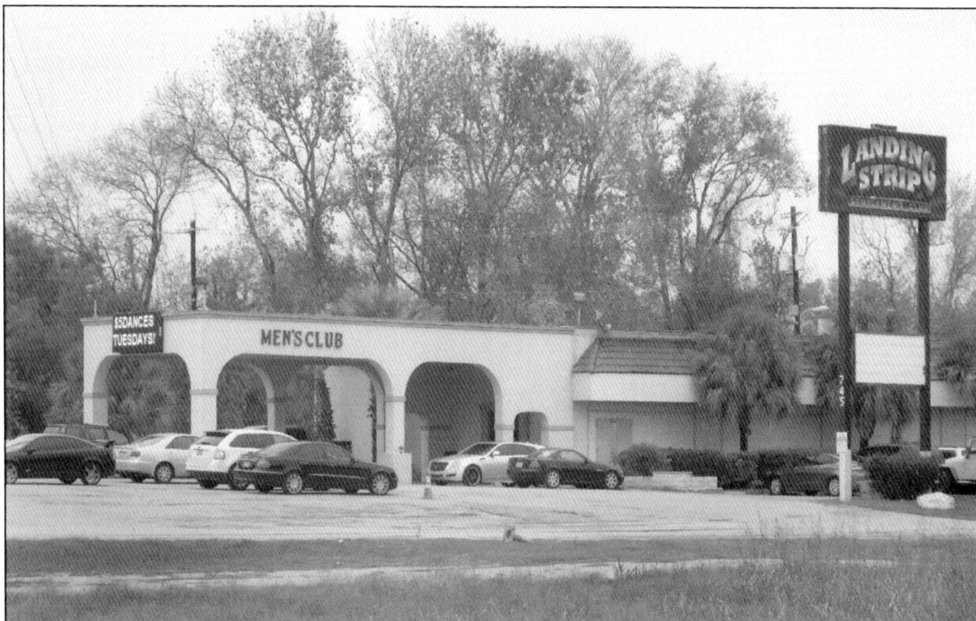

The Landing Strip is a well-known adult entertainment club that catered to a military clientele during the days when Bergstrom Air Force Base was still in operation. (Courtesy of the author's collection.)

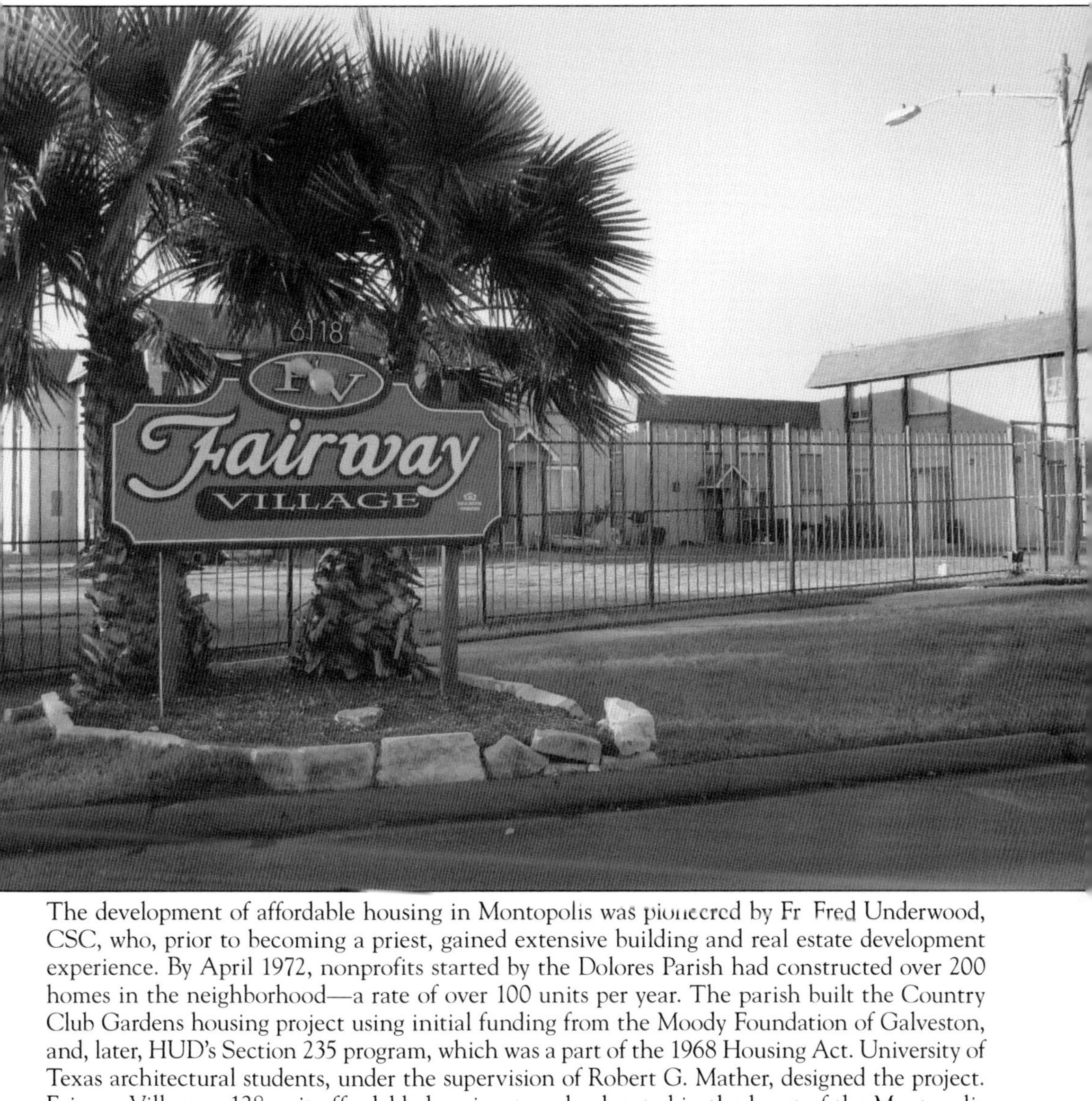


The development of affordable housing in Montopolis was pioneered by Fr. Fred Underwood, CSC, who, prior to becoming a priest, gained extensive building and real estate development experience. By April 1972, nonprofits started by the Dolores Parish had constructed over 200 homes in the neighborhood—a rate of over 100 units per year. The parish built the Country Club Gardens housing project using initial funding from the Moody Foundation of Galveston, and, later, HUD's Section 235 program, which was a part of the 1968 Housing Act. University of Texas architectural students, under the supervision of Robert G. Mather, designed the project. Fairway Village, a 128-unit affordable housing complex located in the heart of the Montopolis neighborhood, is a continuance of this legacy. (Courtesy of the author's collection.)

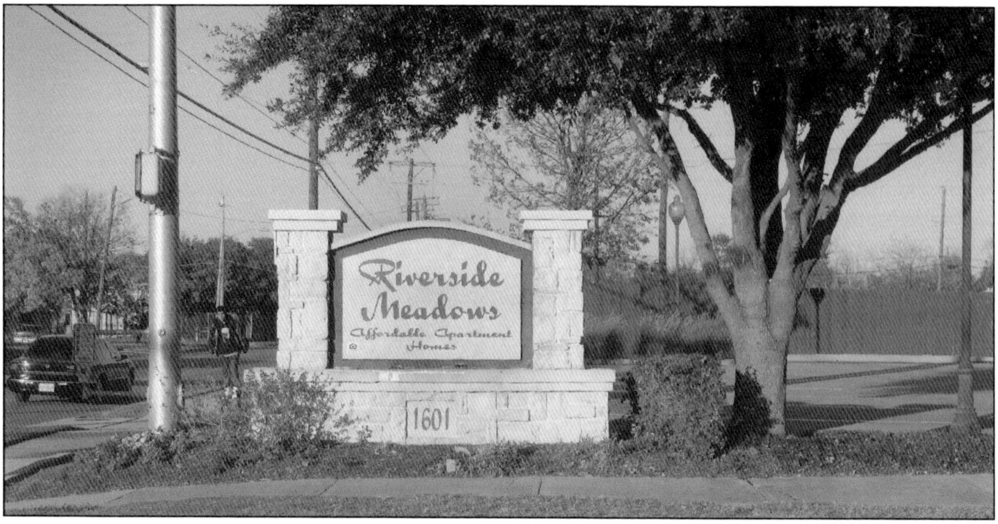


The Montopolis neighborhood contains one of the highest concentrations of "affordable" housing in Austin, especially when one factors in the neighborhood's high concentration of Habitat for Humanity homes (the highest in the city), trailer parks, and its homeless population. An unfortunate consequence of this overconcentration of lower-cost housing has been the ghettoization of Montopolis, which has reinforced residential segregation, particularly on race and class lines. There are numerous reasons for the high concentration of affordable housing developments in Montopolis: real estate is still cheaper than in other parts of Austin, political opposition is generally muted, and there is a pressing need for affordable housing throughout Austin, not just in Montopolis. Riverside Meadows is a 248-unit tax credit and bond-financed property located across the street from Fairway Village, at 1601 Montopolis Drive. (Courtesy of the author's collection.)

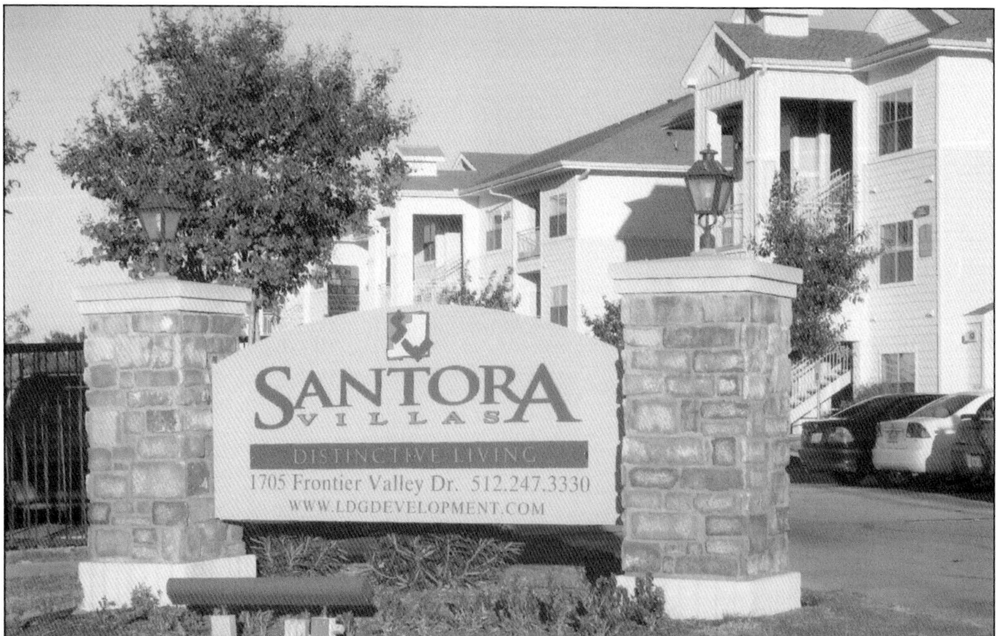


Santora Villas, located on Frontier Drive, is a 192-unit tax credit property constructed by Kentucky-based moderate-income builder LDG Development. (Courtesy of the author's collection.)

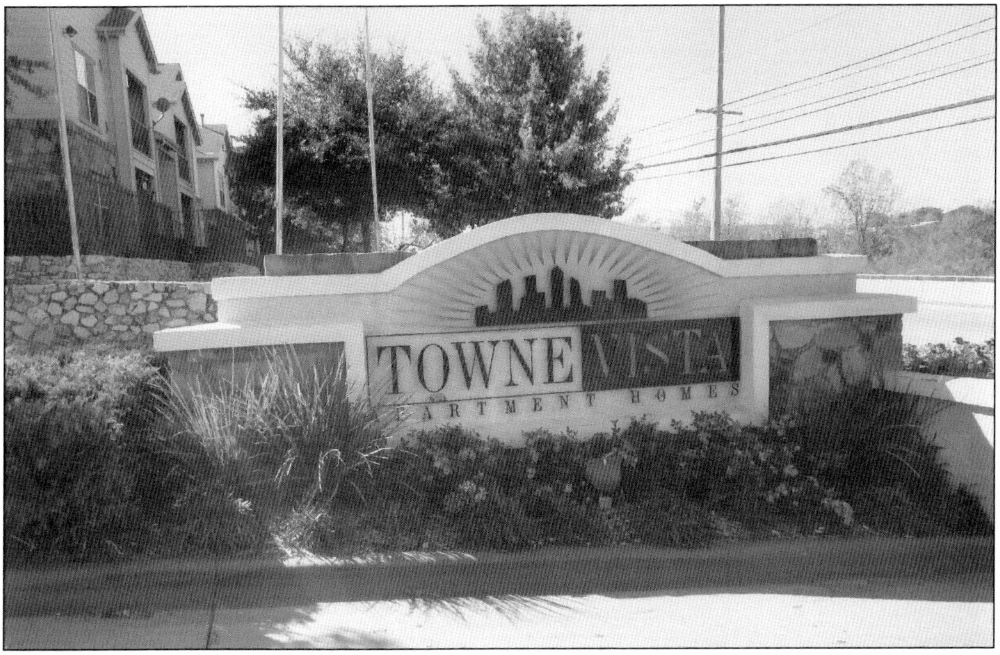

The Towne Vista Apartments, so named because of their terrific views of downtown Austin, is a 280-unit bond and tax credit property located at 2201 Montopolis Drive. It is one of the larger affordable housing developments in the Montopolis neighborhood. (Courtesy of the author's collection.)

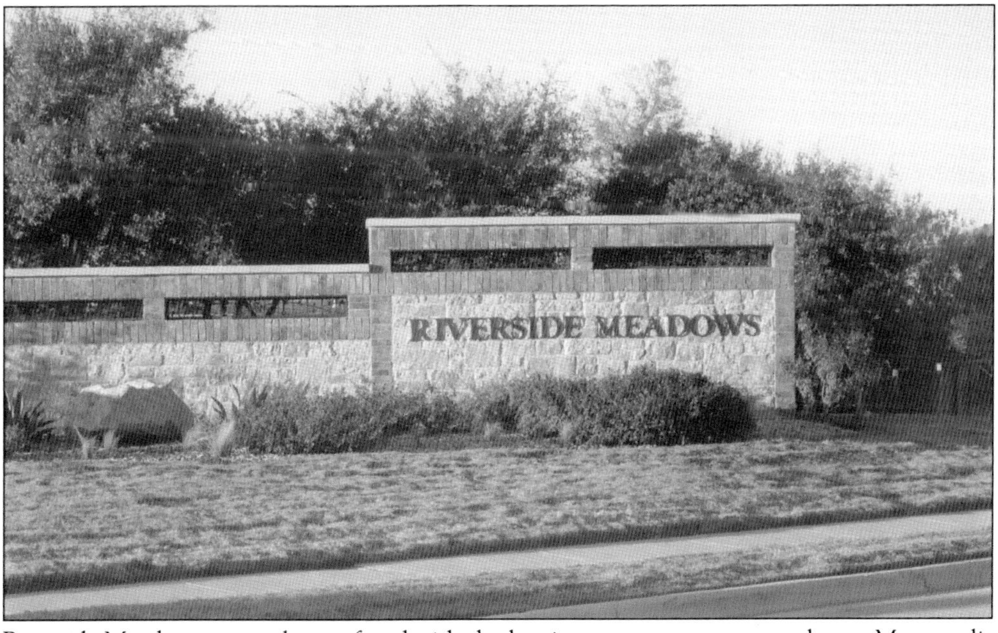

Riverside Meadows, not to be confused with the low-income apartment complex on Montopolis Drive, is a 38-acre Montopolis subdivision containing affordable single-family homes constructed by CENTEX Homes in the early-to-mid-2000s using city bond financing. Its construction altered the demographics of Montopolis somewhat, as most of the people who purchased homes in the new subdivision were not from the neighborhood, and their presence initially produced some tension. (Courtesy of the author's collection.)

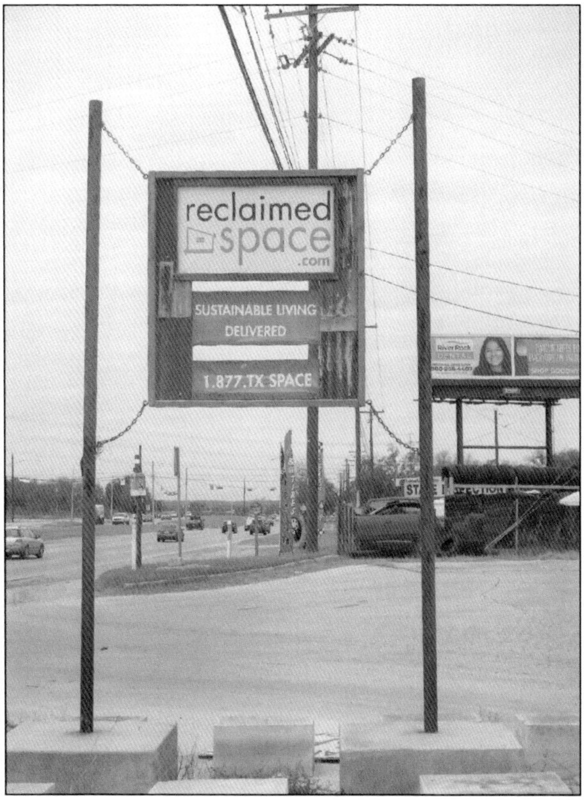


Reclaimed Space/Dirtco Construction green builds modular custom homes using reclaimed materials. New to the Montopolis area, the company has begun to develop real estate in the neighborhood. (Courtesy of the author's collection.)

When SEMATECH and Advanced Micro Devices came to Montopolis in the 1980s and established an industrial zone located dangerously close to single-family-zoned properties, Wilson Oxygen Supply/Praxair Distribution set up shop across the street. In the early 2000s, a city-sponsored plan to locate affordable housing near the business was scuttled due to environmental concerns. (Courtesy of the author's collection.)

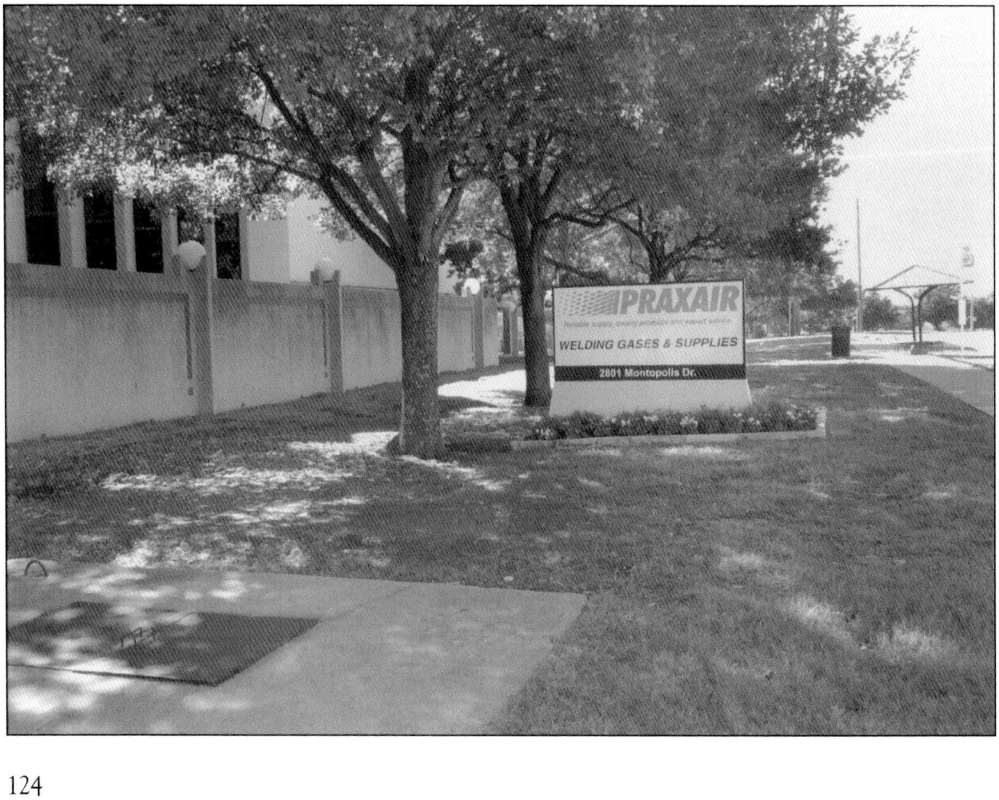

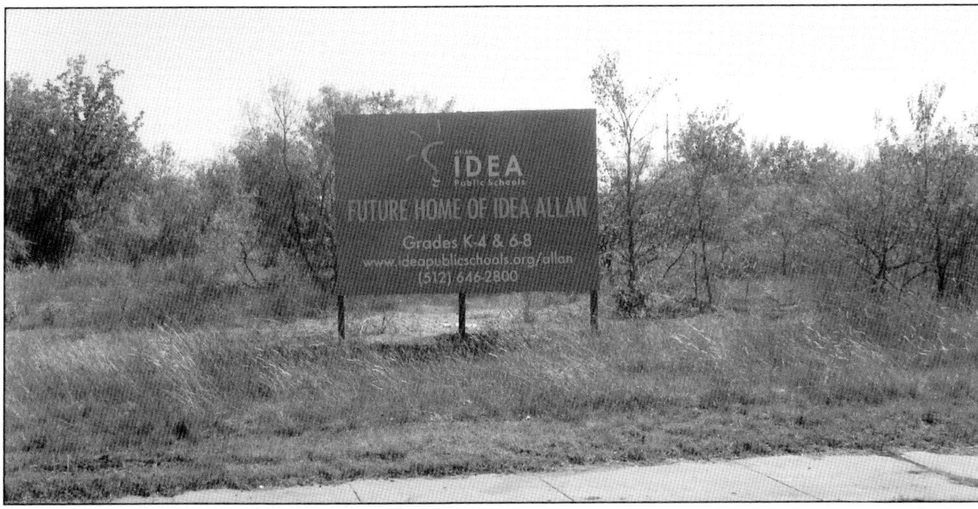


In 2010, IDEA Public Schools, a charter school operator from South Texas, was awarded an Austin Independent School District contract to operate at Allan Elementary School, which is located north of the Colorado River. Two years later, a newly elected Austin school board voted to terminate the contract. The controversial relationship between the charter school network and the Austin School District may be heating back up because, as this photograph indicates, IDEA Public Schools intends to build a new charter school in the Montopolis neighborhood and keep the IDEA/Allan name. (Courtesy of the Central Texas Regional Mobility Authority.)

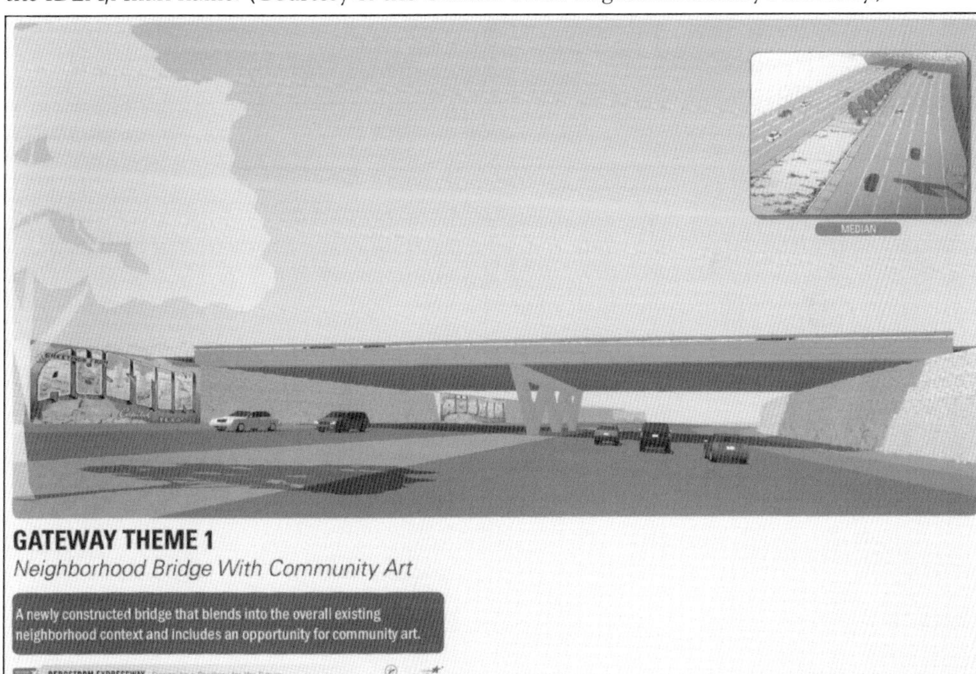


The construction of the Bergstrom Expressway is expected to produce significant changes in Montopolis: Not only will the intersection between Vargas Drive and Highway 183 be closed, but an upper deck along 183 will also be constructed. Perhaps most notably, new bridges will also be constructed. This conceptual photograph depicts a "neighborhood bridge" with community art. (Courtesy of the Central Texas Regional Mobility Authority.)

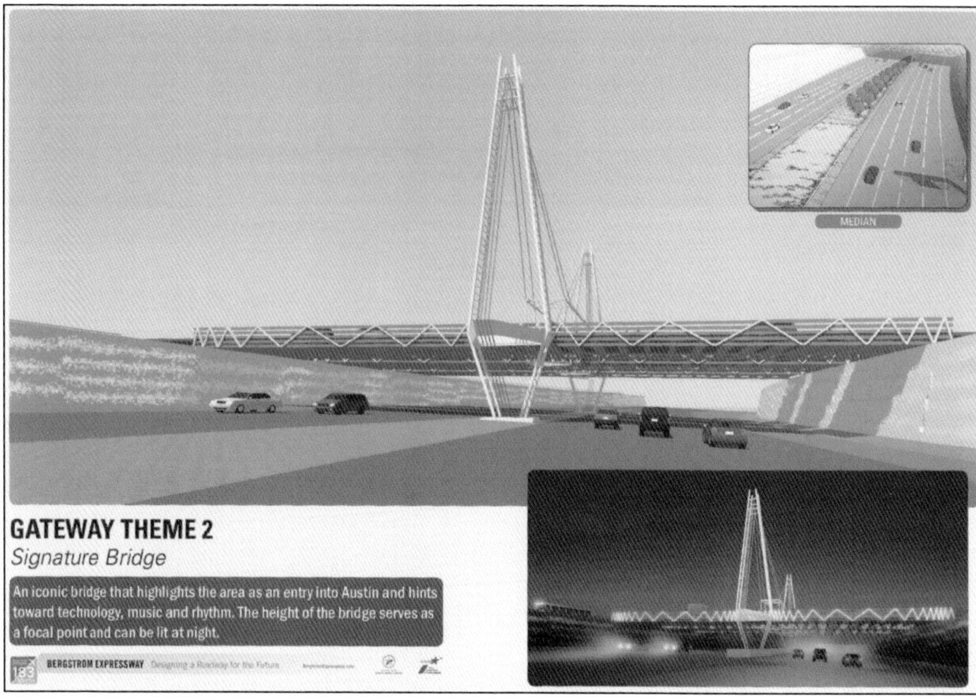


The "signature bridge" concept entails extensive illumination designed to highlight Austin's reputation as a high-tech hot spot and entertainment destination. (Courtesy of the Central Texas Regional Mobility Authority.)

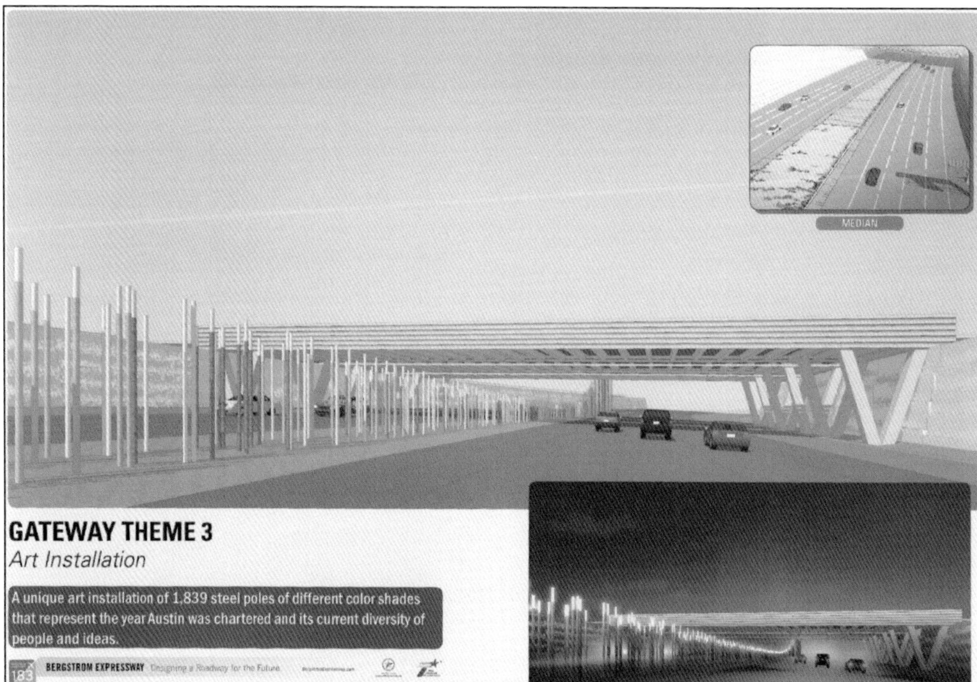


The "art installation" theme entails the installation of 1,839 steel poles of different color shades, signifying the year of Austin's founding.

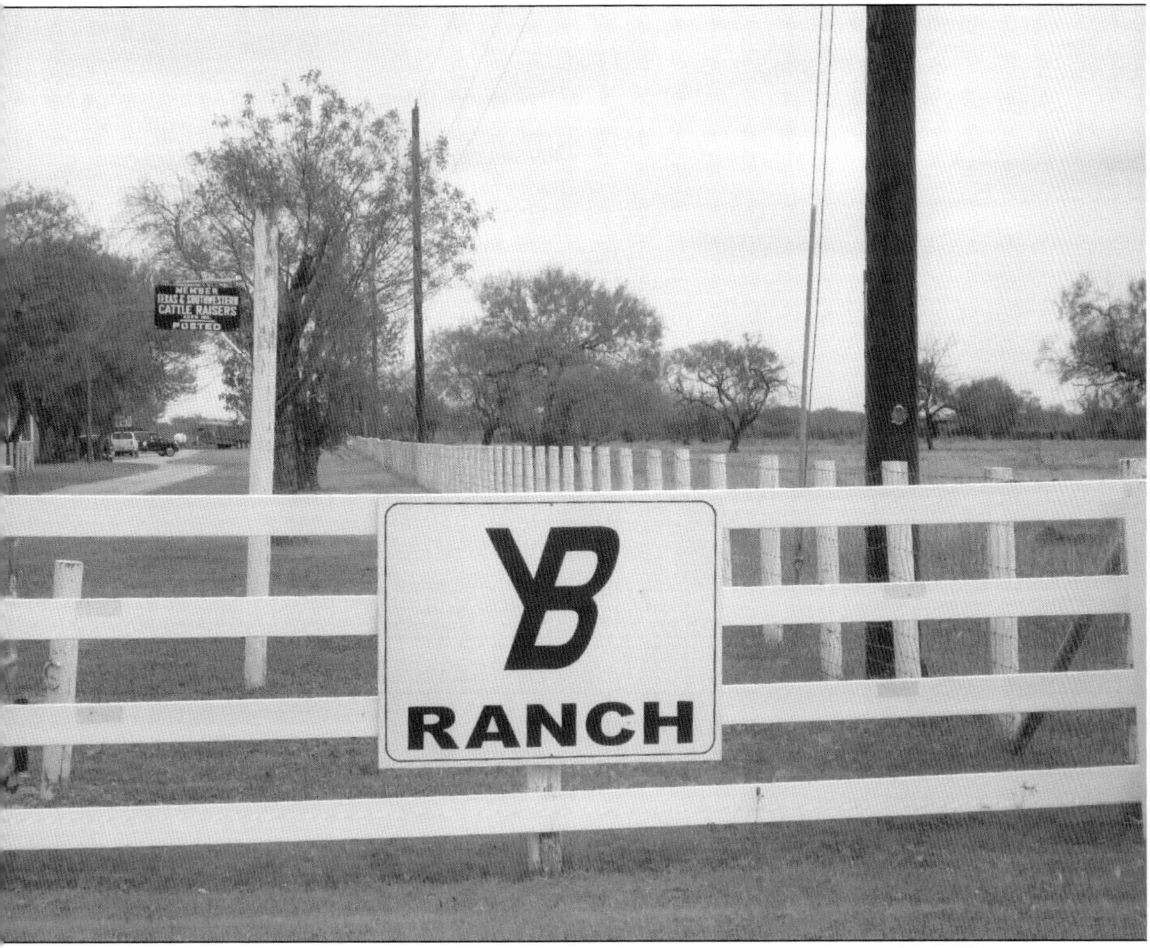


Located along the banks of the Colorado River past the old Jones Plantation, the Bailey Ranch serves as a reminder of the rural origins of the Montopolis area. The post-emancipation transition from cotton to cattle ranching has not only left its historical imprint on the area, it is also an economic and cultural activity that continues to define much of the neighborhood's character.

## Discover Thousands of Local History Books Featuring Millions of Vintage Images

Arcadia Publishing, the leading local history publisher in the United States, is committed to making history accessible and meaningful through publishing books that celebrate and preserve the heritage of America's people and places.

Find more books like this at
**www.arcadiapublishing.com**

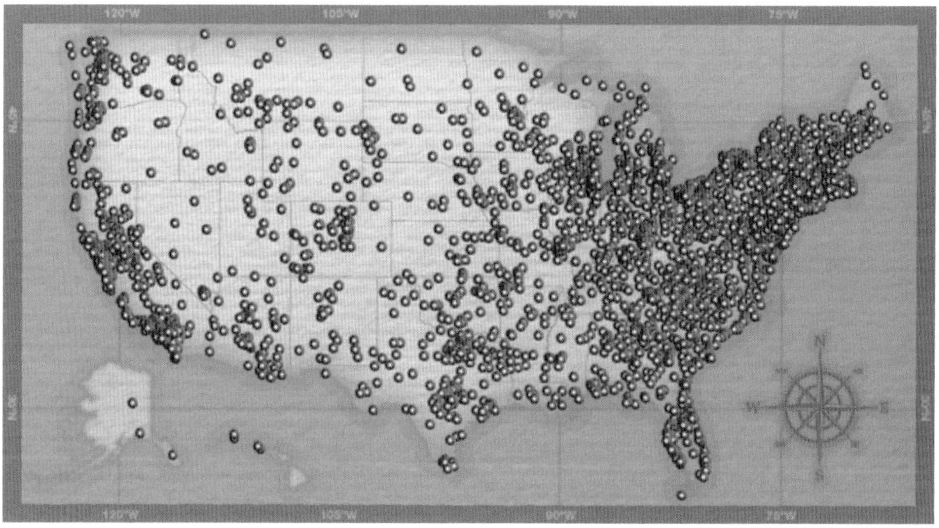

Search for your hometown history, your old stomping grounds, and even your favorite sports team.

Consistent with our mission to preserve history on a local level, this book was printed in South Carolina on American-made paper and manufactured entirely in the United States. Products carrying the accredited Forest Stewardship Council (FSC) label are printed on 100 percent FSC-certified paper.

MADE IN THE USA